Societies and Political Orders in Transition

This book series presents scientific and scholarly studies focusing on societies and political orders in transition in Central and Eastern Europe but also elsewhere in the world, contemporary and historical. By comparing established societies, characterized by well-established market economies and well-functioning democracies, with post-socialist and other societies, often characterized by emerging markets and fragile political systems, the series identifies and analyzes factors influencing change and continuity in societies and political orders. These factors include state capacity to establish formal and informal rules, democratic institutions, forms of social structuration, political regimes, levels of corruption, specificity of political cultures, as well as types and orientation of political and economic elites.

Societies and Political Orders in Transition welcomes monographs and edited volumes with diverse empirical and theoretical approaches from a variety of disciplines, including political science, economics and social sciences in general, as well as comparative politics, political history, political theory, comparative social research, and comparative economics in particular.

Topics may include, but are not limited to, democratization, regime change, changing social norms, migration, etc.

All titles in this series are peer-reviewed.

This book series is indexed in Scopus.

For further information on the series and to submit a proposal for consideration, please contact Johannes Glaeser (Senior Editor Economics and Political Science) Johannes.glaeser@springer.com.

Paskal Zhelev

Bulgaria in the Global Economy

Dynamics, Challenges, and Opportunities

Springer

Paskal Zhelev
Department of International Economic Relations and Business,
Faculty of International Economics and Politics
University of National and World Economy
Sofia, Bulgaria

ISSN 2511-2201 ISSN 2511-221X (electronic)
Societies and Political Orders in Transition
ISBN 978-3-031-87922-7 ISBN 978-3-031-87923-4 (eBook)
https://doi.org/10.1007/978-3-031-87923-4

This work was supported by American-Bulgarian Fulbright Commission

This Springer imprint is published by the registered company Springer Nature Switzerland AG
The registered company address is: Gewerbestrasse 11, 6330 Cham, Switzerland

Acknowledgments

Special acknowledgment goes to the **Fulbright Commission** for the Fulbright Bulgaria Alumni Grant, whose support has been instrumental in the realization of this academic monograph, as well as to those who offered invaluable insights and feedback on the manuscript, including the anonymous reviewers.

Competing Interests The author declares the following as potential competing interests: This book was supported by the Fulbright Bulgaria Alumni Grant. The author has no other conflicts of interest to declare that are relevant to the content of this book.

Contents

Abbreviations

CBA	Currency Board Arrangement
GDP	Gross Domestic Product
EU	European Union
COMECON	Council for Mutual Economic Assistance
FDI	Foreign Direct Investment
GVC	Global Value Chains
ICT	Information and Communication Technology
BPO	Business Process Outsourcing
R&D	Research and Development
DESI	Digital Economy and Society Index
IUS	Innovation Union Scoreboard
GHG	Greenhouse Gas
JTM	Just Transition Mechanism
AI	Artificial Intelligence
IoT	Internet of Things
SME	Small- and Medium-sized Enterprises
S3	Smart Specialization Strategy
EV	Electric Vehicle

List of Figures

List of Tables

Chapter 1
Introduction

The global economy of the twenty-first century is defined by unprecedented complexity, shaped by the dual forces of integration and fragmentation. Technological progress and digitalization have intensified interdependence and reshaped production networks, while geopolitical tensions—exemplified by the US-China rivalry and the ramifications of Russia's war in Ukraine—have propelled economic nationalism, regional realignments, and a renewed emphasis on self-sufficiency. In parallel, worldwide commitments to sustainability and the push for green energy underscore the urgency of low-carbon transitions, which demand substantial investment in infrastructure, innovation, and workforce retraining. These overlapping trends generate both opportunities and risks, particularly for smaller economies that must adapt swiftly or risk marginalization.

For countries like Bulgaria, a limited market size and a legacy of reliance on dominant partners amplify external vulnerabilities. Yet this very environment also presents opportunities: Bulgaria's integration into the European Union grants it access to extensive markets and resources, while the rapid digital shift can spark local innovation. Moreover, the green agenda can serve as a catalyst for diversifying the economy and developing new industries. The interplay of these forces prompts fundamental questions about the best strategies for small states to achieve competitiveness, strengthen resilience, and ensure forward-looking development amid shifting global alliances and market transformations.

Bulgaria in the Global Economy: Dynamics, Challenges, and Opportunities examines these questions through a comprehensive analysis of Bulgaria's past transitions, current realities, and future prospects. The volume explores how global megatrends—geopolitical realignment, climate imperatives, and digitalization—intersect with national-level strategies, shedding light on potential pathways for sustainable development. Utilizing robust data, detailed graphs, and insightful case studies, this volume charts Bulgaria's economic evolution and its integration into global trade in goods and services, investment flows, and labor markets while also

P. Zhelev, *Bulgaria in the Global Economy*, Societies and Political Orders in Transition, https://doi.org/10.1007/978-3-031-87923-4_1

examining its role in regional economic integration and cooperation, particularly within the European Union and the Black Sea region.

Bulgaria's experience offers a unique window into the challenges of small-state integration in the global economy. Historically, the country has alternated between different external partnerships and economic paradigms in its pursuit of development. Initially centered on agrarian production and aligned with German markets, Bulgaria shifted toward heavy industry and later electronics under Soviet-style planning—only to undergo swift liberalization and rapid deindustrialization in the years of systemic transformation and European Union integration. These abrupt transitions—from rigid central planning to market-driven reforms and from one dominant partner to another—have heightened vulnerability to external shocks and limited the cultivation of a diversified, resilient economy. Further, Bulgaria's tendency to adopt external economic models without fully tailoring them to local conditions has often resulted in uneven growth, institutional fragility, and persistent obstacles to achieving long-term dynamism.

This monograph contends that neither isolation and protectionism nor blind liberalization has adequately served Bulgaria's long-term interests. Instead, it argues for a measured, strategic approach that combines the advantages of global participation with policies aligned to local capacities and development priorities. By critically reviewing Bulgaria's historical missteps and successes, the book underscores the value of aligning foreign economic relations with national strengths, suggesting that innovative, adaptive policymaking is key to unlocking sustainable growth.

Nor does the analysis shy away from addressing institutional weaknesses or missed opportunities. Yet this is not solely a narrative of challenges. Bulgaria enjoys distinct advantages: a strategic location linking Europe and Asia, a budding ICT sector, and a workforce that adapts quickly to global demands. Learning from its own history and investing in consistent, forward-thinking policies can help Bulgaria forge a more resilient path, offering broader lessons for other small economies grappling with the complexities of the global economic landscape.

1.1 Structure and Roadmap

The monograph is organized into 13 chapters, each addressing a critical aspect of Bulgaria's economic evolution and interactions with the global economy.

After the Introduction, Chap. 2, *Dependent Pathways: The Historical Evolution of Bulgaria's Economy*, outlines Bulgaria's economic trajectory from independence through the socialist period to the transition to a market economy. This historical foundation is essential for understanding the persistent structural challenges and opportunities that shape Bulgaria's current economic landscape. It argues that Bulgaria's overreliance on dominant external partners and the adoption of misaligned economic models have hindered sustainable growth.

Chapter 3, *Macroeconomic Foundations*, analyzes Bulgaria's macroeconomic environment, including key indicators such as GDP growth, inflation, and public debt within the current framework of the Currency Board Arrangement. It analyzes the fiscal and monetary policies in the face of global disruptions and Bulgaria's path toward Eurozone accession.

Chapters 4, 5, and 6 focus on Bulgaria's foreign economic relations. Chapter 4, *Bulgaria's Integration in the EU*, evaluates the benefits and challenges of EU membership, emphasizing that while EU integration has catalyzed economic transformation, it is not a guarantee of convergence without sustained national efforts. Chapter 5, *Bulgaria and Regional Cooperation in the Black Sea Region*, explores Bulgaria's role in regional economic initiatives and the geopolitical complexities of the area. Chapter 6, *Foreign Economic Relations with Key Global Players*, examines Bulgaria's strategic partnerships with global actors such as the EU, the USA, and China, highlighting how these relationships influence the country's economic prospects.

Chapters 7, 8, 9, 10, and 11 delve into specific aspects of Bulgaria's international economic engagement. *Bulgarian Foreign Trade in Goods* (Chap. 7) and *Services* (Chap. 8) provide comprehensive analyses of trade patterns, competitiveness, and structural transformation. Chapter 9, *Bulgaria's Participation in Global Value Chains (GVCs)*, assesses the country's role in international production networks, while Chap. 10, *Foreign Direct Investment in Bulgaria*, critiques the passive approach toward FDI and calls for proactive policies to maximize benefits. Chapter 11, *Bulgaria's Participation in International Labor Migration*, addresses the dual nature of labor migration, balancing the challenges of brain drain with the opportunities presented by remittances and returning talent.

The final chapters focus on emerging trends and future opportunities. Chapter 12, *Technological Advancement of the Bulgarian Economy in the Era of Digitalization*, evaluates the progress and challenges in digital transformation, while Chap. 13, *Green Transformation: Bulgaria's Path in the Energy Transition Process*, examines the opportunities and barriers in transitioning to a green economy. The concluding chapter synthesizes these threads, offering policy recommendations for enhancing Bulgaria's global competitiveness.

1.2 Significance of the Book

This monograph offers a thorough, structured analysis that spans Bulgaria's historical legacies, contemporary challenges, and forward-looking opportunities. By situating Bulgaria's journey within broader global debates on state intervention, trade dependencies, and technological change, the book enriches our understanding of how small states can navigate an increasingly complex international landscape.

For scholars, it fills a gap by presenting empirical data and comparative analyses that connect macro-level processes with sectoral developments, providing a detailed case study of a small economy grappling with external realignments. For policymakers, it underlines the risks inherent in relying too heavily on dominant partners or oversimplified market solutions and highlights instead the need for calibrated, context-sensitive policies.

In a world where shifting geopolitical fault lines, sustainability imperatives, and digital disruption are redefining economic paradigms, *Bulgaria in the Global Economy* offers timely insights into how a strategically balanced approach—rooted in both domestic strengths and international cooperation—can enable smaller countries to become more resilient, innovative, and competitive on the global stage.

Chapter 2
Dependent Pathways: The Historical Evolution of Bulgaria's Economy

2.1 Introduction

Bulgaria's economic history provides a crucial foundation for understanding its evolving role in the global economy. Over the past century and a half, the country has undergone profound transformations, repeatedly reorienting its economic policies in response to shifting geopolitical and economic forces. A recurring theme throughout this trajectory has been Bulgaria's reliance on a dominant external economic partner—first Germany before WWII, then the Soviet Union during the socialist period, and later the European Union. At the same time, Bulgaria has frequently adopted foreign economic models that were not always suited to its domestic realities, leading to structural inefficiencies and significant economic disruptions.

This chapter examines three critical phases in Bulgaria's economic evolution. The first section explores the postliberation period (1878–1945), when Bulgaria sought to establish an independent economic foundation but became increasingly dependent on Germany as its primary trade and industrial partner. The second section analyzes the socialist era (1945–1989), during which Bulgaria operated a centrally planned economy as a member of the Council for Mutual Economic Assistance (COMECON). While this period saw significant industrial development, particularly in machinery and electronics, it also deepened the country's structural dependence on the Soviet system. The final section examines the post-1989 transition to a market economy, characterized by rapid liberalization and integration into global markets. While these reforms spurred economic modernization, they also resulted in severe economic volatility, deindustrialization, and social upheaval.

By providing a historical perspective on Bulgaria's economic transformations, this chapter offers deeper insight into the long-term structural factors shaping the country's contemporary economic landscape. Moreover, it highlights recurring challenges that remain relevant today, particularly as the global economic

P. Zhelev, *Bulgaria in the Global Economy*, Societies and Political Orders in Transition, https://doi.org/10.1007/978-3-031-87923-4_2

environment faces increasing uncertainty. Bulgaria's experience underscores the risks associated with both economic isolation and unprepared liberalization—lessons that are especially pertinent in an era of rising protectionism and shifting global trade dynamics.

2.1.1 Bulgarian Economy After the Liberation in 1878 Till the End of WWII

The period from 1878 to 1945 was transformative for Bulgaria, marking its reemergence as an independent state after five centuries under Ottoman rule. During this time, Bulgaria navigated the complexities of postliberation economic reconstruction, urgent need for modernization, two world wars, and interwar economic challenges. The trajectory of Bulgaria's economic development was shaped by protectionist policies, failed industrialization attempts, and an increasing dependence on Germany in the 1930s. These structural transformations had lasting implications for Bulgaria's position in the global economy.

At the outset of its Liberation from the Ottoman Empire, Bulgaria was confronted with a starkly underdeveloped economy. The country's economic foundation was predominantly based on agriculture, which even saw a decline of large-scale farming operations and shift toward subsistence agriculture as the Liberation reduced the burdens on the peasantry and gave it greater access to land. While the remnants of Bulgarian proto-industry did provide a basis for factory manufacturing, this sector was, at the time, of minimal significance (Palairet, 1997).

Bulgaria's early trade policies were constrained by the Treaty of Berlin (1878), which imposed the so-called "trade capitulations"—commercial agreements that the Ottoman Empire had previously signed with European powers. These treaties enforced a free trade regime, limiting ad valorem duties to a maximum of 8% (Lozanov, 2014). As a result, Bulgaria was unable to implement protectionist policies in its formative economic years, leaving domestic producers extremely vulnerable to foreign competition. The influx of manufactured goods from Western Europe led to the decline of traditional crafts, further entrenching Bulgaria's agricultural dependency.

The expiration of these obligations in 1890 marked a turning point. Bulgaria pursued bilateral agreements with major European powers, securing most favored nation (MFN) status with England, Germany, Belgium, Switzerland, France, Austro-Hungary, Italy, Russia, Greece, and Turkey. This allowed the imposition of higher import duties (10.5–14%), providing some protection for domestic industries (Berend, 2003).

By the late 1890s, Bulgaria further escalated its protective measures, imposing duties of 14–25% on goods that directly competed with local products (Lozanov, 2014). The drive for protectionist policies stemmed from the quest to create a modern economy virtually from scratch. Moreover, there was a stark necessity of diversifying the production structure and overcoming the critical reliance on a small number of commodities. The economy's overdependence on the export of one or two staples made it extremely vulnerable to global market fluctuations and poor harvests, hampering long-term economic growth and stability. The volatile and worsening terms of trade put under heavy pressure the income of the peasant population and their demand for basic goods. Primary commodities constituted 95.7% of all exports, and almost 91% were grains in 1886–1900, characterizing Bulgaria as a "wheat and maize economy" (Ivanov & Kopsidis, 2023, p. 176).

Challenges to Industrialization: Structural Weaknesses and Policy Failures

A key debate in Bulgaria's economic policy in the late nineteenth and early twentieth centuries revolved around the distribution of state support between the agricultural and industrial sectors. While agriculture was the backbone of the economy, policymakers recognized the necessity of industrialization to reduce its vulnerability to external market fluctuations. The prevailing strategy sought to create a symbiotic relationship where the growth of one sector would stimulate development in the other, with a rough consensus that industrialization is a necessary step toward economic modernization, influenced by the ideas of Friedrich List and the German example. Policymakers agreed to try to support the development of modern industry while safeguarding agriculture and artisanal interests (Lampe, 1986).

Bulgaria's industrialization efforts were significantly hampered due to a combination of structural economic weaknesses, insufficient capital, and ineffective state policies. The industrial sector suffered from limited access to credit, as the banking system prioritized short-term commercial lending rather than long-term industrial investment (Gerschenkron, 1962). The absence of a robust financial sector meant that businesses lacked the necessary funding for modernization, forcing many enterprises to remain small and technologically outdated (Dimitrov, 2018b).

Foreign capital, though present, was insufficient to drive Bulgaria toward a significant industrial breakthrough. It remained concentrated in low-value-added industries such as sugar, brewing, milling, cement, and textiles rather than fostering a diversified industrial base (Milkova, 2018). Foreign investors prioritized quick returns over long-term development, neglecting sectors that required substantial investment and technological advancement. As a result, while some industries benefited, the broader industrial sector remained underdeveloped and dependent on outdated production methods.

A key limiting factor was the very small domestic market, composed of subsistence farmers with limited purchasing power, that hindered the ability of industrial enterprises to achieve economies of scale. The widespread land ownership, while preventing extreme poverty, hindered the development of a labor market necessary for industrial growth (Sabev, 2024). Unlike other late-industrializing European countries, Bulgaria lacked a substantial urban working class that could serve as both producers and consumers of manufactured goods, further constraining industrial growth.

To address these challenges, successive Bulgarian governments combined trade protectionism with direct industrial support, using tariff barriers to shield domestic industries while granting state incentives to encourage industry. The Law on the Promotion of Local Industry (1895) was the first major legislative attempt to stimulate industrial growth. It offered tax exemptions for 15 years, duty-free imports of machinery and raw materials unavailable in Bulgaria, reduced freight rates by 35%, free government land for factory construction, and preferential treatment in state procurement, allowing Bulgarian goods to be 15% more expensive than foreign competitors (Georgieva, 2021, p. 125).

The industrial promotion law was expanded in 1905, 1909, and 1928, with each iteration maintaining similar incentives but increasing their magnitude while imposing stricter requirements for capital investment, workforce size, technological modernization, and social protection compliance to qualify for state support (Dimitrov, 2018b). Despite these refinements, Bulgaria's industrial policies failed to strategically prioritize industries capable of driving sustainable economic growth. Instead, they continued to reinforce traditional sectors, leading to overcapitalization in industries such as flour milling, textiles, ceramics, and construction materials. This misallocation of resources created inefficiencies, with production capacity exceeding market demand in some industries while others remained underdeveloped. Economists like Konstantin Bobchev criticized these distortions, advocating for a reallocation of state incentives toward new industries to foster diversification and technological advancement (Parvanova, 2018). However, these recommendations were largely ignored as powerful industrial lobbies resisted the removal of privileges, further undermining the state's ability to establish clear industrial priorities.

Instead of fostering innovation and competitiveness, these laws often created industries reliant on state intervention, unable to withstand external shocks or integrate effectively into global markets (Dimitrov, 2018b). Bulgaria's industrialization thus remained fragmented, with the absence of a coherent long-term strategy hampering its ability to transition to a more modern and resilient economy.

Besides structural weaknesses and inefficient state intervention, Bulgaria's industrialization efforts were further undermined by unfavorable external conditions, particularly the Balkan Wars (1912–1913) and WWI (1914–1918), which diverted resources toward military expenditures and disrupted trade. During the war years, the state imposed export and import bans to ensure economic self-sufficiency, yet the postwar settlement left Bulgaria economically vulnerable. The Treaty of Neuilly (1919) forced the country to pay reparations, revert to prewar import rates, and extend MFN treatment on a nonreciprocal basis for 5 years (Lozanov, 2014).

In response, the Stamboliyski government pursued agricultural protectionism, exemplified by the Corn Consortium, which controlled grain trade to safeguard farmers (Lampe & Jackson, 1982). By 1926, Bulgaria had returned to highly protectionist policies, with tariff levels rising three to five times above prewar levels. The Great Depression reinforced this stance, prompting increased export bonuses, higher tariffs, exchange restrictions, and licensing systems (Berend, 2006). State intervention intensified with the creation of the Directorate of Grain Export (1930)

Table 2.1 Structure of Bulgarian exports, 1907–1930 (in %)

Products/period	*1907–1911*	*1921–1925*	*1926–1930*
Grains	55.7	23.4	14.5
Grain products	7.5	4.1	3.0
Other unprocessed crops	17.2	5.6	6.4
Tobacco	1.3	26.5	38.5
Rose essence	4.1	1.4	3.5
Eggs	7.6	8.1	12.4
Livestock	5.6	3.1	4.4
Crude hides	2.2	2.0	4.4
Other	8.8	25.8	12.9

Source: Lampe and Jackson (1982, p. 368)

and the Bulgarian Agrarian Cooperative Bank's monopoly over tobacco and rose oil exports.

This prolonged reliance on trade restrictions and state monopolies shielded domestic industries but failed to foster competitive industrialization, keeping Bulgaria locked into low-value-added production while limiting technological advancement and economic diversification. The outcomes of the government's trade and industrial promotion endeavors are manifest in the transformation of the nation's export composition (see Table 2.1).

Although there was a significant reduction in the proportion of grain exports, from 55.7% during 1907–1911 to 14.5% by 1926–1930, the shift in export dynamics primarily highlighted a reorientation toward higher-value and more market-responsive crops within the agricultural sector rather than a substantial move toward the industrial sector. The remarkable increase in tobacco exports, rising to 38.5% of the country's total exports by the end of the 1920s, signifies a strategic adaptation to global market demands. However, this adaptation did not equate to industrial advancement. Instead, the economy continued to be characterized by its agricultural base, with the export list prominently featuring agricultural goods such as eggs, livestock, and crude hides, alongside the dominant tobacco. This continued agricultural orientation shaped Bulgaria's trade patterns, setting the stage for an increasing dependence on Germany as a key trading partner.

The Shift in Trade Relations and Dependence on Germany

The aftermath of WWI heralded a pivotal shift in the geographical orientation of Bulgaria's foreign trade. Prior to the conflict, Western European countries followed by the neighboring countries were Bulgaria's primary trading partners, but afterward, there was a profound redirection toward Central European countries and mostly Germany.

This pronounced reorientation reflects several underlying factors including both economic imperatives and political affinities that emerged during the interwar

Table 2.2 Bulgaria's trade dependence on Germany in the 1930s (in % of total)

	Exports		Imports	
	1933	*1939*	*1933*	*1939*
Bulgaria	36.0	71.1	38.2	69.5
Hungary	11.2	52.4	19.6	52.5
Romania	16.6	43.1	18.6	56.1
Yugoslavia	13.9	45.9	13.2	53.2

Source: Berend (2006, p. 127)

period. The mutual economic interests of Bulgaria and Germany were reinforced by shared political and strategic interests, which included Germany's search for reliable sources of agricultural products and raw materials as well as Bulgaria's need for a strong economic partner to aid its own economic recovery and industrial ambitions. Furthermore, during the Great Depression, many countries have instituted various trade and payment restrictions, which made the clearing agreement signed by Bulgaria and Germany in 1932[1] more beneficial for both parties. This agreement allowed for bilateral trade to continue smoothly despite the challenging economic conditions, ultimately strengthening the economic ties between the two countries.

Table 2.2 shows that between 1933 and 1939, Bulgarian exports to Germany nearly doubled as a percentage of total exports, surging from 36.0% to an overwhelming 71.1%.[2] Similarly, imports from Germany saw a substantial increase from 38.2 to 69.5% of total imports in the same period. While other Southeastern European countries also reoriented their trade toward Germany, Bulgaria's reliance was particularly stark. By 1939, Bulgaria had become extremely dependent on German trade, more so than its regional neighbors. This pronounced dependency highlighted Bulgaria's vulnerability to the economic and political dictates of Germany, with far-reaching implications for its sovereignty and economic policy as Europe edged closer to another major conflict.

WWII saw the Bulgarian government assuming full control over foreign trade through various bureaucratic entities, including the Department of Foreign Trade and the Directorate of Civil Mobilization. This move was emblematic of a broader trend throughout the early to mid-twentieth century, where the Bulgarian state exercised substantial intervention in the economy and foreign trade, viewing such measures as essential for national security and economic stability. The establishment of these entities and the centralization of trade controls were indicative of a governmental strategy to manage the economic challenges posed by the war, aiming to streamline resources, prioritize essential imports and exports, and mitigate the impacts of global market disruptions. This period of heightened control was part of a continuum of state intervention that began in the early decades of the twentieth century, reflecting a persistent belief in the necessity of a strong state role in guiding

[1] A second clearing agreement between the two parties was signed in 1940.

[2] It should be noted that part of the increase reflects the accession of Austria and Czechoslovakia to the Third Reich in 1938.

and protecting the nation's economic interests amidst the uncertainties of international conflicts and the fluctuating global economy.

Throughout the decade leading up to the end of WWII, Bulgaria, with its modest, agrarian-based economy, experienced a consistent trade surplus with the technologically superior German economy. This surplus, however, was largely nominal, representing an outflow of goods that contributed to a growing ledger of unsettled accounts, as Germany's wartime endeavors led to accumulating debts rather than immediate payments. The cessation of hostilities left Bulgaria with significant outstanding German debt of 75 billion leva that was never recovered (Lozanov, 2014), showcasing the perils of an excessive dependency on a single partner. This overreliance on the German economy not only exposed Bulgaria to economic vulnerabilities due to the imbalance but also tied its fate closely to the fortunes of Germany. The consequences of such an economic and political relationship served as a cautionary tale for the risks associated with a lack of diversification in foreign trade partners.

2.1.2 Bulgaria in the Socialist Period

Following the conclusion of WWII, Bulgaria found itself within the Soviet sphere of influence, a shift that drastically altered its societal, economic, and political structures. The governance of Bulgaria was firmly in the hands of the Bulgarian Communist Party, which, like its Soviet counterpart, discouraged political pluralism or dissent and maintained a monopoly on power. This allowed implementation of various policies to fully reshape the country, ushering in a new era of socioeconomic reformation and state-led development experimentation.

Economic Model and Industrialization Under Socialism

A centerpiece of this transformative period is the realignment toward the Soviet model of a command economy characterized by centralized planning and stringent top-down governance of the economic decision-making. The industries were nationalized (98% of the companies already in 1947) and operated under the control of the state, while agriculture was organized into collective farms (collectivization started in 1948 and was completed in 1958), eliminating private ownership of production means (Lampe, 1986). The State Planning Committee, reminiscent of the Soviet Union's Gosplan, assumed a pivotal role in this structure, dictating production targets, allocating resources—including labor—and making crucial investment decisions, based on 5-year plans.[3] As in the other centrally planned economies, the mechanisms of the market played a subordinate role, with wages and prices predominantly determined by administrative decisions.

[3] The first 5-year plan, set to be realized in less than 5 years, was for the period 1949–1952.

In 1949 Bulgaria, together with Czechoslovakia, Hungary, Poland, Romania, and USSR, became a founding member of the Council of Mutual Economic Assistance (CMEA, also COMECON)[4]—the economic integration organization of the Eastern bloc. The COMECON tried to promote economic cooperation and coordination of economic plans among its member states, with the goal of developing a socialist international division of labor. It allowed the Soviet Union to exert control over Eastern European countries, including Bulgaria, by centralizing economic planning and redirecting trade toward the Soviet Union. Additionally, the creation of a "ruble zone" standardized financial relations across the region by adopting the ruble as a common unit of account. This insulated Bulgaria and other Eastern European countries from world prices, further consolidating Soviet economic and political control and reinforcing their economic decoupling from the West (Zhu, 2023).

Despite the lack of significant raw materials endowments, capital, and technologies, Bulgaria has started its industrialization process with a strong emphasis on heavy industry. This approach, which involved import substitution policy and massive state investment, was consistent with the Stalinist belief that industrial strength was the backbone of socialist economic independence. The Soviet Union provided extensive economic and technical assistance, which included credits, raw materials, technology transfers, and the dispatch of experts (NATO, 1973). Soviet oil and gas imports played a crucial role in sustaining industrial expansion. The forced collectivization of agriculture led to hasty urbanization and freed up the needed labor, supplying the growing labor demand in factories and construction sites.

The centralized resource allocation combined with Soviet technical support brought about rapid industrialization driven by the expansion of metallurgy, machine-building, and chemical production. By 1960, machinery and equipment had already begun to feature prominently in Bulgaria's exports, constituting 12.9% of total exports, a dramatic shift from 1950 when agricultural commodities and food dominated at over 80% (Table 2.3). Food-processing industries remained a priority due to their importance for the trade balance, maintaining over 30% of Bulgarian exports in the 1960s. The improvement of the production structure toward more sophisticated goods reflected the early success of industrial policies.

However, the remarkable initial industrial growth was mostly based on extensive factors—the large-scale construction of industrial facilities, the expansion of labor inputs, and increased use of natural resources. Moreover, this industrial policy model relied heavily on imported raw materials and energy inputs. While initially manageable, this dependency became a significant burden following the dramatic rise in global oil prices in the mid-1970s. Thus, economic planners realized that there is a need for enhanced productivity through automation and technological modernization in the existing sectors and shift toward higher-value manufacturing. The state sought to increase production in less energy-intensive industries, such as electronics and consumer goods.

[4] COMECON expanded with Albania in 1949 (ceased participating in 1961), East Germany (1950), Mongolia (1962), Cuba (1972), and Vietnam (1978).

Table 2.3 Product structure of Bulgarian exports (1950–1989, in %)

Product groups	1950	1960	1970	1980	1989
Machinery and equipment	0	12.9	29	44.4	59.4
Fuels, minerals, and metals	8.4	9.2	8.1	15	7.7
Chemicals, fertilizers, and rubber	0.4	2.2	3.4	4.1	3.4
Construction materials	1.8	0.6	1.1	2.1	2
Inedible raw materials	7.3	5.8	3.8	1.6	1.8
Livestock	0	0	0	0	0.1
Food inputs	50.5	19.7	8.4	4.9	2.2
Food	30	30.9	31.2	17.9	11.7
Consumer goods	1.6	17.9	14.7	8.8	11.1

Source: Central Statistical Office

Bulgaria's integration into COMECON played a crucial role in shaping its industrial priorities, aligning its economy with the broader socialist division of labor. In the 1960s, COMECON introduced coordinated specialization agreements to enhance efficiency and optimize resource allocation among member states. Within this framework, Bulgaria was designated to focus on agriculture and food processing, chemical fertilizers, and small electrical equipment, reinforcing its role in regional economic integration (Library of Congress, 1992). Leveraging the secured markets and industrial policy shift toward higher-value-added sectors, Bulgaria rapidly expanded its technological sector. By the 1980s, it had emerged as the Eastern Bloc's leading producer of computers and electronics, most notably through the *Pravetz* series (see Box 2.1). Western analysts recognized the advantages of COMECON's framework for Bulgaria, noting that it had developed its technological sector "practically from nothing" (Paraskevov, 2016). By the late 1980s, machinery and equipment accounted for nearly 60% of Bulgaria's total exports, underscoring the depth of its industrial transformation.

Box 2.1 Bulgaria: The Socialist Bloc's Computing Powerhouse

During the socialist period, Bulgaria earned the nickname the "Silicon Valley of the Eastern Bloc" due to its dominant role in computing and electronics production (Lepage & Kolarova, 2005, p. 15). By the late 1980s, the country was responsible for producing approximately 40% of all computers in the Eastern Bloc, with the sector's annual value exceeding $13 billion. Bulgaria also had one of the highest per capita computer ownership rates in the world (BBC News, 2015).

This remarkable transformation from an agrarian economy to a high-tech powerhouse was driven by deliberate state policy, which positioned computing, automation, and cybernetics at the core of Bulgaria's modernization strategy (Petrov, 2023). The government heavily invested in research institutions and STEM education, cultivating a generation of engineers who became the backbone of an expanding electronics industry, producing mainframes, minicomputers, and personal computers that were widely used across COMECON countries. A crucial factor behind this success was Bulgaria's ability to acquire and replicate Western computing technologies, often circumventing Cold War trade restrictions through informal channels. The electronics sector became a showcase of socialist industrialization, solidifying Bulgaria's position within COMECON and enabling it to export technology to nonaligned nations. However, despite these achievements, the industry remained structurally dependent on imported components and was ultimately constrained by the inefficiencies of the planned economy. Nevertheless, the expertise developed during this period laid the foundation for Bulgaria's modern IT sector, which continues to be a key pillar of the country's post-socialist economy.

The industrial expansion in Bulgaria during the socialist period catalyzed profound social and economic transformations, driving economic growth, rapid urbanization, and the development of a highly skilled workforce. The emphasis on technical education and vocational training supplied industries with qualified personnel, fostering technological advancements in sectors such as electronics, engineering, and pharmaceuticals. A key achievement of the socialist model was the establishment of comprehensive social welfare programs, including universal healthcare, free education, and state-provided housing, which contributed to rising living standards and social stability. Industrialization also spurred modern infrastructure development, with improved transportation networks, expanded utilities, and urban modernization projects evident across all regional centers.

Structural Weaknesses of the Planned Economy and the Road to Its Collapse

The economic transformation of Bulgaria under socialism, while achieving rapid industrialization and social progress, came at a significant cost. These accomplishments were largely driven by a rigid system of central planning, extensive state intervention, and heavy reliance on external support from the Soviet Union. However, the same mechanisms that enabled Bulgaria's initial economic progress ultimately became the sources of its collapse.

One of the key weaknesses of the socialist economy was the misallocation of resources (Veleva, 2016). Central planning dictated investment priorities, emphasizing heavy industry and machinery production while neglecting consumer goods and services. Enterprises focused on fulfilling quotas rather than optimizing efficiency. Production continued even when it was unprofitable, sustained by state subsidies and credit extensions. The absence of market-driven incentives meant that inefficiencies became embedded in the system, reducing productivity and economic dynamism.

The lack of competition and reliance on secured markets within the Soviet-led COMECON further deepened inefficiencies. Since Bulgarian products were guaranteed a market in the Soviet Bloc, there was little incentive to improve quality or reduce costs. Unlike in market economies, where competition forces firms to innovate or fail, Bulgarian enterprises had no pressure to modernize. As a result, industries relied on outdated technology, and the quality of goods lagged behind Western standards. While Bulgaria became a significant exporter of machinery and industrial equipment, these products often remained technologically inferior and were intensive in foreign inputs.

The electronics industry particularly struggled with slow restructuring, frequent issues with product dimensions, quality, and reliability, which limited its competitiveness even within COMECON. A major constraint was its dependence on imported Western components, requiring hard currency, while its exports were primarily directed within COMECON and conducted in transferable rubles rather than convertible currencies (Berov & Dimitrov, 1990). This imbalance limited Bulgaria's ability to reinvest in technological advancements and made it difficult to compete outside the Socialist Bloc, where Western and Japanese manufacturers dominated.

A fundamental weakness of Bulgaria's economy was its excessive dependence on the USSR, making it highly vulnerable to external shocks originating from Moscow. The geographical orientation of Bulgarian exports illustrates this dependence as a primary export market (Table 2.4).

Throughout the socialist period, over 50% of Bulgaria's exports went to the USSR. By 1989, this figure had actually increased to nearly 60%, highlighting the country's growing vulnerability to Soviet economic conditions. Despite some trade with Western countries and developing economies, Bulgaria never developed a significant foothold in global markets outside of the Socialist Bloc. This economic dependence meant that any crisis in the Soviet economy or shifts in Soviet policy would have immediate and profound consequences for Bulgaria. As the Soviet Union itself faced economic stagnation and growing inefficiencies in the 1980s, the foundations of Bulgaria's socialist economy began to erode.

Already in the mid-1970s, Bulgaria's economy was severely strained due to the energy crises and oil price shocks. When global oil prices surged, Bulgaria's terms of trade dramatically worsened (Znepolski et al., 2019). This meant that Bulgaria had to export increasing volumes of machinery and industrial goods to afford essential energy imports, exacerbating economic pressures.

Table 2.4 Geographical orientation of Bulgarian exports (1950–1989, in %)

Group of countries	1950	1960	1970	1980	1989
COMECON countries	88.7	80.5	74.1	72.7	79.0
Incl. USSR	52.2	53.1	53.0	53.5	59.2
Other socialist countries	–	3.4	3.7	2.0	1.6
Developed capitalist countries	10.3	13.2	16.6	16.5	12.4
Developing countries	1.0	2.9	5.6	8.8	7.0

Source: Central Statistical Office

To maintain growth and compensate for inefficiencies, Bulgaria increasingly turned to foreign borrowing. By the mid-1980s, Bulgaria had accumulated significant debt to Western financial institutions, further exposing the economy to external vulnerabilities. As shortages of consumer goods became more common and living standards stagnated, public dissatisfaction with the planned economy grew. The inefficiencies of the system became more visible to ordinary citizens, undermining confidence in the state. The external debt of Bulgaria has surged from 2 billion USD in 1975 to 10.7 billion USD in 1989, while the "external debt to exports" ratio increased from 63% in 1981 to staggering 156% in 1989 (Gomes, 2021, p. 10), projecting the collapse of the system.

By the end of 1989, the economic and political pressures culminated in the fall of the socialist regime. The rigidities of central planning, inefficiencies of state enterprises, lack of competition, and dependence on Soviet trade created an economic model that could not sustain itself once external conditions changed. As Bulgaria transitioned to a market economy, it was forced to reckon with the deep-seated inefficiencies and vulnerabilities of its socialist past, setting the stage for the economic and social upheavals of the 1990s.

2.1.3 The Transition to a Market Economy

Bulgaria's transition to a market economy in the early 1990s started under especially unfavorable conditions. The collapse of the Eastern Bloc abruptly cut off its primary export markets within COMECON, leading to a sharp contraction in industrial output and a dramatic fall in foreign exchange earnings. This vulnerability was exacerbated by Bulgaria's reliance on energy-intensive industries ill-prepared for the shift to world market prices. Adding to the crisis was the burden of external debt, which had tripled in the 1980s due to extensive borrowing from Western banks to prop up inefficient industries. By 1989, this debt in hard currencies exceeded three times the value of exports, while servicing costs consumed nearly four-fifths of earnings from convertible currency exports (Levinson, 1995), rendering repayment unsustainable after the loss of COMECON trade.

Shock Therapy vs. Gradualism: The Bulgarian Path

In March 1990, facing an unsustainable external debt burden and a severe shortage of foreign exchange reserves, the Bulgarian government declared a moratorium on foreign debt payments, effectively defaulting on its obligations. The repercussions were immediate and far-reaching—Bulgaria was cut off from international credit markets, exacerbating its financial situation and leaving the country with no independent means of stabilizing its economy. Deprived of access to private capital, Bulgaria had no alternative but to turn to the International Monetary Fund (IMF) for emergency assistance. But this help came at a cost: not a direct one, as IMF loans carried interest rates lower than prevailing market rates, but because of the stringent economic restructuring conditions—commonly referred to as "IMF conditionality."

At the time, both the IMF and the World Bank adhered to the Washington Consensus framework, which prescribed a standard set of neoliberal reforms for distressed economies. In short they required deregulation of prices, privatization of state-owned enterprises, and trade liberalization and prioritized macroeconomic stabilization while neglecting the broader institutional and structural foundations necessary for a functional market economy (Rodrik, 2006). While some CEE countries that did not require IMF assistance were able to choose how to proceed with the transformation process, Bulgaria, constrained by its severe debt crisis and reliance on IMF support, had little room for maneuver.

The transition from centrally planned to market economies in CEE sparked debate over shock therapy versus gradualism. Shock therapy, with rapid liberalization and privatization, aimed for swift market integration but often led to recession, high unemployment, and corruption and institutional failures (Marangos, 2005). In contrast, gradualism emphasized phased reforms, allowing institutions to evolve alongside market mechanisms, as seen in countries like Slovenia and Hungary. This approach minimized social disruptions and facilitated more stable economic transitions. However, its drawbacks included prolonged inefficiencies, slower structural adjustments, and the risk of policy stagnation (Brada, 1993). The CEE experience demonstrates that neither approach is universally superior; rather, long-term success depended on institutional resilience, historical context, and policy coherence. Economic transitions were ultimately path-dependent, meaning that once a country embarks on a particular reform path, it may be more beneficial to continue on that path rather than switching strategies midcourse (Popov, 2010).

However, Bulgaria's early transition was defined by a lack of institutional stability and policy continuity, undermining its shift to a market economy. Following the IMF recommendations, the country initially adopted shock therapy, starting in February 1991. It swiftly liberalized prices, reduced subsidies, dismantled import and export restrictions, and rendered the lev convertible (Djankov & Hoekman, 1998). Despite the tight monetary and fiscal policies adopted, the abrupt changes fueled hyperinflation, which reached 334%, while GDP shrank by 16.7% and unemployment surged from virtually zero to 11% in 1991 (Levinson, 1995). Consumer goods became more available, and private businesses started to emerge, but the social costs were immense, with real wages collapsing and financial uncertainty escalating.

A deeper challenge, however, lays in the rapid dismantling of the communist-era institutional framework without an effective replacement (Dobrinsky, 2013). Rather than a structured transition, Bulgaria's institutional collapse left a vacuum, weakening the state's regulatory functions and encouraging opportunistic behavior, financial mismanagement, and widespread corruption. With no clear framework to support new market institutions, reform efforts became erratic and unpredictable.

At the same time, former elites exploited this institutional breakdown, using their political influence to capture economic resources rather than foster market reforms

(Ganev, 2007). This further undermined the state's ability to regulate markets, enforce property rights, and guide economic transformation, making Bulgaria's transition more chaotic than in Central Europe.

Political instability further exacerbated this institutional fragility. Frequent shifts in government led to conflicting policy directions, preventing long-term economic planning. As different political factions pursued their own short-term agendas, Bulgaria's transition lacked strategic coherence, making structural reforms difficult to sustain.

By mid-1992, Bulgaria abandoned shock therapy in favor of a more gradual approach. Without strong domestic support or an effective implementation strategy, the IMF stabilization programs frequently faltered, and between 1991 and 1996, none of Bulgaria's IMF agreements reached successful completion (Minassian, 2001). While trade and price liberalization were largely achieved, the third pillar of the Washington Consensus—privatization—stalled. By 1995 only 10% of SOEs were privatized (Djankov & Hoekman, 1998).

Political resistance, weak institutional capacity, and widespread corruption hampered the process, leaving many state enterprises in limbo, neither fully restructured nor efficiently managed. Instead of fostering a competitive private sector, delays in privatization prolonged economic inefficiencies, allowed asset stripping by insiders, and created a climate of uncertainty that discouraged foreign direct investment. Unlike other CEE that used FDI to drive economic restructuring and stabilize their balance of payments, Bulgaria saw minimal FDI inflows, averaging just 1% of GDP between 1989 and 1997 (World Bank, 2005).

With a stagnant economy and an underdeveloped private sector, Bulgaria's financial system became increasingly fragile. Banks, often politically connected and poorly supervised, issued risky loans to failing SOEs that had little chance of repayment. Without hard budget constraints or effective bankruptcy procedures, these enterprises continued to operate, deepening financial instability. As bad loans piled up, banks faced liquidity shortages, triggering deposit withdrawals and capital flight. The Bulgarian National Bank (BNB) failed to enforce adequate regulations, allowing these imbalances to grow unchecked, pushing the banking sector toward collapse.

By mid-1996, the banking crisis escalated into a full-scale financial and currency crisis. As depositors lost confidence, they withdrew savings and converted lev holdings into foreign currency, accelerating capital flight and currency depreciation. The government's persistent deficits, financed through domestic borrowing, fueled inflation, while the central bank's conflicting attempts to rescue banks and stabilize the lev drained foreign reserves. By early 1997, hyperinflation surpassed 2000% (Dobrinsky, 2000).

Economic paralysis sparked mass protests, some of which turned violent, culminating in the storming of the National Assembly. Facing mounting unrest and a collapsing economy, the government resigned, paving the way for the implementation of urgent stabilization measures.

In the aftermath of the crisis, Bulgaria secured an IMF-backed stabilization program, enforcing strict fiscal discipline and structural reforms. However, with institutions discredited and inflation unchecked, only a currency board arrangement (CBA) could restore confidence. Introduced in mid-1997, the CBA pegged the lev to the German mark (later the euro), eliminating independent monetary policy and tying money supply to foreign reserves. While rigid and highly conservative, this strict framework was the only way to rebuild trust, curb inflation, and stabilize the financial system.

After the introduction of the CBA, which served as a strong anchor for reform, Bulgaria quickly restored financial stability and brought inflation under control (Nenovsky, 2011). With monetary discipline enforced, fiscal responsibility and structural reforms became the focus. The government strengthened banking regulations, advanced privatization, and improved the business climate to attract investment. In 1999, the decision to start EU membership negotiations provided another powerful anchor, reinforcing Bulgaria's commitment to market economy transformation.

Unprepared for Open Markets: Trade Liberalization Without Industrial Strategy

Throughout Bulgaria's transition to a market economy, the primary objective of its trade policy was the systematic liberalization of its trade regime, pursued across multilateral, regional, and bilateral levels. A key milestone in this process was Bulgaria's accession to the World Trade Organization (WTO) on December 1, 1996, which was achieved under terms similar for other emerging economies (Ognivtsev, 2005). However, the country's most significant liberalization efforts were carried out through an extensive network of regional and bilateral free trade agreements, which played a crucial role in integrating Bulgaria into the global economy.

Bilateral trade liberalization was structured reciprocally, encompassing agreements with Albania, Bosnia and Herzegovina, Estonia, Israel, Latvia, Lithuania, Macedonia, Moldova, Serbia, Montenegro, and Turkey, most of which entered into force in the beginning of the 2000s. Additionally, Bulgaria joined the Central European Free Trade Agreement (CEFTA) in 1999, further strengthening its trade ties within the region. Despite these initiatives, the earliest, most strategic and consequential aspect of Bulgaria's trade policy was its economic relationship with the European Union, which was entirely subordinated to the overarching goal of achieving full EU membership.

Bulgaria's European Association Agreement (EAA) with the EU, signed on March 8, 1993, was meant to facilitate gradual integration into the European economy through a free trade area. Trade liberalization under the EAA was initially asymmetric: the EU committed to eliminating all tariffs on industrial products from Bulgaria by January 1, 1998, while Bulgaria retained some tariffs on EU industrial imports until 2002. This phased approach was intended to provide Bulgaria's industries time to adapt to competition with the EU companies. However, this structure fell short in significantly boosting Bulgarian exports to the EU. While Bulgarian companies gained nominal access to the European market, they faced substantial nontariff barriers, as exports to the EU were conditional upon meeting strict EU standards. For many Bulgarian producers, still hindered by technological and managerial limitations, these standards proved difficult to achieve. In contrast, EU businesses were able to capitalize on access to the Bulgarian market, despite the slower liberalization schedule. Consequently, what was intended as "asymmetric liberalization" resulted in a "reverse asymmetry" with EU producers enjoying a relative advantage and Bulgaria experiencing a growing trade deficit in manufactured goods, which also impacted its global trade balance (Lozanov & Zhivkova, 2017, p. 150). This dynamic undermined the competitiveness of Bulgaria's industrial base, accelerating the decline of key manufacturing sectors and contributing to premature deindustrialization, as domestic industries struggled to compete with the influx of more competitive imports from established EU producers (Zhelev, 2017).

Moreover, Bulgaria deliberately refrained from adopting an active industrial policy, placing unwavering faith in market forces as the primary driver of economic transformation. This approach was not merely a domestic policy choice but was reinforced by the dominant EU economic paradigm at the time, which, unlike today's more interventionist stance, was rooted in neoliberal principles of nonintervention and free market primacy.

Beyond ideological influence, the EU accession process itself imposed structural constraints on Bulgaria's ability to design an industrial strategy capable of mitigating the adverse effects of trade liberalization. As Barlett (2014) highlights, EU conditionality mandated a shift from vertical to horizontal industrial policies, meaning that Bulgaria was expected to dismantle sector-specific industrial support mechanisms in favor of a generic, competition-driven framework. This left the country unable to implement strategic state intervention in key industrial sectors—an approach that had been instrumental in the success of East Asian economies but was largely discouraged in the EU accession process.

An additional factor responsible for Bulgaria's industrial decline during the transition process was the way privatization was carried out. While, unlike trade liberalization, it was significantly delayed, the lack of a clear industrial strategy meant that this postponement did not lead to a more structured or strategic approach to enterprise restructuring. Instead, it was poorly managed and often nontransparent, resulting in asset stripping, speculative ownership changes, and the collapse of once-strategic industries (Michailova, 1997; Ganev, 2007). The absence of state-led modernization efforts meant that many formerly state-owned enterprises were transferred to private ownership without investment in technological upgrading or sectoral development (see Box 2.2). As a result, rather than supporting industrial renewal, in many cases privatization weakened Bulgaria's industrial base.

Box 2.2 CHIMCO: The Fall of a Giant After a Failed Privatization

Chimco, a major chemical plant in Vratsa, was one of Bulgaria's largest industrial enterprises, employing over 10,000 workers even in the market conditions of the mid-1990s. Established in 1968, it became a significant global player in the fertilizer market, specializing in urea and ammonia production.

(continued)

By 1996, Chimco held 3.3% of the global urea market, exporting 85% of its production to over 60 countries, none of which were from the former USSR (Petkov, 2017).

However, Chimco's decline began in the late 1990s, primarily due to flawed privatization and mismanagement. The privatization process, initiated in 1997, was fraught with problems. In 1999, a 57% stake was sold to IBE Trans of New York for just 1 million BGN, with an expectation of $50 million in investments. However, instead of modernizing the plant, the new owners failed to meet their commitments. Weak privatization oversight allowed critical assets—including Chimco's thermal power plant, railway, and port terminal—to be sold off to private entities. This stripped the company of its operational infrastructure, making it unsellable to potential investors.

External conditions further worsened the situation, as natural gas prices surged, raising production costs. Meanwhile, the global fertilizer market shifted, with new modern, cost-efficient plants in the Middle East and North Africa outcompeting Chimco. By 2003, the company had accumulated BGN 150 million in debt. Despite several attempts to revive the plant, including a 2005 rehabilitation plan, Chimco's financial and operational challenges proved insurmountable.

Chimco's collapse was not just the result of changing market conditions but also of poorly executed privatization and the absence of strategic industrial policy. As a capital-intensive and infrastructure-dependent industry, benefiting from economies of scale, its survival required state coordination in energy, transport, and technology investments. Instead, unregulated privatization led to asset stripping and deindustrialization, deepening regional disparities in northwestern Bulgaria, one of the EU's poorest areas. Chimco remains a stark example of how unchecked privatization and the lack of coherent industrial policy can dismantle once-competitive industries, erode regional economies, and accelerate industrial decline.

During the transition process in Bulgaria, the combination of rapid trade liberalization without a coherent industrial strategy and delayed, poorly executed privatization resulted in the following:

- A sharp decline in high-value-added manufacturing, as formerly competitive industries failed to meet EU standards and struggled against established producers, leading to widespread deindustrialization.
- A structural shift toward low-productivity sectors, where trade liberalization reinforced the dominance of low-cost, labor-intensive production, while the absence of targeted industrial policies prevented the growth of high-tech and innovation-driven industries.

- A deeper process of "de-development," in which the collapse of state-supported industries and the failure to develop competitive replacements pushed Bulgaria into a peripheral position within the global economy (Vassilev, 2003). Instead of integrating into high-value production networks, Bulgaria experienced a dramatic deterioration in its position within the international division of labor, leading to the erosion of industrial and technological capacities that had been built up during the years of socialist experimentation.

This trajectory underscores the dangers of rapid liberalization without institutional and strategic preparedness. Rather than facilitating a smooth transition to a competitive market economy, Bulgaria's approach deepened structural weaknesses, reinforcing dependency on low-value-added production and external capital. The transformational shock was so severe that Bulgaria only managed to recover its pre-transition 1989 GDP level in 2006, reflecting the depth of economic collapse and the long road to stabilization. These missteps highlight the critical need for policy consistency, institutional resilience, and a well-defined national economic strategy—lessons that remain relevant for Bulgaria's future development and for other countries undergoing similar transitions.

2.2 Conclusion

Bulgaria's economic history is marked by extreme shifts, swinging from agrarian dependency to forced industrialization and later to rapid market liberalization—each driven more by external pressures than by a coherent national strategy. These abrupt transitions, while intended as modernization efforts, have often resulted in economic instability, inefficiencies, and long-term dependency.

A key lesson is that economic models cannot simply be imported—they must be adapted. Whether supplying raw materials within prewar German trade networks, producing specialized manufacturing for the Soviet Bloc, or undergoing IMF-led shock therapy in the early 1990s, Bulgaria has repeatedly relied on dominant external partners. While these alignments promised growth, they very often deepened structural vulnerabilities instead of fostering self-sustaining development.

Equally crucial is the role of institutions in ensuring stability and long-term progress. While Bulgaria has adopted modern legal and regulatory frameworks, their effectiveness has often been undermined by political fragmentation, elite capture, and short-term policymaking. Institutions that should enforce policy continuity and economic strategy have instead contributed to inefficiency and stagnation. Without strong, independent institutions capable of sustaining long-term policies beyond electoral cycles, economic progress remains fragile.

Another lesson is that economic transformation requires national consensus and policy stability. Decades of polarized decision-making—swinging between state control and laissez-faire extremes—have discouraged investment, weakened public trust, and slowed modernization. Bulgaria's ability to develop a sustainable economy depends on moving beyond reactionary policymaking and ensuring a stable, long-term vision for industrial diversification, infrastructure modernization, and investment in productive sectors.

Bulgaria's history underscores that economic success is not about choosing between state control and free markets but about strategic pragmatism. A balanced approach—combining institutional strength, competitive markets, and well-calibrated government policies—offers the best path to long-term stability and growth.

References

Barlett, W. (2014). *Shut out?* South East Europe and the EU's New Industrial Policy. LSE 'Europe in Question' Discussion Paper Series, LEQS Paper No. 84/2014.

BBC News. (2015, April 18). *Could Bulgaria become Europe's Silicon Valley?* https://www.bbc.com/news/av/world-europe-32352370

Berend, I. (2003). *History Derailed: Central and Eastern Europe in the Long Nineteenth Century*, University of California Press.

Berend, I. (2006). *An Economic History of Twentieth-Century Europe: Economic Regimes from Laissez-Faire to Globalization*, Cambridge University Press.

Berov, L., & Dimitrov, D. (1990). *Razvitie na industriyata v Balgariya: 1834, 1947, 1989 [The development of industry in Bulgaria: 1834, 1947, 1989]*. Nauka i izkustvo.

Brada, J. (1993). The transformation from communism to capitalism: How far? How fast? *Post-Soviet Affairs, 9*(2), 87–110. https://doi.org/10.1080/1060586X.1993.10641361

Central Statistical Office. (n.d., various years). *Foreign trade of the People's Republic of Bulgaria*. Statistical Data.

Dimitrov, M. (2018a). *Zakonite za nasarchavane na industriyata v Balgariya (1879–1912 godina) [Laws for the promotion of industry in Bulgaria (1879–1912)]*. https://www.researchgate.net/publication/322569405_Marko_Dimitrov_ZAKONITE_ZA_NASRCAVANE_NA_INDUSTRIATA_V_BLGARIA_1879-1912_godina

Dimitrov, M. (2018b). *Industria, protoindustrializaciya, industrializaciya [Industry, proto-industrialization, industrialization]*. University of National and World Economy. https://www.researchgate.net/publication/322569652_Marco_Dimitrov_INDUSTRIA_PROTOINDUSTRIALIZACIA_INDUSTRIALIZACIA

Djankov, S., & Hoekman, B. (1998). Trade reorientation and postreform productivity growth in Bulgarian enterprises. *The Journal of Policy Reform, 2*(2), 151–168.

Dobrinsky, R. (2000). The transition crisis in Bulgaria. *Cambridge Journal of Economics, 24*, 581–602.

Dobrinsky, R. (2013). Bulgaria and political economy of transition. In P. Hare & G. Turley (Eds.), *Handbook of the economics and political economy of transition* (pp. 217–227). Routledge.

Ganev, V. (2007). *Preying on the state—The transformation of Bulgaria after 1989*. Cornell University Press.

Georgieva, S. (2021). Predpriemachestvo i industrialna politika v Bŭlgariya sled Osvobozhdenieto do Balkanskite voĭni (1878–1912) [Entrepreneurship and industrial policy in Bulgaria after the liberation until the Balkan wars (1878–1912)]. *Proceedings of CEHR, 6*, 121–135.

Gerschenkron, A. (1962). Some aspects of industrialization in Bulgaria, 1878–1939. In *Economic backwardness in historical perspective. A book of essays* (pp. 198–234).

Gomes, L. (2021). *Economic trajectory of the People's Republic of Bulgaria (1946–1990)*. MPRA Paper No. 111182. https://mpra.ub.uni-muenchen.de/111182/

Ivanov, M., & Kopsidis, M. (2023). Industrialisation in a small grain economy during the first globalisation: Bulgaria c. 1870–1910. *Economic History Review, 76*, 169–198. https://doi.org/10.1111/ehr.13185

Lampe, J. (1986). *The Bulgarian economy in the twentieth century*. Croom Helm.

Lampe, J., & Jackson, M. (1982). *Balkan economic history, 1550–1950: From imperial borderlands to developing nations*.

Lepage, L., & Kolarova, D. (2005). *Knowledge society and transition economies -The Bulgarian challenge*.

Levinson, A. (1995). Bulgaria's transition to a market economy. *Demokratizatsiya: The Journal of Post-Soviet Democratization, 3*(1), 103–109.

Library of Congress. (1992). *Bulgaria country study*. In Encyclopedia of the Nations. http://www.country-data.com/cgi-bin/query/r-1939.html

Lozanov, O. (2014). *Vanshnoikonomicheski otnosheniya na Republika Bulgaria [Foreign economic relations of the Republic of Bulgaria]*. Avangard-Prima.

Lozanov, O., & Zhivkova, S. (2017). Development and structure of the Bulgarian export after the country's accession to the EU. *European Journal of Economics and Business Studies, 3*(3), 147–155.

Marangos, J. (2005). Shock therapy and its consequences in transition economies. *Development, 48*, 70–78.

Michailova, S. (1997). The Bulgarian experience in the privatization process. *Eastern European Economics, 35*(3), 75–92. http://www.jstor.org/stable/4380090

Milkova, K. (2018). The first hundred years: A spatial analysis of foreign direct investment in Bulgaria (1879–1989). *Geopolitics, 6*. https://geopolitica.eu/spisanie-geopolitika/165-2017/broi6-2017/2749-parvite-sto-godini-prostranstven-analiz-na-prekite-chuzhdestranni-investitsii-v-balgariya-prez-1879-1989

Minassian, G. (2001). Bulgaria and the International Monetary Fund, Russian and East European Finance and Trade, 37(2), 7–35.

NATO. (1973). *The economy of Bulgaria: Notes by the German delegation (AC/127-D/434-REV1)*. NATO Economic Committee.

Nenovsky, N. (2011). Bulgarian economic thought since 1989: A personal perspective. *In The History of Economic Thought in Transitional Countries, 52*, 1–26. https://doi.org/10.5362/JSHET.52.2_1

Ognivtsev, V. (2005). *Bulgaria: Experience in systemic transition and reforms*. UNCTAD Project Study: Coping with Trade Reforms: A Developing–country Perspective on the WTO Industrial Tariff Negotiations (pp. 139–160).

Palairet, M. (1997). *Balkan economies c. 1800–1914: Evolution without development*. Cambridge.

Paraskevov, V. (2016). Drugata polovina na Evropa: Spisanie „Ikonomist" za vatreshnata i vanshnata politika na Balgariya (1985–1989g.) [The other half of Europe: The economist for Bulgarian internal and external affairs, 1985–1989]. *Journalism History, 3*, 129–139.

Parvanova, R. (2018). The parliament, business and professional organizations and passing of the local industry encouragement act (1928). *Proceedings of the Centre for Economic History Research, 3*, 139–150.

Petkov, K. (2017). Hroniki za Himco—sazidanie, razvitie, likvidatsiya [Chronicles of Himko—Creation, development, liquidation]. *BG*. Print-Vratsa.

Petrov, V. (2023). *Balkan Cyberia: Cold war computing, Bulgarian modernization, and the information age behind the iron curtain*. The MIT Press.

Popov, V. (2010). Putting the success stories in the post-communist world into a broader perspective. *Society and Economy, 32*(1), 83–102.

Rodrik, D. (2006) Goodbye Washington Consensus, Hello Washington Confusion? A Review of the World Bank's Economic Growth in the 1990s: Learning from a Decade of Reform, *Journal of Economic Literature* Vol. XLIV, pp. 973–987.

Sabev, D. (2024). Not enough poor: Agricultural and industrial development of Bulgaria, 1878–1939. *Proceedings of the Centre for Economic History Research, 9*, 221–232.

Vassilev, R. (2003). The "third-worldization" of a "second-world" nation: De-development in post-communist Bulgaria. *New Political Science, 25*, 112–199. https://doi.org/10.1080/0739314032000077400

Veleva, L. (2016). Kam vaprosa za industrializatsiyata v Balgariya (1944–1989): Diskusionni aspekti [The question for the industrialization in Bulgaria (1944–1989)]. *Proceedings of the Centre for Economic History Research, 1*, 85–109.

World Bank. (2005). *Bulgaria: The road to successful EU integration—The policy Agenda*. Report No. 34233-BG.

Zhelev, P. (2017). Structural transformation and industrial competitiveness of Bulgaria after 10 years of EU membership. *Yearbook of UNWE, 1*(1), 87–103.

Zhu, X. (2023). Western studies on the Sovietization of Eastern Europe. *Chinese Journal of Slavic Studies, 3*(1), 15–32. https://doi.org/10.1515/cjss-2023-0008

Znepolski, I., Gruev, M., Metodiev, M., Ivanov, M., Vatchkov, D., Elenkov, I., & Doynov, P. (2019). *Bulgaria under communism*. Routledge.

Chapter 3
Bulgaria's Macroeconomic Foundations in a Turbulent Global Context

3.1 Introduction

Bulgaria stands at a pivotal moment in its economic development, balancing domestic reforms with global uncertainties. As a small, open economy, it has shown resilience in the face of significant disruptions, including the COVID-19 pandemic and geopolitical tensions arising from the war in Ukraine. These challenges have tested the adaptability of its policies and institutions, highlighting both the strengths and vulnerabilities of its economic framework.

Central to Bulgaria's economic strategy is its distinctive monetary policy choice, defined by the Currency Board Arrangement (CBA) adopted in 1997. This framework has ensured economic stability but has also resulted in conservative macroeconomic policies. The country's ongoing efforts to transition from the CBA to membership in the Eurozone—a step toward full participation in the European Monetary Union—represent a crucial turning point, albeit one accompanied by significant challenges.

This chapter begins with an overview of the Bulgarian economy, providing a foundational understanding of its development level, economic structure, and key indicators. This contextualization sets the stage for an analysis of macroeconomic dynamics over the past decade, focusing on GDP growth, inflation, unemployment, and public debt. Particular attention is given to the role of monetary and fiscal policies in addressing external pressures and preparing for forthcoming monetary union membership.

The chapter concludes by addressing the critical challenges facing Bulgaria's economy. These include persistently low labor productivity, a demographic crisis that threatens long-term growth, insufficient investment in physical and human capital, and institutional weaknesses. By examining these structural issues, the chapter underscores the need for strategic reforms to ensure sustainable growth and resilience in an increasingly turbulent global environment.

P. Zhelev, *Bulgaria in the Global Economy*, Societies and Political Orders in Transition, https://doi.org/10.1007/978-3-031-87923-4_3

3.1.1 *Bulgaria's Economic Landscape: Key Features and Structure*

Bulgaria represents a typical example of a small economy, characterized by its compact territorial expanse of 111,000 square kilometers (105th rank in the world) and a population of 6.5 million (117th rank). Over the past decade, Bulgaria's economy has shown impressive growth, but it faces significant demographic challenges, with its population steadily declining from 7.25 million in 2014 (Table 3.1). This demographic shift has reduced Bulgaria's share of the EU population to just 1.44% in 2023, emphasizing the urgency of addressing labor shortages and maintaining economic dynamism.

In terms of economic output, Bulgaria's GDP nearly doubled from €43 billion in 2014 to €93.9 billion in 2023, reflecting robust performance despite global disruptions like the COVID-19 pandemic and the war in Ukraine. GDP per capita rose significantly during this period, reaching €14,580 in 2023, or 64% of the EU average. While Bulgaria still lags behind wealthier EU peers, this upward trajectory demonstrates ongoing progress in closing the income gap within the Union.

Trade plays a central role in Bulgaria's economy, underlining its openness and integration into global markets. In 2023, exports of goods and services accounted for 60.9% of GDP, slightly outpacing imports at 57.7%. The steady trade balance highlights the growing competitiveness of Bulgarian products, with the EU serving as the country's main trading partner. However, Bulgaria's reliance on external markets also exposes it to global economic fluctuations, underscoring the need for resilience in its economic policies.

The structure of Bulgaria's economy is broadly in line with trends across the EU, with services dominating the landscape. In 2023, services accounted for 71.3% of gross value added (GVA), closely aligning with the EU average of 72.5% (Table 3.2). Key drivers include wholesale and retail trade, real estate, and the rapidly growing

Table 3.1 Bulgaria's economy at a glance (2014–2023)

Indicator/year	2014	2015	2016	2017	2018	2019	2020	2021	2022	2023
Population (mln.)	7.25	7.20	7.15	7.10	7.05	7.00	6.95	6.92	6.84	6.45
Population (share in the EU's pop, %)	1.64	1.62	1.61	1.59	1.58	1.57	1.55	1.55	1.53	1.44
Territory	111, 000 sq. km.									
GDP, bln. euro	43.0	45.8	48.8	52.5	56.2	61.5	61.6	71.1	85.8	93.9
Share in EU GDP (%)	0.37	0.37	0.39	0.40	0.42	0.44	0.46	0.49	0.54	0.55
GDP per capita, current prices in euro	5960	6380	6840	7420	8000	8820	8880	10,330	13,270	14,580
GDP per capita (EU-27 = 100)	47	48	49	50	51	53	55	57	62	64
Exports (% of GDP)	64.6	63.8	63.9	67.0	65.7	63.9	56.1	61.4	69.2	60.9
Imports (% of GDP)	65.7	62.9	59.0	62.7	63.2	60.7	54.2	59.6	69.0	57.7

Source: Eurostat

Table 3.2 Structure of the economy of Bulgaria and the EU-27 (GVA by sector as a share of GDP, %)

	Bulgaria			EU-27		
Sector/year	2014	2019	2023	2014	2019	2023
Agriculture	5.3	3.7	2.9	1.9	1.8	1.8
Industry	27.0	24.9	25.8	25.0	25.3	25.7
Manufacturing	15.0	15.4	15.3	16.4	16.7	16.3
Services	67.7	71.4	71.3	73.1	72.9	72.5
Information and communication	*5.5*	*7.6*	*8.2*	*4.6*	*5.0*	*5.3*

Source: Eurostat

information and communication technologies (ICT) sector, which has become a standout performer in recent years. However, the industrial sector, and specifically manufacturing, has struggled to achieve its potential.

Manufacturing contributed just 15.3% of GVA in 2023, falling below the EU average of 16.3%. This shortfall highlights Bulgaria's inability to achieve meaningful reindustrialization, a process that many European countries have embraced to strengthen industrial bases and increase economic resilience. Moreover, Bulgaria remains far from the European Commission's indicative goal of increasing the share of manufacturing to 20% of GDP, a target set as part of the EU's industrial strategy (European Commission, 2014).

3.1.2 *Bulgaria's Development Status in a Global Context*

To effectively analyze the Bulgarian economy, it is crucial to consider its classification within global economic frameworks. This provides a foundational background for understanding its economic status and structure compared to other nations, helping to inform domestic policy decisions and international investment strategies by highlighting the country's potential, challenges, and opportunities for growth and development.

A major distinction in global economic analysis is between advanced economies and less developed countries, reflecting disparities in income levels, technological advancement, and institutional quality. However, classifications such as "developed" or "developing" lack universal definitions as international organizations apply varied criteria, creating ambiguity in discussions about Bulgaria's status.

In 2024, the World Bank designated Bulgaria as a high-income country, marking a significant milestone in its economic progress. However, this raises a broader debate: can Bulgaria, despite this achievement, truly be considered a developed country?

The World Bank bases its classification on gross national income (GNI) per capita, with Bulgaria surpassing the 14,005 USD threshold in 2023 (WB, n.d.-a). This attainment follows years of categorization as an upper-middle-income country, which used to classify Bulgaria into the developing countries category together with the other middle- and low-income economies.

The IMF, in its *World Economic Outlook* (WEO), groups Bulgaria within the emerging market and developing economies category. This flexible classification, which considers market dynamics and institutional quality rather than strict income thresholds, places Bulgaria alongside regional peers such as Romania, Hungary, and Poland (IMF, 2023). Notably, all other EU member states are classified as advanced economies, highlighting Bulgaria's differing positioning within the Union.

In contrast, the United Nations and UNCTAD include Bulgaria in the developed economies group, emphasizing its alignment with socioeconomic benchmarks typical of advanced nations and its EU membership (UN, 2023; UNCTAD, 2023). The UNIDO classification, focusing on industrial development, designates Bulgaria as a middle-income industrial economy, reflecting its industrial base relative to global standards and its need for further progress to align with advanced economies (UNIDO, 2024).

Table 3.3 illustrates Bulgaria's classifications across major frameworks, offering a comparative view of its positioning in the global economy. While the classifications vary, they collectively underline Bulgaria's unique place as a country straddling the line between emerging and developed economies.

Bulgaria's ambition and ongoing efforts to join the Organization for Economic Cooperation and Development (OECD) is a pivotal marker of its development aspirations. OECD membership is widely regarded as a benchmark for advanced economic governance and institutional quality (Peters, 2023). It would signal Bulgaria's alignment with advanced economic governance and policy standards, enhance its international credibility, attract foreign investment, and provide access to a network of best practices in economic policy and governance. Achieving this goal will foster deeper integration into the global economy; however, the process is rigorous and requires significant alignment with OECD standards and values.

A more holistic way to evaluate a country's level of development is by using the human development index (HDI). Bulgaria's HDI performance further reflects its

Table 3.3 The Bulgarian economy according to various classification systems in various years

Institution	Year	Country group	Developing country status
WB	1978	Centrally planned economies	No
	2022	Upper middle-income economies	Yes
	2023	High-income economies	No
IMF	1991	Emerging market and developing economies	Yes
	2023	Emerging market and developing economies	Yes
UNCTAD	1981	Socialist countries of Eastern Europe	No
	2004	Southeast Europe and CIS	No
UNIDO	1988	Industrialized socialist economy	No
	2015	Emerging industrial economy	Yes
	2022	Middle-income industrial economy	No

Source: Hoffmeister (2020), IMF (2024), UNIDO (2024), WB (n.d.-b)

mixed development status. Between 1990 and 2022, Bulgaria's HDI value rose by 14.5%, from 0.698 to 0.799, placing it in the high human development category (Table 3.4). However, this growth has been slower compared to regional peers like Romania. While Bulgaria made substantial gains in mean years of schooling (rising from 6.8 in 1990 to 11.4 in 2022) and GNI per capita (up by 73.2%), its life expectancy at birth saw minimal improvement of just 0.1 years over 1990–2022. This stagnation contrasts sharply with Romania, which increased life expectancy by 4.4 years during the same timeframe.

Bulgaria's development status illustrates a story of progress tempered by persistent challenges. While the country has achieved remarkable economic growth and integration into the global economy, addressing structural weaknesses will be critical to ensuring sustained convergence with its EU counterparts and improving the well-being of its population.

3.1.3 Macroeconomic Performance of Bulgaria Over 2014–2023

Bulgaria experienced steady economic growth during the pre-pandemic years (2014–2019), with an average annual growth rate of 2.8%, closely aligning with EU-27 trends. This growth was underpinned by EU structural funding, robust export performance, and rising domestic consumption. However, the 2020 COVID-19 pandemic caused a sharp contraction of −4.0%, reflecting disruptions in trade, tourism, and industrial activity. The subsequent recovery in 2021 was stronger than the EU average (7.7 vs. 6.0%), driven by fiscal stimulus measures and pent-up consumer demand. Nevertheless, growth moderated in 2022 and 2023 (3.9 and 1.8%, respectively) amid global economic headwinds, including inflationary pressures and energy price volatility (Table 3.5).

Unemployment in Bulgaria declined significantly from 12.4% in 2014 to 5.2% in 2019, surpassing EU averages in terms of improvement. This decline was attributed to strong labor demand in manufacturing, information technology, and construction, coupled with ongoing structural reforms. However, the pandemic reversed these gains, pushing unemployment to 6.1% in 2020. Recovery was swift, with the rate falling back to 4.2% by 2022. Despite this progress, labor market challenges persist, including skills mismatches, regional disparities, and the impact of emigration on workforce availability.

Inflation in Bulgaria remained subdued and even negative in 2014–2016, reflecting weak domestic demand and alignment with the ECB's low inflationary environment. This stability persisted through 2019, with inflation averaging 1.2%. However, it surged to 13.0% in 2022, driven by global supply chain disruptions, energy price spikes, and the post-pandemic rebound. Although it moderated to 8.6% in 2023, inflation remained above EU averages, straining household budgets. Under

Table 3.4 Human development index in Bulgaria and Romania (1990–2022, selected years)

	Bulgaria					Romania				
	1990	2000	2010	2022	2022–1990 change	1990	2000	2010	2022	2022–1999 change
HDI value	0.698	0.723	0.790	0.799	14.5%	0.709	0.721	0.813	0.827	16.6%
Life expectancy at birth (years)	71.4	71.6	73.8	71.5	0.2	69.7	71.3	74.0	74.1	4.4
Expected years of schooling (years)	12.3	12.8	14.5	13.9	1.6	12.5	12.2	16.2	14.5	2.0
Mean years of schooling (years)	6.8	9.7	10.7	11.4	4.6	8.5	9.5	10.7	11.4	2.9
GNI per capita (constant 2017 PPP $)	14,970	10,280	17,799	25,921	73.2%	13,364	12,128	20,192	31,641	136.8%

Source: UNDP (n.d.)

Table 3.5 Dynamics of basic macroeconomic indicators of Bulgaria and the EU-27 (2014–2023)

Indicator	2014	2015	2016	2017	2018	2019	2020	2021	2022	2023
Real GDP growth rate (%)										
BG	0.9	3.4	3.0	2.7	2.7	4.0	−4.0	7.7	3.9	1.8
EU	1.6	2.3	2.0	2.8	2.1	1.8	−5.6	6.0	3.5	0.4
Inflation (%)										
BG	−1.6	−1.1	−1.3	1.2	2.6	2.5	1.2	2.8	13.0	8.6
EU	0.4	0.1	0.2	1.6	1.8	1.4	0.7	2.9	9.2	6.4
Unemployment rate (%)										
BG	12.4	10.1	8.6	7.2	6.2	5.2	6.1	5.3	4.2	4.3
EU	11.0	10.2	9.3	8.3	7.4	6.8	7.2	7.1	6.2	6.1

Source: Eurostat

Bulgaria's Currency Board Arrangement, the country lacks discretionary monetary policy and passively follows the ECB. While the Eurozone responded with interest rate hikes, Bulgaria had no direct influence, and the effects of ECB policies reached the economy with a lag, contributing to the delayed inflation slowdown (Zlatinov et al., 2024).

Bulgaria's macroeconomic trajectory over the past decade highlights a dual narrative of progress and vulnerability. The country demonstrated resilience through steady GDP growth and a swift recovery from the COVID-19 pandemic. However, its higher-than-average inflation in 2022 and 2023, driven by global energy price shocks, exposed significant structural vulnerabilities. This challenge underscores the importance of enhancing resilience to external price pressures, particularly as Bulgaria seeks to align with Eurozone inflation criteria.

3.1.4 Fiscal and Monetary Policies in Bulgaria: Stability amid Constraints

Bulgaria's macroeconomic framework has been shaped by its Currency Board Arrangement (CBA), which has provided stability and credibility but has also imposed structural constraints on economic flexibility. Established in 1997 as a response to severe financial instability, the CBA effectively pegs the Bulgarian lev to the euro and mandates that the Bulgarian National Bank (BNB) maintain full foreign exchange reserves to back the money supply. While this system has successfully reduced inflation and strengthened investor confidence, it has also eliminated the BNB's ability to engage in discretionary monetary policy, leaving fiscal policy as the primary tool for macroeconomic management (Houbenova-Delisivkova, 2019).

Box 3.1 Bulgaria's Currency Board Arrangement

The Currency Board Arrangement (CBA) has been the backbone of Bulgaria's monetary policy since 1997, designed to prevent inflation and ensure financial discipline. The Bulgarian lev is pegged to the euro at a fixed exchange rate of 1.95583 BGN/EUR, and the Bulgarian National Bank (BNB) is legally required to maintain full foreign exchange reserves to back the monetary base. This system eliminates the ability to conduct independent monetary policy, effectively outsourcing monetary decision-making to the European Central Bank (ECB) (Nenovsky et al., 2013).

Key Features

- No discretionary monetary policy: The BNB cannot set interest rates, conduct open market operations, or implement quantitative easing.
- Full foreign exchange backing: Every lev in circulation is covered by foreign reserves.
- No lender of last resort: The BNB cannot provide emergency liquidity to commercial banks.

Advantages

- Low inflation and currency stability
- Strong investor confidence and credibility in financial markets
- Facilitates Bulgaria's long-term goal of Eurozone accession

Disadvantages

- No monetary flexibility in times of crisis
- Economic dependence on ECB policies without representation in monetary policymaking

Vulnerable to external shocks, as fiscal policy bears the full burden of economic stabilization

Under the CBA, Bulgaria's fiscal policy has been constrained by the need to maintain strict budgetary discipline. This is not only an inherent requirement of the CBA—where excessive deficits could threaten foreign reserve backing and undermine currency stability—but is also reinforced by Bulgaria's commitments under the EU's fiscal governance framework, particularly the Stability and Growth Pact (SGP).

The SGP mandates that EU member states maintain budget deficits below 3% of GDP and public debt below 60% of GDP, ensuring long-term fiscal sustainability. As a member of the EU but not yet in the Eurozone, Bulgaria adheres to these rules to maintain macroeconomic stability and signal readiness for future euro adoption. The European Semester and Excessive Deficit Procedure (EDP) also serve as key oversight mechanisms, requiring Bulgaria to align its fiscal policies with EU

Table 3.6 Public deficit and public debt in Bulgaria and the EU (2014–2023, % of GDP)

Indicator	2014	2015	2016	2017	2018	2019	2020	2021	2022	2023
Public deficit										
BG	−5.4	−1.9	0.3	1.6	1.7	2.1	−3.8	−3.9	−2.9	−1.9
EU	−2.5	−1.9	−1.4	−0.9	−0.4	−0.4	−6.7	−4.7	−3.4	−3.5
Public debt										
BG	27.0	25.9	29.1	25.1	22.1	20.0	24.6	23.9	22.6	23.1
EU	87.2	85.4	84.3	82.0	79.9	77.8	90.0	87.4	83.4	81.7

Source: Eurostat

economic coordination frameworks (Paliova, 2021). Compliance with these rules has reinforced Bulgaria's conservative fiscal stance, driven by the CBA, but it has also restricted its ability to engage in countercyclical spending during economic downturns.

The commitment to fiscal discipline of Bulgaria has ensured low borrowing costs and maintained financial credibility (Petkov, 2014). However, the trade-off has limited public investment in key sectors such as infrastructure, healthcare, and education. While Bulgaria's conservative fiscal policies have shielded it from the debt crises experienced by many EU peers, the lack of strategic investments in high-impact areas has constrained Bulgaria's ability to foster economic growth and reduce regional and social disparities.

The COVID-19 pandemic was the most significant test of Bulgaria's monetary and fiscal framework, revealing both its strengths and limitations. Entering the crisis with one of the lowest public debt levels in the EU, Bulgaria had some fiscal space but, constrained by the CBA, was unable to implement monetary stimulus, relying solely on fiscal measures (Magnin & Nenovsky, 2022).

Bulgaria's fiscal response focused on wage subsidies (60/40 scheme), pension supplements, healthcare funding, and state-backed credit guarantees. As a result, the country's public deficit widened from 2.1% in 2019 to −3.8% in 2020, while public debt rose to 24.6% of GDP (Table 3.6). Although this represented a deterioration, Bulgaria's fiscal position remained more stable than the EU average, where the deficit reached −6.7% and debt surged to 90%. While fiscal discipline ensured stability, it also limited Bulgaria's ability to stimulate recovery, unlike neighboring countries like Romania and Serbia, which introduced large-scale liquidity measures. Their central banks implemented interest rate cuts, government bond purchases, and direct credit support. Instead, Bulgaria relied on a €2 billion ECB swap line to stabilize its banking system (Nenovsky & Marinova, 2023).

Lacking monetary flexibility, Bulgaria's recovery lagged behind regional peers, reinforcing concerns about the CBA's limitations in responding to economic crises. Despite its long-standing role in ensuring stability, the CBA was never intended as a permanent framework. Successive Bulgarian governments have viewed it as a transitional mechanism to support macroeconomic discipline and prepare the country for Eurozone accession. Yet, the path to Eurozone membership is not without obstacles, requiring careful assessment of its economic and institutional implications.

3.1.5 Bulgaria and the Euro

Bulgaria is legally committed to joining the European Monetary Union (EMU) under the terms of its EU Accession Treaty (there is no opt-out provision), though no specific timeline is mandated. Membership is contingent upon fulfilling the Maastricht criteria, which include benchmarks for price stability (an average inflation no more than 1.5 percentage points over the three best-performing member states), public finances (the country is not subject to excessive deficit procedure during the assessment), exchange rate stability (participation of at least 2 years in the ERM-II), and long-term interest rates (should not exceed 2 percentage points over the three best-performing member states in price stability) (European Council, n.d.). The ongoing debate, however, questions whether meeting these nominal convergence criteria is sufficient or whether the country should first achieve a higher degree of real economic convergence before transitioning from the CBA.

Some contend that as long as business cycles are synchronized, convergence in per capita income levels is not necessary for the operation of a monetary union and that macroeconomic stabilization mechanisms can work well even if cross-country variations in income levels exist (Franks et al., 2018). Moreover, full euro adoption is a powerful mechanism to accelerate real convergence (Todorov, 2023). Others claim that Bulgaria should address productivity gaps and wage convergence before joining the eurozone and caution that entering prematurely may lead to economic difficulties (Stefanov, 2020). Admitting Bulgaria with its low level of real convergence, deep social disparities, and institutional weaknesses could not only destabilize its economy but also pose significant risks to the broader stability of the euro area (Moździerz, 2019).

The question of whether Bulgaria is ready to join the eurozone must be assessed within the framework of the Optimum Currency Area (OCA) theory, which evaluates whether countries forming a monetary union benefit from it. According to the traditional OCA criteria set by Mundell, McKinnon, and Kenen, an OCA should ideally consist of member economies that experience similar economic shocks. If that is not the case, then they should have high factor mobility (especially labor), price and wage flexibility, strong fiscal integration, high trade openness, a diversified economic structure, and similar production and trade patterns to mitigate the effects of asymmetric shocks (Baldwin & Wyplosz, 2019; Dellas & Tavlas, 2009; Yotzov, 2023).

Here's how Bulgaria measures up:

- Economic shock similarity (*moderate to strong*): Bulgaria's aggregate demand and supply shocks have become more aligned with those of the Eurozone, particularly in the post-EU accession period, reflecting increasing synchronization (Todorov, 2023). However, past divergences were notable, especially during the 2008 financial crisis and the European debt crisis, when Bulgaria experienced delayed and prolonged recessions compared to the Eurozone (Karamisheva, 2021).
- Factor mobility (*moderate*): Many Bulgarian workers have relocated to EU countries, but labor mobility is constrained by linguistic and regulatory barriers

making this a weaker aspect of OCA compliance. Capital mobility, particularly in terms of FDI, is relatively strong and supports economic stability.

- Price and wage flexibility (*moderate but constrained*): Bulgaria's labor market exhibits moderate flexibility, with wages responding to labor demand and economic cycles but constrained by sectoral agreements and administrative policies. Productivity-wage misalignment persists, indicating structural rigidities (Loukanova & Houbenova-Delisivkova, 2024). Price flexibility remains limited due to market concentration, regulated utility prices, and government interventions, reducing the economy's adaptability to shocks.
- Fiscal integration (*moderate*): Bulgaria meets the Maastricht criteria, with low public debt and a history of fiscal prudence, reducing macroeconomic risks. However, the absence of significant fiscal transfer mechanisms within the Eurozone raises concerns about its ability to absorb asymmetric shocks effectively (Gechev et al., 2020).
- Trade openness and integration (*strong*): Bulgaria is a highly open economy, with a trade-to-GDP ratio exceeding 100% and strong commercial ties with the Eurozone which absorbs around 50% of Bulgarian exports.
- Economic diversification (*moderate*): Bulgaria's product Herfindahl-Hirschman Index (HHI) declined from 0.126 in 2007 to 0.084 in 2023, indicating decreasing concentration (UNCTAD, n.d.). However, its economy remains reliant on specific export sectors, while high energy dependence and foreign demand sensitivity continue to expose it to external shocks.
- Trade similarity (*moderate to strong*): Bulgaria's structural convergence with Eurozone exports has increased, with declining dissimilarity and divergence indices, particularly in food, chemicals, and manufactured goods. However, gaps remain in high-value-added sectors, requiring further alignment (Pirimova, 2021).

Bulgaria demonstrates moderate compliance with the OCA criteria, showing increasing alignment with the Eurozone in areas such as trade integration and economic shock synchronization, while still facing structural challenges related to labor mobility, price flexibility, and exposure to external shocks. This mixed assessment suggests that while euro adoption could bring economic benefits, it also carries potential risks if adjustment mechanisms remain underdeveloped. In this context, the starting position is crucial. Unlike countries such as Czechia, Poland, Hungary, and Romania which maintain monetary independence and delay euro adoption until achieving higher real convergence, Bulgaria operates under a CBA, effectively giving up autonomous monetary policy. This unique monetary framework shapes the dynamics of euro adoption and requires a distinct evaluation of Bulgaria's readiness. To fully assess the implications of EMU membership, it is essential to compare Bulgaria's current monetary framework—the CBA—with the mechanisms of the Eurozone (Table 3.7).

Bulgaria's transition from the CBA to full Eurozone membership is expected to be economically beneficial, with minimal disruptions in monetary policy, enhanced financial stability, and lower borrowing costs. While the shift introduces new fiscal obligations, these are moderate and manageable, providing Bulgaria with access to Eurozone-wide financial safety nets. The most significant economic gains include

Table 3.7 Projected implications for Bulgaria's Euro adoption

Category	Currency Board Arrangement (Bulgaria today)	Eurozone membership (what changes)	Implications for Bulgaria
Monetary Policy, Exchange Rate, and Sovereignty	No monetary policy flexibility; fixed peg to the euro	No independent monetary policy, ECB-controlled	No major change in monetary autonomy, as Bulgaria already follows ECB policies under the CBA. Full integration into ECB decision-making
Inflation Control	Inflation is stable but vulnerable to external shocks	ECB-driven stability	Minimal long-term impact
Public Debt and Fiscal Rules	Fiscal policy is independent but subject to EU oversight	Becomes fully subject to Stability and Growth Pact enforcement	No major new constraint, as Bulgaria already follows strict fiscal policies
Interest Rates and Borrowing Costs	Higher borrowing costs due to risk premiums	Lower borrowing costs, improved credit rating	Expected decline in borrowing rates for government, businesses, and households
Financial Stability, Banking, and Crisis Support	Part of the European Banking Union but no ECB liquidity support	Gains full ECB liquidity access and Eurozone-wide financial stability mechanisms	Stronger financial resilience; lower systemic risk, reducing chances of banking crises
Official Reserves	Large reserves required to maintain currency stability	No requirement for large reserves; ECB provides liquidity	Bulgaria can repurpose some reserves for investment or debt reduction
Liabilities and Financial Contributions	No contributions to Eurozone stabilization funds	Contributions to ECB capital and the European Stability Mechanism (ESM)	Financial obligations increase, but Bulgaria gains access to crisis support mechanisms
Trade, Investment, and Transaction Costs	No exchange rate fluctuations but transaction costs	Fully eliminates BGN/EUR risk, enhances trade and investment attractiveness	Expected increase in FDI and lower transaction costs for businesses operating within the Eurozone
Public Perception and Inflation Fears	Strong public trust in CBA	Public concerns over price increases. Minor price rounding effect in the short term	Transparency and public awareness campaigns needed to address inflation misconceptions

lower transaction costs, increased trade efficiency, and higher FDI inflows, which will support Bulgaria's long-term economic growth.

Despite public concerns over inflation, historical evidence suggests that inflationary fears are largely psychological, reinforcing the need for public awareness campaigns and regulatory safeguards to ensure a smooth transition. In this context, Bulgaria has taken a decisive step forward with the recently adopted Law on Euro Adoption, which establishes the legal and technical framework for the shift from the lev to the euro. The law mandates dual price display for 12 months, a 1-month dual circulation period, and a 6-month window for free currency exchange, ensuring transparency and consumer protection. Coordinated with the ECB and the EC, this legislation leaves meeting the inflation criterion as the final hurdle, with the government aiming for compliance around the start of 2025 to enable euro adoption on January 1, 2026.

3.1.6 Assessing Bulgaria's External Vulnerabilities

Bulgaria's external sector is critical to its macroeconomic stability, particularly in an increasingly volatile global economic environment. Key indicators such as the current account balance, net international investment position (NIIP), and net external debt provide insights into the country's ability to sustain external financing, mitigate risks from global shocks, and maintain economic resilience.

The current account balance reflects the net flows of goods, services, income, and transfers between Bulgaria and the rest of the world, serving as a measure of its external sustainability. From 2014 to 2019, Bulgaria recorded consistent surpluses, peaking at 3.3% of GDP in 2017, supported by a positive trade balance in goods and services, strong remittance inflows, and EU structural funds (Table 3.8). The pandemic in 2020 disrupted this trajectory, with the current account balance turning negative (−1.7% in 2021 and −1.4% in 2022). The deficits were largely attributable to negative balances in income flows, including profit repatriation by foreign-owned companies and increased payments on foreign liabilities. Rising energy import costs also widened the goods trade deficit during this period. By 2023, the CA deficit narrowed to −0.3% of GDP, signaling partial stabilization but underscoring vulnerabilities related to income outflows and energy dependency.

The NIIP reflects the net balance of Bulgaria's external assets and liabilities. Between 2014 and 2023, the NIIP has improved significantly from −€31 billion (72% of GDP) to −€6.4 billion (6.9% of GDP). While the country continues to be a net debtor in the global economy, this marked reduction in net liabilities indicates a substantial enhancement in Bulgaria's external sustainability. The improvement is largely attributed to sustained current account surpluses during the earlier years, prudent external debt management, and the accumulation of foreign assets.

Table 3.8 Current account balance and net international investment position (NIIP) of Bulgaria (2014–2023)

Indicator	2014	2015	2016	2017	2018	2019	2020	2021	2022	2023
Current account balance (% of GDP)	1.2	0.0	3.1	3.3	0.9	1.9	0.0	−1.7	−1.4	−0.3
Net international investment position (billion EUR)	−31.0	−28.2	−23.2	−22.9	−21.1	−18.9	−14.5	−11.1	−8.8	−6.4
Net external debt (% of GDP)	18.2	3.3	−7.8	−10.1	−16.0	−21.1	−27.0	−28.8	−30.5	−33.6

Source: Eurostat

A crucial component of this adjustment has been the transition in the composition of Bulgaria's external liabilities. The reduction in net external debt, which fell from 18.2% of GDP in 2014 to a net creditor position of −33.6% of GDP in 2023, highlights the country's shift away from debt-financed external obligations toward more stable and growth-oriented forms of financing, such as equity and FDI. This shift reduces vulnerability to external shocks, such as rising global interest rates or fluctuations in capital flows, enhancing the robustness of Bulgaria's external position.

Despite these improvements, some vulnerabilities persist. The recent current account deficits suggest emerging pressures on the trade balance and income outflows. Bulgaria's ability to sustain its external position will depend on addressing structural challenges, such as enhancing export competitiveness and diversifying its economic base.

3.1.7 Bulgaria's Economic Challenges

For Bulgaria to achieve sustainable long-term growth and successfully converge with more advanced EU economies, it must overcome deep-rooted structural constraints that risk trapping it in the middle-income trap—a situation where a country experiences stagnating growth after reaching a certain income level, unable to transition to a high-income economy. Macroeconomic stability has been maintained, and this is widely recognized as a crucial condition, yet not sufficient. International assessments, including those from the OECD, the World Bank, and the IMF, consistently highlight *low labour productivity, weak investment, governance deficiencies,* and *demographic and regional disparities* as the most pressing economic challenges for Bulgaria's development (OECD, 2023; Nikolova et al., 2023; IMF, 2024).

Labor productivity remains a critical constraint on Bulgaria's economic convergence with more developed EU economies. As shown in Fig. 3.1, Bulgaria's labor productivity per person employed has improved gradually but remains significantly

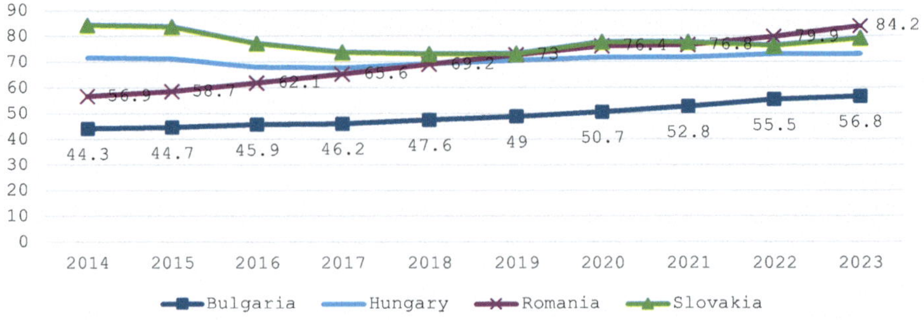

Fig. 3.1 Labor productivity per person employed in Bulgaria and selected comparator countries (EU27 in 2020 = 100). (Source: Eurostat)

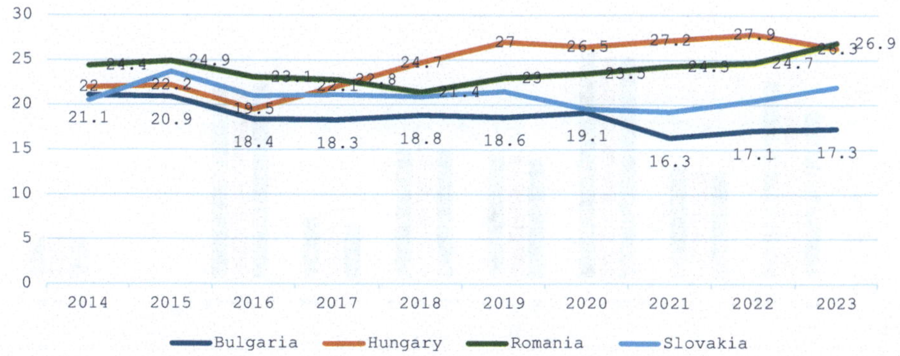

Fig. 3.2 Gross fixed capital formation in Bulgaria and selected comparator countries (% of GDP). (Source: Eurostat)

below comparator countries such as Hungary, Slovakia, and Romania. While Romania has witnessed a sharp increase in productivity, overtaking Slovakia in 2023, Bulgaria continues to lag behind, reaching only 56.8% of the EU27 average. This persistent productivity gap reflects structural inefficiencies, limited technological adoption, and weaknesses in workforce skills.

Investment levels, measured by gross fixed capital formation (GFCF) as a percentage of GDP (Fig. 3.2), highlight another structural challenge. Bulgaria's GFCF has stagnated at relatively low levels, averaging around 17–18% of GDP in recent years, whereas Romania and Hungary have consistently maintained investment rates above 23%. This disparity suggests a weaker capacity for capital deepening and modernization, which further exacerbates productivity constraints. Insufficient public and private investment in infrastructure, innovation, and high-value-added industries continue to hinder Bulgaria's economic transformation.

Bulgaria's demographic crisis presents one of the most severe long-term challenges to its economic sustainability. The country has one of the fastest-declining populations in the EU due to low birth rates, high emigration, and an aging workforce (Table 3.1). This demographic trend exacerbates labor shortages, places additional strain on social security systems, and limits economic growth potential.

Compounding the demographic crisis, regional disparities are widening, with economic activity and investment heavily concentrated in Sofia, while many peripheral regions face industrial decline. Figure 3.3 illustrates this growing imbalance, showing that Bulgaria has one of the highest and fastest-increasing concentrations of urban population in its capital compared to regional peers. The deepening divide between Sofia and the rest of the country is entrenching a two-speed economy, where peripheral regions struggle to retain talent, attract businesses, and sustain development. If left unaddressed, these demographic and regional imbalances will continue to undermine economic cohesion and Bulgaria's long-term growth prospects.

Finally, governance deficiencies remain one of Bulgaria's most fundamental obstacles to long-term economic development, affecting nearly every aspect of the

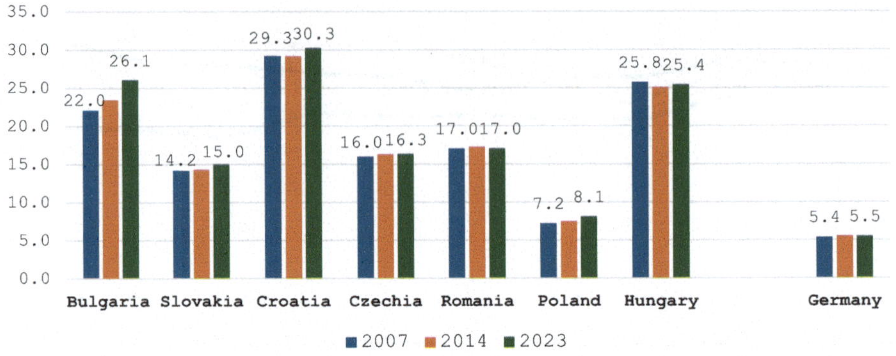

Fig. 3.3 Population in the largest city in Bulgaria and selected comparator countries (% of urban population). (Source: World Bank)

Table 3.9 Worldwide Governance Indicators scores for Bulgaria and select comparator countries

	Government effectiveness		Rule of law		Control of corruption	
	2007	*2023*	*2007*	*2023*	*2007*	*2023*
Bulgaria	51.94	53.30	52.63	53.77	50.97	50.00
Croatia	67.96	75.47	54.55	59.43	58.25	59.91
Hungary	73.79	62.74	80.38	63.21	73.30	54.72
Romania	44.17	46.70	52.15	64.15	51.46	56.13
Slovakia	73.30	58.96	63.16	68.87	64.56	61.32

Source: The Worldwide Governance Indicators, 2024 update
Note: Percentile rank among all countries [ranges from 0 (lowest) to 100 (highest) rank]

country's ability to enhance productivity, attract investment, and transition to a high-income economy (Milatovic et al. 2019). Institutional inefficiencies, lack of transparency, and persistent corruption have seen little improvement over the past decade, with Bulgaria ranking among the worst regional performers in the Worldwide Governance Indicators (Table 3.9). While peers like Croatia and Romania have improved in governance metrics, Bulgaria's scores remain stagnant or have slightly declined, particularly in control of corruption (falling from 50.97 in 2007 to 50.00 in 2023), deterring investment and eroding public trust.

3.2 Conclusion

Bulgaria's aspiration to join the ranks of high-income countries has long been underpinned by a conservative macroeconomic stance. The CBA, introduced in 1997, has served as a bulwark against inflationary threats and fiscal mismanagement, thereby enabling Bulgaria to post some of the lowest public debt levels in Europe. Yet, this stability comes with inherent trade-offs. Limitations on monetary and fiscal flexibility restrain Bulgaria's capacity to respond proactively to changing economic conditions and to leverage policy stimuli for more ambitious growth initiatives.

Significantly, this reliance on conservative macroeconomic policies is not merely a strategic preference but also a consequence of the institutional landscape. Historically weak governance structures and suboptimal administrative capacities have necessitated rigid rules-based mechanisms like the CBA to maintain economic discipline and investor confidence. However, striving for sustainable long-term development will require Bulgaria to address these institutional limitations head-on. The impending adoption of the euro further amplifies the importance of such reforms: aligning fully with Eurozone standards is not solely about meeting nominal convergence criteria but also about strengthening administrative efficiency, ensuring transparency, and bolstering regulatory oversight.

Ultimately, resolving Bulgaria's structural challenges—ranging from shrinking population and labor force to growing regional inequalities—will hinge upon more robust governance. Only by elevating institutional quality can the country effectively harness the benefits of Eurozone membership, augment its competitiveness, and safeguard its macroeconomic stability in an uncertain global landscape. Bulgaria's path to high-income status thus rests on a delicate balance: sustaining the credibility gained through conservative policies while investing in the institutional revitalization essential to unlock more dynamic and inclusive economic growth.

References

Baldwin, R., & Wyplosz, C. (2019). *The economics of European integration*. McGraw-Hill Education.

Dellas, H., & Tavlas, G. (2009). An optimum-currency-area odyssey. *Journal of International Money and Finance, 28*, 1117–1137.

European Commission. (2014). *Communication from the commission—For a European industrial renaissance*. COM (2014) 14 final.

European Council. (n.d.). *Conditions for joining the euro area: Convergence criteria*. https://www.consilium.europa.eu/en/policies/join-the-euro-area/convergence-criteria/

Franks, M. J. R., Barkbu, M. B. B., Blavy, M. R., Oman, W., & Schoelermann, H. (2018). *Economic convergence in the Euro area: Coming together or drifting apart?* International Monetary Fund.

Gechev, R., Beev, I., & Hristozov, Y. (2020). Expected effects of the Euro adoption in Bulgaria. *Economic Studies, 29*(2), 19–44.

Hoffmeister, O. (2020). *Development status as a measure of development*. UNCTAD Research Paper No. 46. UNCTAD.

Houbenova-Delisivkova, T. (2019). The fiscal policy of Bulgaria in the process of integration to the European Union. *Finance, Accounting and Business Analysis, 1*(1), 91–113.

IMF. (2023). *World economic outlook: A rocky recovery, statistical appendix*. International Monetary Fund.

IMF. (2024). *Bulgaria: 2024 article IV consultation staff report*. IMF Country Reports 24/163.

Karamisheva, T. (2021). Measuring the business cycle in Bulgaria. *Economic Studies, 30*(3), 17–38.

Loukanova, P., & Houbenova-Delisivkova, T. (2024). *Labour market flexibility*. Prof. Marin Drinov Publishing House of Bulgarian Academy of Sciences.
Magnin, E., & Nenovsky, N. (2022). *Diversity of capitalism in Central and Eastern Europe: Dependent economies and monetary regimes*. Palgrave Macmillan.
Milatovic, J., Szczurek, M., & Meshulam, D. (2019). *Bulgaria country diagnostic*. European Bank for Reconstruction and Development.
Możdzierz, A. (2019). Macroeconomic stability as the condition for Bulgaria to join the euro area. *Equilibrium. Quarterly Journal of Economics and Economic Policy, 14*(2), 295–315.
Nenovsky, N., & Marinova, E. (2023). Diversity of monetary regimes and reactions to the COVID-19 pandemic: Crisis in the Balkan countries. In M. Yağıcı (Ed.), *Central banking in a post-pandemic world: Challenges, opportunities and dilemmas*. Routledge.
Nenovsky, N., Tochkov, K., & Turcu, C. (2013). Monetary policies and European integration: The case of two Balkan countries. *Revue d'études comparatives Est-Ouest, 44*(2), 141–162.
Nikolova, D., Schiffbauer, M., Fazekas, M., Drozd, M., Pennings, S., Vaughan, K., & Kilinc, U. (2023). *Bulgaria country economic memorandum: A path to high income*. World Bank Group.
OECD. (2023). *OECD economic surveys: Bulgaria 2023*. OECD Publishing. https://doi.org/10.1787/5ca812a4-en
Paliova, I. (2021). European Union's fiscal rules and new financial instruments for 2021–2027: Bulgaria's case study. *Bulgarian Journal of International Economics and Politics, 1*(1), 26–35.
Peters, B. (2023). Good governance. In *The Elgar companion to the OECD* (pp. 256–265).
Petkov, V. S. (2014). Advantages and disadvantages of fiscal discipline in Bulgaria in times of crisis. *Contemporary Economics, 8*(1), 47–56.
Pirimova, V. (2021). Structural convergence of Bulgarian foreign trade and exports to the Euro area. *Economic Studies, 30*(5), 93–117.
Stefanov, G. (2020). Mundell optimality of the Bulgarian accession to the euro area. *Izvestiya. Journal of Varna University of Economics, 3*, 297–315.
Todorov, I. (2023). Is Bulgaria ready to join the euro area—Income convergence or similarity of shocks criteria? *Yearbook of UNWE, 2*, 95–105.
UN. (2023). *World economic and social prospects*.
UNCTAD. (2023). *Handbook of statistics 2023*. Annex: Classifications. https://hbs.unctad.org/classifications/
UNCTAD. (n.d.). *Merchandise: Product concentration and diversification indices of exports and imports*. https://unctadstat.unctad.org/datacentre/dataviewer/US.ConcentDiversIndices
UNDP. (n.d.). *Human development index*. https://hdr.undp.org/data-center/specific-country-data#/countries/BGR
UNIDO. (2024). *UNIDO country classification—Methodological document*. https://stat.unido.org
WB. (n.d.-a). *World development indicators*. The World Bank Group. https://data.worldbank.org/indicator/NY.GNP.PCAP.CD
WB (n.d.-b) World Bank Country and Lending Groups, retrieved from: https://datahelpdesk.worldbank.org/knowledgebase/articles/906519-world-bank-country-and-lending-groups
Yotzov, V. (2023). The Euro and Bulgaria—Fears and Hopes. *Economic Studies, 32*(3), 3–18.
Zlatinov, D., Loukanova, P., Yotzov, V., Sariisky, G., Paliova, I., & Georgieva, S. (2024). Bulgarian economy in 2023—Structural challenges and medium-run perspectives. *Economic Studies, 33*(6), 3–35.

Chapter 4
Bulgaria's Integration in the EU: Benefits and Challenges

4.1 Introduction

The European Union (EU), widely considered to be the most advanced regional economic bloc, has been described by the World Bank as a "convergence machine" due to its ability to integrate poorer countries and aid their transition into high-income economies. Through a combination of market access, structural funds, policy alignment, and institutional support, the EU fosters economic development and rise of living standards of its member states (Gill & Raiser, 2012). This chapter looks at Bulgaria's experience with the EU integration and aims to ascertain to what extent the country has taken advantage of this process to advance economic prosperity.

Bulgaria's journey toward EU membership began in the beginning of the 1990s, marked by a strategic shift from a centrally planned economy to a market-based one, driven by the strategy of "returning to Europe" with an overarching goal accession to the EU (Nitoiu & Moga, 2020). This strategy was driven by the desire to reintegrate with the Western European partners and enjoyed unprecedented consensus among Bulgaria's major political parties and widespread and firm societal support. It was widely hoped that integrating in the club of rich European countries would provide all the necessary conditions for a fast catching-up economic growth through improved governance, substantial investments, technology transfer, and infrastructural upgrades. Therefore, the EU accession has been widely considered as a panacea to the specific Bulgarian problems.

Indeed, Bulgaria has made significant progress in economic catching-up following its EU membership. However, Bulgaria's EU integration has been fraught with complexities and challenges. While the country has made strides in reducing gaps in GDP per capita with other EU nations, it continues to be the poorest member state and continues to lag in productivity. The export list is still dominated by raw-material-intensive industries, with limited presence of technologically-driven activities. The income disparity and regional divergence within the country have been

P. Zhelev, *Bulgaria in the Global Economy*, Societies and Political Orders in Transition, https://doi.org/10.1007/978-3-031-87923-4_4

growing. Demographic challenges such as emigration and an aging population exacerbate these economic difficulties, posing a risk of stagnating the national economy in a middle-income trap. Furthermore, there is a growing perception that Bulgaria is treated as a second-tier EU member, with unequal access to benefits such as Schengen Area membership. Despite meeting the necessary criteria in 2011, it took 13 years for Bulgaria to achieve partial entry, with sea and air border participation beginning on March 31, 2024, and full accession completed on January 1, 2025.

Some scholars, such as Stoyanova and Raichev (2017), assess the EU integration impacts in a narrow sense by calculating the net financial position—specifically, the difference between the funds received from the EU budget and the contributions made to it. However, others, like Boneva (2005), recognize the multidimensional nature of EU membership, categorizing its effects into economic, political, and social dimensions at both macro and micro levels.

This chapter will adopt a comprehensive approach to elucidate the broad spectrum of impacts on Bulgaria's economy and society. It will explore the substantial benefits and significant challenges of regional economic integration as identified in existing literature, focusing on the economic effects and employing a comparative methodology that includes the performance of other similar EU and non-EU countries. Seventeen years after Bulgaria's accession to the EU, enough time has elapsed to provide an up-to-date evaluation of what the country has gained and lost. By analyzing Bulgaria's experience, this chapter will present valuable insights into the broader implications for other small countries undergoing similar processes at advanced stages of regional integration. This will not only help understand Bulgaria's unique position but also offer a clear understanding of the varied effects of regional integration.

4.1.1 Regional Economic Integration and Its Effects

Regionalization, characterized by an intensification of cross-border economic transactions among a specific subset of countries, is a defining feature of today's global economy. This phenomenon may emerge as a natural, market-driven outcome due to increased social and economic interactions among non-state actors across geographically, politically, or culturally adjacent states. However, it is often propelled by economic regionalism—a deliberate, state-led initiative aimed at crafting formal regional institutions that bind separate national economies, thereby fostering their interdependence and culminating in the formation of regional trading and economic blocs (Börzel & Risse, 2016; Robson, 1998).

Economic regionalism is used by some authors interchangeably with regional economic integration (Pelkmans, 2006). However, others believe that we can talk about regional economic integration only when states transfer at least some authority giving up part of their sovereignty to the community level (Börzel & Risse, 2016).

Economic regionalism is advanced through regional trade agreements, where treaties establish two or more states as preferential trade and economic partners. Initially, these agreements focus on "negative integration," which involves the reduction or elimination of tariffs, quotas, and other barriers to trade (Tinbergen, 1965). As integration evolves, the scope extends to "positive integration" or "deep integration," which not only removes trade barriers but also includes the creation of new institutional frameworks to enable effective market operations and support broader policy goals within the union.

Regional economic integration can evolve into various forms, each representing a different level of cooperation and depth. The most common typology of the stages of integration is introduced by Balassa (1962). Starting with a free trade area, countries eliminate internal tariffs and quotas but maintain distinct external trade policies. Moving to a customs union, members abolish internal trade barriers and adopt a common external tariff against nonmember countries. More advanced is a common market, which permits the free movement of goods, services, capital, and labor, effectively erasing production factor borders between member states. An economic union goes further by integrating some economic policies alongside the features of a common market, introducing positive integration measures. The most integrated form is a full economic union, where countries unify their monetary, fiscal, social, and countercyclical policies. Each level of integration demands greater commitment and often the concession of sovereignty, providing substantial economic benefits but also posing significant challenges.

The effects of regional economic integration are usually analyzed using the standard theoretical framework developed by Viner (1950) on the example of customs unions. It relates to two effects—trade creation and trade diversion. Trade creation is the positive result of trade liberalization within the union and occurs when higher-cost domestic production is replaced with lower-cost imports from member countries, thus increasing overall economic efficiency and consumer welfare. Conversely, trade diversion happens due to the discrimination versus third countries and occurs when lower-cost imports from nonmember countries are replaced by higher-cost imports from member countries due to preferential treatment within the union, which is welfare decreasing. The net effect of the integration depends on the relative magnitude of these two effects and the specific economic context of the member countries (Viner, 1950).

These, however, are allocative efficiency effects, static by nature. Much more important are the dynamic effects, which include factors such as economies of scale, increased competition, and technological innovation spurred by the integration process. These elements can lead to sustained economic growth, improved productivity, and long-term development benefits for member countries (Balassa, 1962). They have a cumulative, long lasting, and deep effect but it is hard to be quantified.

Viner's framework is insufficient to analyze the integration effects as the EU represents the most advanced form of regional integration, going far beyond a customs union. According to Balassa's stages of integration, the EU has evolved from a customs union achieved in 1968, to a common market in 1993, and finally to an economic and monetary union with the introduction of the common currency and the euro area in 1999. Additionally, the Schengen Area, which allows for passport-free travel across the participating countries, exemplifies the EU's commitment to deepening integration beyond economic measures to include significant political and social dimensions. Therefore, membership in the European Union involves a greater level of obligations and anticipated outcomes compared to joining other integration groups.

Furthermore, it is important to note that the fifth EU enlargement included new member states with a significant income per capita divergence compared to the incumbents. This phenomenon is referred to in economic literature as heterogeneous integration. Unlike homogeneous integration, which involves countries with similar socioeconomic levels, heterogeneous integration often faces challenges due to disparities in economic structures, differing market maturity levels, and gaps in technology, institutions, and infrastructure. To effectively assess the benefits and costs of integration in such a context, it is advisable to consider the specific stages of economic development, the structure of the economy, production characteristics, and demand preferences of each member state (Marinov, 2015). A case-by-case analysis is essential to understand and address the unique challenges and opportunities presented by each country's integration into the EU as country experiences vary depending on initial conditions and adjustment capacities.

In the absence of a singular theoretical framework capable of fully capturing the multifaceted effects of regional economic integration, this chapter draws upon a broad spectrum of existing literature to distill key themes and insights particularly within the European Union context (Baldwin & Wyplosz, 2020; Pelkmans, 2006). By integrating these scholarly perspectives, we aim to illuminate both the economic benefits and potential costs associated with EU membership from the perspective of the acceding country (Pasimeni, 2024; Kundera, 2016; Boneva, 2005; Breuss, 2002; Mortensen & Richter, 2000; Baldwin et al., 1997). The synthesized findings highlight not only the opportunities for market expansion, regulatory alignment, and capital inflows but also the challenges of economic dependency, regulatory burdens, and socioeconomic disparities. These dynamics are encapsulated in Table 4.1, which outlines both the positive and negative dimensions of EU membership alongside potential indicators that can offer a more detailed understanding of the integration's impact.

4.1.2 Effects of the EU Integration on Bulgaria's Economy

Bulgaria's accession to the European Union in 2007 significantly influenced its economic and institutional development, driving growth through market access, foreign investments, and regulatory reforms. However, persistent challenges such as income disparities, regional inequalities, and demographic decline have tempered these gains. This section examines the multifaceted effects of EU integration on Bulgaria, highlighting both the benefits and the ongoing challenges.

Table 4.1 Economic impact of EU membership

Dimension	Benefits	Costs	Potential indicators
Market access	Greatly increased size of the marketplace allows firms to produce at optimal scale and enjoy lower average costs of production. Increased competition disciplines domestic firms to become more efficient. Welfare gains from lower prices and better quality/variety of goods and services	Meeting EU product standards and regulations imposes adjustment costs, disproportionately burdening SMEs Increased competition from established TNCs leading to loss of certain technologically intensive industries and premature deindustrialization Trade diversion from nonmembers	Intra-bloc trade volume, trade balance, medium- and high-tech net exports
Regulatory alignment	Adherence to the EU acquis communautaire enhances the legal framework, governance standards, and institutional quality	Some national sovereignty relinquished to the community level and loss of important policy tools	World Bank governance indicators
Capital flows and technology transfer	Increased FDI inflows and access to new technologies	Potential overreliance on foreign investments, crowding out of local investors, and technology dependence	FDI inflows, R&D spending by foreign-controlled enterprises
Labor market	Integration leads to new job opportunities and greater mobility for workers within the bloc	Wage differentials induce large amount of emigration, depopulation, and severe "brain drain"	Unemployment rate, migration rate
Fiscal transfers	Fiscal support through cohesion and structural funds for upgrading infrastructure, human capital, and productive capacities	Contribution to the EU budget and growing budgetary pressures for cofinancing of EU projects Inefficient use of the funds leading to distortions	Net budgetary transfers
Overall economic performance	The dynamic effects of integration lead to faster GDP growth and higher individual consumption	Economic benefits can be unevenly distributed, with some regions or sectors benefiting more than others, exacerbating regional and income inequalities	GDP per capita, individual consumption, GINI coefficient, regional disparities

Source: Own elaboration

Market Access

Bulgaria's trade dynamics reflects the dual impacts of EU integration, which began well before formal accession in 2007 with the European Association Agreement

(EAA), signed in 1993. This early alignment with EU markets promptly turned the EU as the primary export and import market for Bulgaria. Over the years, trade volumes expanded significantly, as shown in Fig. 4.1, with exports surpassing €30 billion by 2023. Access to a larger marketplace allowed Bulgarian firms to scale production and improve efficiency, while consumers benefited from greater product variety and quality. However, imports consistently outpaced exports, resulting in a persistent trade deficit. Though this deficit narrowed post-accession—thanks to incoming FDI and EU structural funds—it underscores Bulgaria's economy high import intensity.

The benefits of market access came with costs. Bulgarian firms faced significant challenges adapting to EU standards and increased competition from transnational corporations (TNCs), leading to the erosion of many technologically intensive industries. Figure 4.2 illustrates this shift: Bulgaria initially maintained a positive trade balance in medium-technology goods in the mid-1990s but quickly lost this advantage following the EAA, reflecting premature deindustrialization (Zhelev, 2017). High-technology sectors remained consistently in deficit, highlighting struggles to compete in innovation-driven industries.

Post-2007, EU membership facilitated gradual improvements. Medium-technology exports, especially in machinery and automotive parts, began to recover due to deeper integration into EU supply chains and foreign investment. High-technology exports also grew modestly but continue to lag, underscoring the challenge of transitioning from low-value, assembly-based production to high-value industries. Bulgaria's experience therefore highlights both the opportunities of EU market access and the enduring structural adjustments required to fully leverage membership benefits.

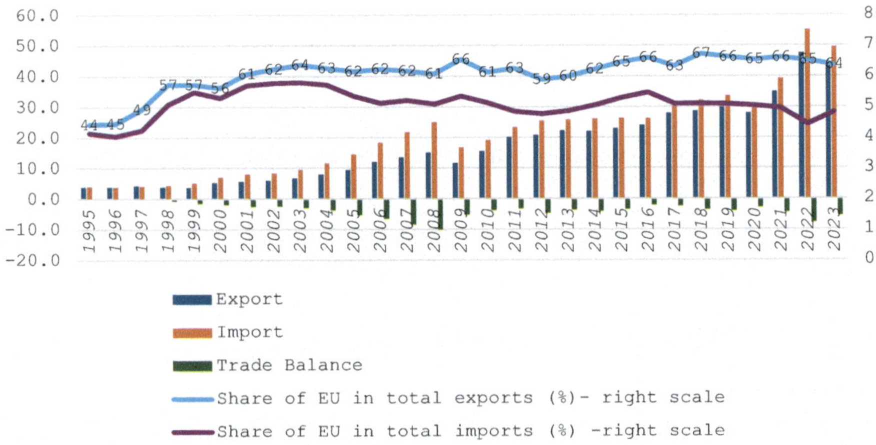

Fig. 4.1 Export, import, and trade balance of Bulgaria (1995–2023, billion euro). (Source: BNB, accessed on 27.06.2024)

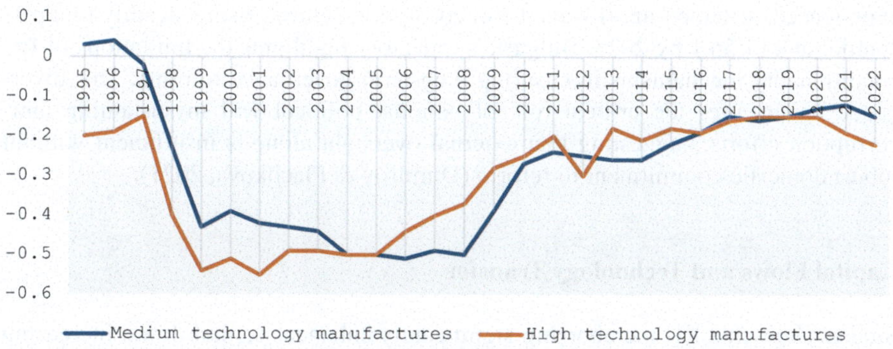

Fig. 4.2 Relative trade balance of Bulgaria's trade with medium- and high-technology manufactures (1995–2022). (Source: UNCTAD, accessed on 27.06.2024)

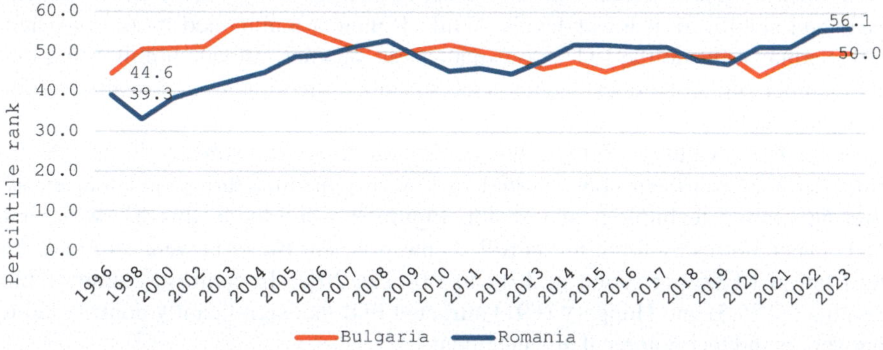

Fig. 4.3 Control of corruption in Bulgaria and Romania (0–100 percentile rank with 0 as lowest and 100 as highest; selected years of the 1995–2023 period). (Source: Worldwide Governance Indicators, accessed on 15.12.2024)

Regulatory Alignment

Bulgaria's integration into the European Union initially spurred significant regulatory reforms, driven by adherence to the acquis communautaire, which strengthened legal frameworks and governance standards. This alignment with EU norms acted as a catalyst for anti-corruption efforts, with Bulgaria's control of corruption percentile rising from 44.6 in 1996 to a peak of 56.6 in 2005 (Fig. 4.3). However, this momentum proved unsustainable after accession, as post-accession reform fatigue set in, leading to stagnation and eventual regression in anti-corruption efforts. By 2015, Bulgaria's corruption control had declined to around 45, reflecting a broader pattern of stalled institutional reform.

The EU's Cooperation and Verification Mechanism (CVM), designed to maintain reform pressure post-accession, had limited efficacy in Bulgaria, in contrast to its relative success in Romania (Lacatus & Sedelmeier, 2020). While Romania experienced sustained improvements in corruption control, rising steadily to a percentile rank of 56.1 by 2023, Bulgaria's trajectory highlights the limitations of EU conditionality mechanisms in ensuring long-term governance reforms. This divergence underscores the critical role of national political will in sustaining anti-corruption efforts, suggesting that external oversight alone is insufficient without robust domestic commitment to reform (Dimitrov & Plachkova, 2021).

Capital Flows and Technology Transfer

Studies show that EU membership significantly enhances capital flows, increasing non-EU FDI by 60% and intra-EU FDI by 50%, thereby promoting investment and technological transfer (Bruno et al., 2021). Bulgaria experienced this surge, with FDI peaking at $1605 per capita in 2007, just after EU accession (Fig. 4.4). However, this growth was short-lived, as inflows dropped sharply following the 2008 financial crisis and stabilized at lower levels. While Romania maintained more consistent FDI, Serbia—outside the EU—saw smaller but steadier inflows, highlighting that EU membership alone doesn't guarantee sustained investment, and diversification strategies matter.

Beyond the volume of FDI, the quality of these investments is critical. In Bulgaria, FDI has been concentrated in low-cost manufacturing and real estate, offering limited technological transfer. Figure 4.5 highlights this, showing that R&D expenditures by foreign-controlled enterprises in Bulgaria were minimal, rising from just €3.6 per capita in 2011 to €10.3 in 2019. In contrast, countries like Czechia (€175.5) and Hungary (€91) attracted FDI that significantly contributed to innovation and technological advancement.

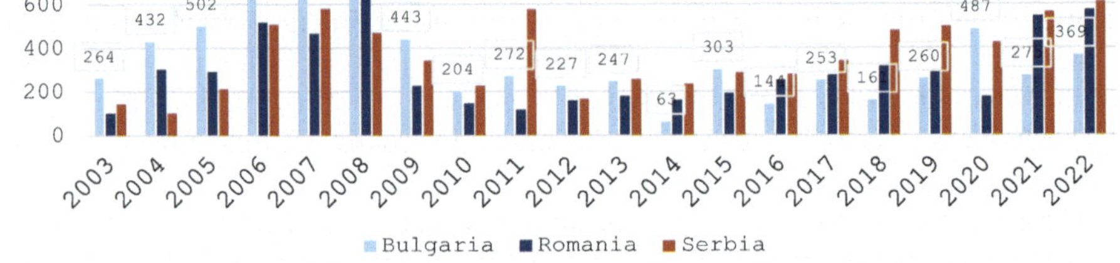

Fig. 4.4 Inward FDI flows in Bulgaria, Romania, and Serbia (2003–2022, US dollar per capita). (Source: UNCTAD, accessed on 27.06.2024)

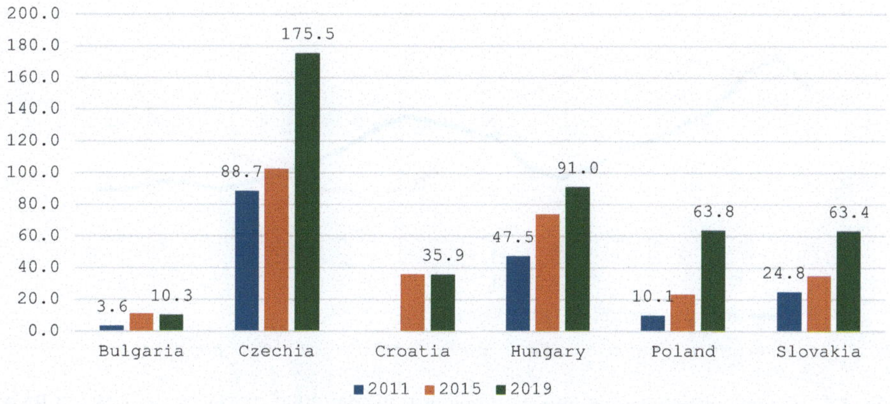

Fig. 4.5 Intramural business enterprise R&D expenditures by foreign-controlled enterprises in Bulgaria and selected comparator countries (euro per capita, 2011, 2015, and 2019). (Source: Own calculations based on Eurostat, accessed on 27.06.2024)

While EU integration significantly stimulated capital inflows, the limited contribution of foreign investment to technological transfer in Bulgaria highlights the need to attract higher-quality, innovation-driven FDI and strengthen domestic R&D capacity for sustainable growth.

Labor Market

EU integration has created new job opportunities and increased worker mobility in Bulgaria, but it has also intensified challenges like emigration, depopulation, and a severe brain drain due to wage differentials with Western Europe.

Figure 4.6 shows that while unemployment fell from 20% in 2001 to around 4% by 2023, net migration remained persistently negative. Even as job opportunities improved post-EU accession, many Bulgarians continued to emigrate in search of higher wages, with the net migration rate dropping to nearly −2.1 per 1000 population by 2014. Although there was a certain recovery after 2015, the rate remained negative at around −0.5 per 1000 by 2023.

The massive emigration has triggered a demographic crisis, depleting Bulgaria's workforce and contributing to one of the EU's steepest population declines. The loss of young, skilled workers hampers long-term growth and strains public finances. While EU integration spurred economic growth, addressing wage disparities and improving domestic opportunities are crucial to reversing this trend and mitigating its impact on Bulgaria's labor market.

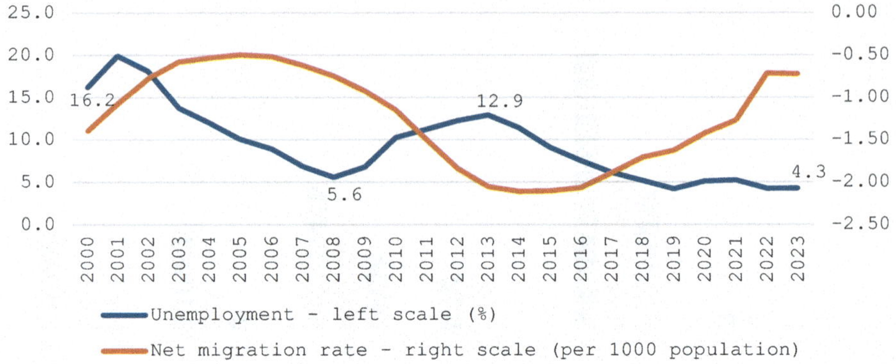

Fig. 4.6 Unemployment and net migration rate in Bulgaria (2000–2023). (Source: World Bank and UNSD)

Fiscal Transfers

One of the most tangible and anticipated effects of Bulgaria's EU membership was access to EU structural funds. These fiscal transfers have been pivotal for Bulgaria's economic development, providing crucial support for structural reforms, infrastructure projects, and growth initiatives. Following accession, Bulgaria gained significant EU resources, aimed at reducing regional disparities and modernizing key sectors (Christova-Balkanska, 2016). These funds were expected to drive economic convergence, boost private investment, and strengthen state capacity. They became a primary source of public investment, especially during economic downturns when domestic resources were limited (Surubaru, 2021). However, these benefits come with growing challenges, including contributions to the EU budget, cofinancing requirements, and the need for higher efficiencies in fund utilization.

Figure 4.7 shows Bulgaria's contributions to the EU budget rising from BGN 595 million in 2007 to BGN 1.85 billion in 2023. Despite this increase, Bulgaria remains a clear net beneficiary, with over €20 billion received between 2007 and 2020 and an additional €11.2 billion allocated for 2021–2027 (Table 4.2). Major investments were directed toward transport, regional development, and human resources, with regional development funding alone more than doubling over successive periods. However, it should not be forgotten that Bulgaria's accession required significant concessions, such as the closure of Kozloduy Nuclear Power Plant units, which, despite EU compensation, resulted in considerable economic losses and energy challenges (see Box 4.1).

According to the Ministry of Finance (2022), EU funds contributed to GDP growth, infrastructure improvements, and job creation, with the 2014–2020 period yielding a 10.6% GDP increase and a 16.6% rise in employment by mid-2022 in Bulgaria. Beyond economic gains, EU funds also influenced governance, promoting strategic public investments and institutional reforms.

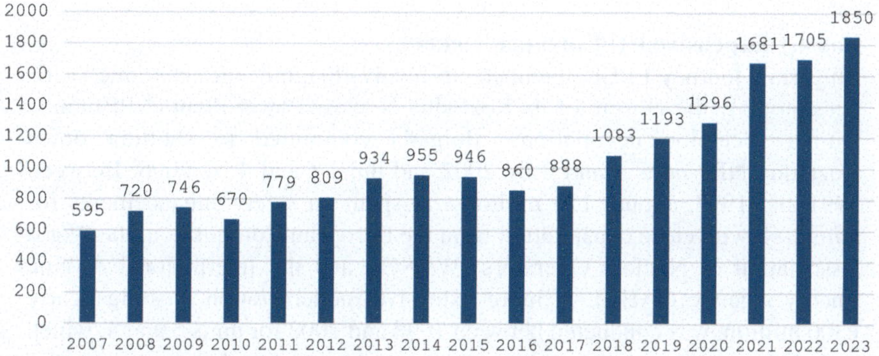

Fig. 4.7 Contribution of Bulgaria to the EU budget (2007–2023, in million BGN). (Source: Ministry of Finance)

Table 4.2 EU funding of the Bulgarian operational programs (in million EUR)

2007–2013		2014–2020		2021–2027	
Transport	1624.5	Transport and transport infrastructure	1520.8	Transport connectivity	1616.0
Environment	1466.4	Environment	1440.0	Environment	1531.6
Regional development	1361.1	Regions in growth	1359.7	Development of the regions	2894.5
Human resources development	1031.8	Human resources development	1206.9	Human resources development	1648.9
Competitiveness of the Bulgarian economy	987.9	Innovation and competitiveness	1443.4	Competitiveness and innovation in enterprises	1228.2
Administrative capacity	153.7	Good governance	238.4	Research, innovation, and digitalization for smart transformation	885.5
Technical assistance	48.3	Science and education for smart growth	595.1	Education	786.8
		Foods	143.4	Food and basic material support	189.5
		SME initiative	102.0	Technical assistance	100.3
Rural development	2642.2	Rural development	2487.7	Migration and security (AMIF+BMVI+ISF)	264.1
Fisheries	75.9	Maritime and fisheries	80.8	Maritime, fisheries, and aquaculture	84.9
Total	9391.8	Total	10618.1	Total	11230.3

Source: UMIS, accessed on: 21.07.2024

Box 4.1 Expensive EU Entrance Ticket

Bulgaria's journey to EU membership involved significant economic sacrifices, notably the closure of its Kozloduy Nuclear Power Plant (NPP) units. During accession negotiations, Bulgaria committed to shutting down Kozloduy NPP units 1 and 2 by 2002 and units 3 and 4 by 2006. Between 1991 and 1997, about €129 million was spent on safety enhancements for units 1–4, with close consultation from the European Commission, the World Association of Nuclear Operators (WANO), and the International Atomic Energy Agency (IAEA). A more extensive modernization, costing nearly €300 million, was conducted between 1998 and 2002 for units 3 and 4, which included control systems replacements and operational safety upgrades (Wuppertal Institute for Climate, Environment and Energy, 2007).

In 2003, after scrutiny by international inspectors, WANO confirmed that units 3 and 4 met all necessary international safety standards for operation, a finding supported by the 2002 IAEA Safety Review Mission at Kozloduy (ibid.). Despite this, Bulgaria proceeded with the shutdowns to meet EU requirements, with the EU contributing approximately €850 million for reactor decommissioning. This decision reflected Bulgaria's strategic prioritization of EU integration. The total costs and lost profits from these closures were estimated at $14 billion (Angelov, 2015), highlighting the significant trade-offs in energy security and economic stability required to comply with EU safety regulations.

Nonetheless, challenges like administrative inefficiencies, uneven regional development, and fund absorption issues have limited their effectiveness (Medve-Bálint & Šćepanović, 2020). While some regions thrived, others lagged, revealing disparities in fund distribution and utilization. Moreover, Surubaru (2021) highlights unintended consequences, such as fostering clientelism and corruption, where political actors exploited funding mechanisms for personal or party gain. Additionally, the reliance on EU funds has at times substituted for domestic investment, reducing incentives for comprehensive national policy reforms and creating a dependency on external financial support.

Similarly, Bulgaria's experience with the Common Agricultural Policy (CAP) has been mixed. While CAP subsidies have modernized agriculture, they disproportionately favored large-scale farms, marginalizing smaller producers and skewing production toward cash crops like wheat and maize, which require less labor and offer lower added value. This shift has transformed Bulgaria, once a major fruit and vegetable producer, into a net importer of these products, undermining agricultural diversity and labor-intensive farming sectors (Sabev, 2019).

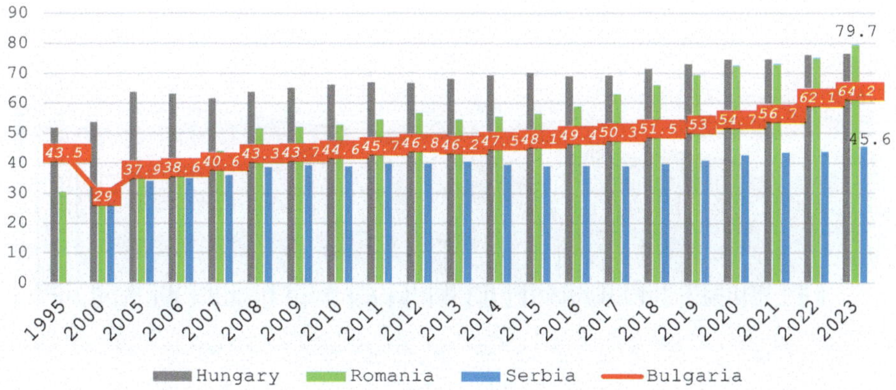

Fig. 4.8 GDP at market prices of Bulgaria and comparator countries (per capita in PPS EU-27 = 100, selected years of the 1995–2023 period). (Source: Eurostat, accessed on 27.06.2024)

Overall Economic Performance

Finally, to truly evaluate the effects of EU integration, it is essential to examine how the standard of living in Bulgaria has evolved. Exports, investment, and fiscal transfers, after all, hold little meaning if they do not translate into tangible improvements in the lives of citizens. While Bulgaria has made notable progress in terms of GDP per capita and actual individual consumption, deeper analysis reveals persistent regional disparities and rising income inequality that temper the broader success story.

Figure 4.8 shows Bulgaria's GDP per capita at market prices (in PPS) compared to regional peers. Since joining the EU in 2007, Bulgaria's GDP per capita has steadily increased, rising from 43.5% of the EU average in 1995 to 64.2% by 2023. This reflects Bulgaria's successful macroeconomic stabilization and integration into the single market. Notably, Bulgaria has outpaced Serbia, which remains outside the EU, highlighting the positive role of EU membership in accelerating economic growth. However, Bulgaria still lags behind Hungary and Romania, with Romania surpassing Bulgaria post-2006 and reaching nearly 80% of the EU average by 2023.

Figure 4.9 reveals a striking rise in Bulgaria's actual individual consumption, from just 4.3 thousand PPS in 1995 to 17.9 thousand PPS in 2023. This fourfold increase highlights not only the expansion of Bulgaria's economy but also a meaningful improvement in citizens' ability to spend on goods and services. The importance of this indicator cannot be overstated: while GDP figures reflect broader economic activity, individual consumption speaks directly to the quality of life, capturing how economic growth translates into tangible benefits for households.

What makes Bulgaria's progress even more noteworthy is that it has not only outpaced non-EU neighbors like Serbia but has also surpassed Hungary in 2023. This shift signals that Bulgaria has effectively leveraged EU integration to boost household consumption, moving ahead of countries that were traditionally more economically advanced. While Romania continues to maintain a lead, Bulgaria's

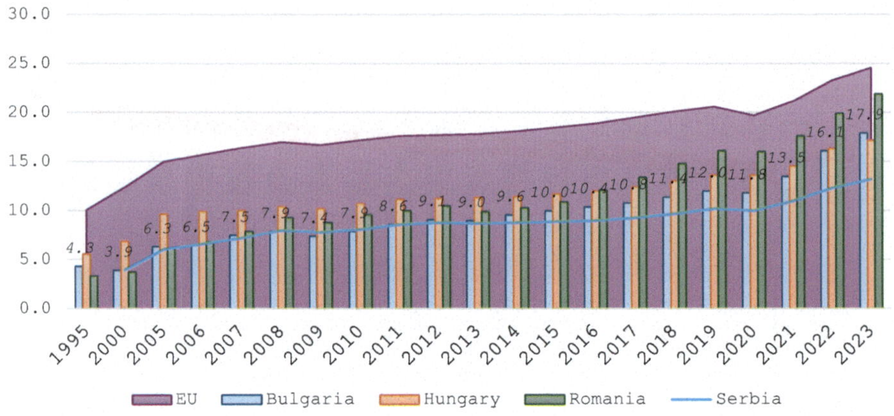

Fig. 4.9 Actual individual consumption of Bulgaria and comparator countries (real expenditure per capita in thousand PPS EU-27, selected years of the 1995–2023 period). (Source: Eurostat, accessed on 19.06.2024)

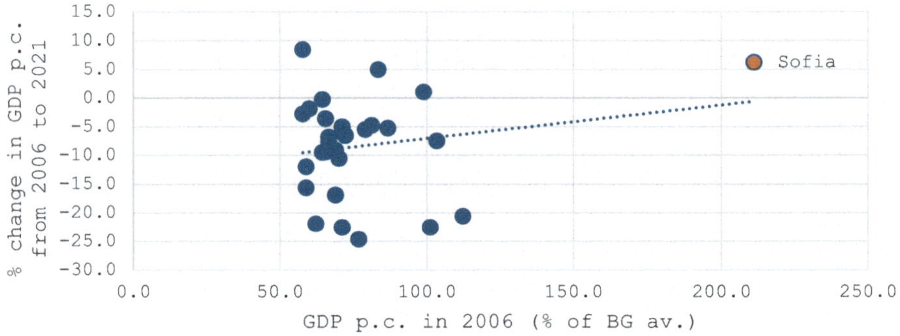

Fig. 4.10 Regional income divergence among Bulgaria's NUTS 3 regions in PPS per inhabitant. (Source: Eurostat, accessed on 19.06.2024)

rapid rise demonstrates the concrete gains of increased investment, job creation, and wage growth stemming from its EU membership.

Despite these achievements, challenges remain—chief among them, Bulgaria's growing regional inequalities. Figure 4.10 paints a clear picture of this divide, comparing GDP per capita across NUTS 3 regions from 2006 to 2021 and revealing how some areas have flourished while others have fallen further behind.

Sofia stands out as the undeniable winner. Already more than double the national average in 2006, Sofia continued to grow, solidifying its role as Bulgaria's economic engine. With better infrastructure, investment, and job opportunities, the capital has become a magnet for talent and resources, leaving other regions struggling to keep up.

Most other regions tell a different story. Clustered on the left side of the graph, many had GDP per capita below the national average in 2006 and saw further declines over the next 15 years. Some regions experienced drops of over 15–20%. This highlights how EU integration and structural funds have not been enough to reverse economic stagnation in regions of industrial decline and peripheral areas (Hadjinikolov, 2020).

Adding to Bulgaria's regional disparities is a persistent and troubling trend in income inequality. The Gini index, a key measure of income distribution where higher values indicate greater inequality, highlights how unevenly the benefits of economic growth have been shared.

Between 2006 and 2021, Bulgaria's Gini coefficient rose from 35.7 to a peak of 41.3 in 2018, before slightly declining to 39 in 2021 (Table 4.3). This makes Bulgaria one of the most unequal countries in the region, despite consistent GDP growth and rising individual consumption. The data reveals a serious concern: while the country has advanced economically, wealth has become increasingly concentrated, with many Bulgarians seeing limited improvements in their living standards.

When compared to regional peers, the contrast is stark. Romania, despite starting with higher inequality (Gini of 39.6 in 2006), managed to reduce it to 33.9 by 2021, suggesting more inclusive growth. Hungary and Slovakia maintained significantly lower Gini levels, both under 30 throughout the period, indicating more equitable income distribution.

This persistent inequality suggests that, although EU funds and integration have spurred economic progress, they have not effectively tackled the underlying structural factors driving income disparity. To mitigate Bulgaria's high levels of inequality, the IMF (2024) has recommended implementing a progressive taxation system. The current flat tax structure restricts fiscal redistribution and exacerbates social disparities, limiting the broader benefits of economic growth.

4.2 Conclusion

Bulgaria's EU integration stands as one of the most significant milestones in the country's contemporary history, coinciding with its complex transition from a centrally planned economy to a market-driven system. This dual challenge—navigating both post-socialist reforms and the rigorous demands of EU accession—presented unprecedented opportunities and formidable obstacles. On one hand, EU membership has opened doors for export expansion, attracted foreign investment, improved infrastructure, and strengthened institutional frameworks. It has facilitated Bulgaria's integration into global markets, contributed to macroeconomic stability, and driven tangible improvements in living standards, evidenced by the nearly fourfold rise in individual consumption since 1995.

Yet, EU membership has not been a panacea for Bulgaria's deep-rooted challenges. Corruption remains pervasive, undermining public trust and institutional efficiency. Socioeconomic and territorial disparities have persisted, with rural and peripheral regions lagging significantly behind urban centers like Sofia. While the largest cities have benefited from investment and infrastructure development, many

Table 4.3 Gini index for Bulgaria and selected comparator countries (2006–2021)

	2006	2007	2008	2009	2010	2011	2012	2013	2014	2015	2016	2017	2018	2019	2020	2021
BG	35.7	36.1	33.6	33.8	35.7	34.3	36	36.6	37.4	38.6	40.6	40.4	41.3	40.3	40.5	39
HU	28.3	27.9	27.5	27	29.4	29.2	30.8	31.5	30.9	30.4	30.3	30.6	29.6	30	29.7	29.2
SK	25.8	24.7	26	27.2	27.3	26.5	26.1	28.1	26.1	26.5	25.2	23.2	25	23.2	24.2	24.1
RO	39.6	37.5	36.4	35.6	35.5	35.9	36.5	36.9	36	35.9	34.4	36	35.8	34.8	34.6	33.9

Source: World Development Indicators, Date accessed: 20.07.2024

smaller towns and rural areas have struggled to attract the same level of economic activity and opportunity. The expected economic convergence with more developed EU countries has been uneven—some sectors and regions have thrived, while others remain stagnant.

Moreover, EU integration has, in some cases, intensified Bulgaria's existing problems. The freedom of movement within the EU, coupled with wage disparities, has led to increased emigration, particularly among young and skilled workers, further deepening the country's population decline and contributing to labor shortages in key sectors.

What emerges from this complex picture is a critical insight: the benefits of EU integration are neither automatic nor evenly distributed. While the EU provides a framework for growth and modernization, the extent to which Bulgaria can capitalize on these opportunities depends on sustained domestic efforts. Addressing persistent inequalities, investing in regional development and innovation is essential for ensuring that growth is both inclusive and sustainable. Without decisive action, Bulgaria risks entrenching the very divides that EU membership was expected to bridge.

In the end, EU integration has offered Bulgaria a powerful set of tools—but the responsibility to wield them effectively lies within the country's own hands. The future of Bulgaria's development will depend on its ability to translate the opportunities of integration into meaningful, widespread prosperity for all its citizens.

References

Angelov, I. (2015). *Bulgaria plati nai-skapiya vhoden bilet za Evropeiskiya sayuz [Bulgaria paid the most expensive entrance ticket to the European Union].* https://www.iki.bas.bg/english/CVita/angelov/No268.htm

Balassa, B. (1962). *The theory of economic integration*. Allen & Unwin.

Baldwin, R., & Wyplosz, C. (2020). *The economics of european integration* (6th ed.). McGraw-Hill Education.

Baldwin, R. E., Francois, J. F., & Portes, R. (1997). The costs and benefits of eastern enlargement: The impact on the EU and Central Europe. *Economic Policy, 12*(24), 125–176.

Boneva, S. (2005). Classification of the main economic costs and benefits of the EU enlargement. *Economic Thought Journal, Bulgarian Academy of Sciences—Economic Research Institute, 1*, 86–99.

Börzel, T., & Risse, T. (2016). Introduction. In T. A. Börzel & T. Risse (Eds.), *The oxford handbook of comparative regionalism* (pp. 4–15). Oxford University Press.

Breuss, F. (2002). Benefits and dangers of EU enlargement. *Empirica, 29*(3), 245–274.

Bruno, R., Campos, N., & Estrin, S. (2021). The effect on foreign direct investment of membership in the European Union. *Journal of Common Market Studies, 59*(4), 802–821.

Christova-Balkanska, I. (2016). *Bulgarian economic development and EU integration: How FDI and EU structural funds could help this process?* Economic Research Institute at BAS. https://www.researchgate.net/publication/378213133

Dimitrov, G., & Plachkova, A. (2021). Bulgaria and Romania, twin Cinderellas in the European Union: How they contributed in a peculiar way to the change in EU policy for the promotion of democracy and rule of law. *European Politics and Society, 22*(2), 167–184. https://doi.org/10.1080/23745118.2020.1729946

Gill, I., & Raiser, M. (2012). *Golden growth: Restoring the lustre of the european economic model (Vol. 2). Europe and Central Asia studies*. World Bank Group.

Hadjinikolov, D. (2020). Achieving the objectives of EU cohesion policy—The case of intra-regional disparities in Bulgaria. *Romanian Journal of European Affairs, 20*(2), 86–99.

IMF. (2024). *Bulgaria: 2024 article IV consultation staff report*. IMF Country Reports 24/163.

Kundera, J. (2016). The main economic effects of Poland's entrance into the European Union. In S. Katsikides & H. Hanappi (Eds.), *Society and economics in Europe* (pp. 95–112). Springer. https://doi.org/10.1007/978-3-319-21431-3_5

Lacatus, C., & Sedelmeier, U. (2020). Does monitoring without enforcement make a difference? The European Union and anti-corruption policies in Bulgaria and Romania after accession. *Journal of European Public Policy*. https://doi.org/10.1080/13501763.2020.1770842

Marinov, E. (2015). Economic determinants of regional integration in developing countries. *International Journal of Business and Management, 3*(3), 22–39.

Medve-Bálint, G., & Šćepanović, V. (2020). EU funds, state capacity and the development of transnational industrial policies in Europe's eastern periphery. *Review of International Political Economy, 27*(5), 1063–1082. https://doi.org/10.1080/09692290.2019.1646669

Ministry of Finance of Bulgaria. (2022). *EU funds in Bulgaria: Assessment of macroeconomic effects from programs co-financed by EU resources (2014–2020)*. https://www.minfin.bg/bg/1168

Mortensen, J., & Richter, S. (2000). *Measurement of costs and benefits of accession to the European Union for selected countries in Central and Eastern Europe (No. 263)*. WIIW Research Report.

Nitoiu, C., & Moga, T. (2020). Change and continuity in Bulgaria and Romania's foreign policies post-EU accession. *European Politics and Society, 22*(2), 277–294. https://doi.org/10.1080/23745118.2020.1729053

Pasimeni, P. (2024). Twenty years after the big enlargement: Integration within the single market. *Intereconomics, 59*(4), 222–230.

Pelkmans, J. (2006). *European integration: Methods and economic analysis*. Pearson Education Limited.

Robson, P. (1998). *The economics of international integration*. Routledge.

Sabev, D. (2019). *Bulgaria: In the realm of big leaseholders. In where does the EU money go?* A Report Commissioned by the Greens/EFA Group in the European Parliament.

Stoyanova, D., & Raichev, S. (2017). EU integration effects on Bulgaria and Romania. In I. Christova-Balkanska & E. Marinov (Eds.), *International scientific conference proceedings "Bulgaria and Romania: Country members of the EU, part of the global economy"* (pp. 31–40). ERI-BAS.

Surubaru, N.-C. (2021). European funds in CEE: Drivers of change or mere funding transfers? *European Politics and Society, 22*(2), 203–221.

Tinbergen, J. (1965). *International economic integration*. Elsevier.

Viner, J. (1950). *The customs union issue*. Carnegie Endowment for International Peace.

Wuppertal Institute for Climate, Environment and Energy. (2007). *Comparison among different decommissioning funds methodologies for nuclear installations: Country report Bulgaria*. On behalf of the EC DG Energy and Transport, H2 Service Contract TREN/05/NUCL/S07.55436.

Zhelev, P. (2017). Structural transformation and industrial competitiveness of Bulgaria after 10 years of EU membership. *Yearbook of UNWE, 1*(1), 87–103.

Chapter 5
Bulgaria and the Regional Cooperation in the Black Sea Region

5.1 Introduction

The Black Sea region, a critical juncture connecting Europe, Asia, and the Middle East, is a dynamic area of geopolitical and economic significance. Comprising a diverse set of countries with varying levels of economic development and political alignment, the region has historically been a hub for trade, energy, and cultural exchange. For Bulgaria, the Black Sea represents not only a vital corridor for economic cooperation but also a platform for advancing its strategic interests as a European Union member and a regional stakeholder. The stability and integration of the Black Sea area are not merely regional priorities but fundamental to the country's national security and economic development.

The war in Ukraine has profoundly altered the geopolitical and economic landscape of the Black Sea region, introducing new challenges and uncertainties that have redefined Bulgaria's trade and investment relationships with its neighbors. Traditional supply chains have been disrupted, energy routes recalibrated, and markets reshaped, necessitating a reassessment of economic priorities and partnerships (Toygar & Yildirim, 2023). For Bulgaria, the war reaffirms the importance of a peaceful and cooperative subregion to mitigate the spillover effects of conflict, secure trade routes, and enhance regional stability.

This chapter opens with a concise overview of the Black Sea region, highlighting its strategic and economic significance while acknowledging the diversity of its constituent countries. It then explores overlapping regional initiatives, often shaped by competing priorities and external influences, underscoring the region's complex dynamics, where progress is often hindered by divergent interests and global players' competition (Oğan, 2006).

P. Zhelev, *Bulgaria in the Global Economy*, Societies and Political Orders in Transition, https://doi.org/10.1007/978-3-031-87923-4_5

The analysis then shifts to Bulgaria's evolving trade and investment relationships with its Black Sea neighbors, focusing on how these ties are being redefined in response to ongoing geopolitical shifts, particularly the profound impact of the war in Ukraine. By doing so, the chapter emphasizes the critical role of peaceful and stable economic relations in transforming the Black Sea into a region of shared prosperity and integration. Bulgaria's active engagement in regional initiatives and its commitment to strengthening economic ties reflect its broader vision for a resilient and interconnected Black Sea region, firmly aligned with the European Union's strategic goals.

5.2 Black Sea Geopolitics and Regional Cooperation Frameworks

5.2.1 Defining the Black Sea Region

With declining multilateralism, countries around the world are increasingly engaging in regional cooperation to gain economic and political competitive advantages and improve their international standing. The unprecedented disruption of world economic activity caused by the COVID-19 pandemic has further enhanced the trend toward regionalization (Enderwick & Buckley, 2020). In response to the fragilities of globalization making global value chains shorter and more resilient through reshoring and nearshoring, there would be finer regional specialization and increased intraregional flows. Regionalization is oftentimes market-driven, but it also depends on the purposeful efforts of the states to eliminate existing barriers and create conditions for frictionless exchange. Currently, over 350 regional trade agreements are in force that institutionalize regionalization and form the global competitive landscape.

Regional integration is greatly facilitated when participating countries possess a high degree of similarity—geographical, economic, political, cultural. The Black Sea region's distinct characteristic is its heterogeneity. The sea basin brings the countries together, but besides geographical closeness, they are remote in so many ways—in terms of territory, population, economic structure, and political orientation—that it is doubtful whether they represent a region at all.

Another ambiguity is related to which countries are part of the region. From an economic perspective, it is sensible besides the littoral states (Bulgaria, Romania, Ukraine, Russia, Georgia, and Türkiye) to consider also adjacent countries that are linked together and have established or exhibit potential and interest in intensive trade relations (like Azerbaijan Armenia, Greece and Moldova). This is the approach used by the EU which in 2007, acknowledging the importance of the Black Sea region as "a distinctive geographical area, strategically located at the junction between Europe, Asia and Africa and rich in human and natural resources," has initiated the Black Sea Synergy (BSS) with the aim to foster regional cooperation with and between the countries surrounding the Black Sea (Zhelev, 2021). The countries covered by the BSS initiative and therefore considered by the EU to be part of the Black Sea region are Armenia, Azerbaijan, Bulgaria, Georgia, Greece, Romania, Moldova, Russia, Türkiye, and Ukraine. The same notion of the region is posited by the Commission on the Black Sea, a civil society initiative started jointly in 2009 by the Bertelsmann Stiftung, Gütersloh; the Black Sea Trust for Regional Cooperation, Bucharest; the Economic Policy Research Foundation of Türkiye (TEPAV), Ankara; and the International Centre for Black Sea Studies (ICBSS), Athens (Commission on the Black Sea, 2010).

Moreover, participation in regional organizations is often used as a criterion for being a part of a region. Thus, in addition to the abovementioned states, the other members of the Black Sea Economic Cooperation (BSEC)—Albania, Serbia, and North Macedonia—could be considered to form the wider Black Sea region. Nonetheless, many authors stress on the fact that it would be erroneous to perceive the Black Sea countries as a region since even their most comprehensive and advanced initiative the BSEC focuses on economic cooperation rather than integration and pursues low security instead of high politics agenda. Therefore, the Black Sea pursues subregionalism rather than regionalism and should be conceived as a subregion (Manoli, 2016; Andreev, 2009; Dungaciu & Dumitrescu, 2019).

In this chapter, the most straightforward and unambiguous approach is used to identify the Black Sea region (BSR) by looking at the geographical area determined by the Black Sea catchment as a center of gravity and the six riparian states. Without downgrading the functional and geographical ties with adjacent countries and their political and economic interest to take part in regional cooperation, the BSR is deemed to encompass Bulgaria, Georgia, Romania, Russia, Türkiye, and Ukraine. Furthermore, the terms "Black Sea area," "Black Sea region," "Black Sea space," "Black Sea zone," and "Black Sea countries" (BSCs) are used interchangeably.

5.2.2 Regionalization Challenges

The end of the Cold War has removed a critical divisive line between the countries around the Black Sea that belonged to two rival ideological systems and made possible mutual cooperation. While the breakup of the Eastern Bloc paved the way for the shaping up of the Black Sea region but at the same time has opened new challenges and uncovered long-lasting downtrodden problems. Ethnic confrontation, historical remnants, and emergence of new independent players pursuing their sovereign interests very often clashing with the ones of their former metropolitan state have triggered antagonism and major conflicts with the steady participation of Russia. The postimperial power found it difficult to adapt to the new realities of adjacent countries being attracted by other geopolitical and economic actors and models. Unable to retain these countries under its sphere of influence, Russia has adopted aggressive policies to the post-Soviet BSCs aspiring for NATO membership and EU integration. First in 2008 Russia invaded Georgia supporting separatists in South Ossetia and Abkhazia. Then in 2014, after Ukraine has chosen the path of European instead of Eurasian integration, Russia violated Ukrainian sovereignty and territorial integrity by an unprecedented act of annexation of the Crimean Peninsula (Zhelev, 2021).

Large number of mostly developed countries led by the USA and the EU have imposed international sanctions on Russian businesses and individuals which besides slightly weakening the Russian economy has done little to stop the seizure. In 2022, Russia launched a "special military operation" in Ukraine, which, although not formally declared as a war by either side, has effectively escalated into a full-scale conflict (Stoilov, 2023). This war has caused widespread death, displacement, and devastation, severely disrupting trade, investment, and economic stability in the Black Sea region. The ongoing hostilities have underscored the vulnerabilities of a region where mutual cooperation has struggled to take root, revealing the fragility of regionalization efforts.

While the notion that intensified trade could have prevented conflict is now often criticized, the reality is more subtle. In the Black Sea region, intraregional trade had already begun declining before the onset of the war (Table 5.1). This decline reflected the region's inability to develop the level of economic interdependence that could serve as a strong deterrent to conflict. Interdependence, which requires robust economic ties and shared interests, was hindered by structural challenges that long predated the current crisis.

Key among these challenges are the divergent political systems across the region, ranging from EU-aligned democracies to authoritarian regimes, which have created significant barriers to trust and policy alignment. Additionally, economic asymmetries, such as disparities in market size, development levels, and resource endowments, have limited the scope for mutually beneficial trade. These asymmetries have often translated into competitive rather than cooperative economic relationships.

Furthermore, unresolved historical disputes, many of which are tied to ethnic tensions and territorial claims, continue to weigh heavily on regional dynamics. These disputes have not only fueled mistrust but also diverted attention and resources away from efforts to build cohesive economic frameworks.

Table 5.1 Intraregional exports of the Black Sea countries (2011–2023, %)

	2011	2012	2013	2014	2015	2016	2017	2018	2019	2020	2021	2022	2023
Black Sea Basin	11.5	10.7	10.3	9.2	10.5	9.5	9.9	9.4	9.4	9.5	9.8	12.7	12.3
Russia	7.4	7.2	6.6	5.9	9.8	8.8	9.0	8.5	8.2	8.1	8.5	12.8	11.9
Türkiye	9.9	9.1	9.9	8.9	7.2	6.5	7.2	7.6	8.1	8.6	8.7	10.5	11.0
Romania	14.3	14.1	13.9	12.3	10.0	9.1	9.5	8.8	9.4	9.4	9.9	9.4	10.6
Bulgaria	23.2	22.7	22.1	21.4	20.0	19.3	20.5	18.9	19.4	18.3	19.1	20.0	18.6
Ukraine	37.9	33.4	32.5	27.8	23.6	19.7	18.8	16.8	15.5	14.4	15.2	20.3	20.1
Georgia	22.4	17.3	24.5	28.1	33.6	35.8	40.1	43.0	48.7	41.6	42.2	38.2	41.3

Source: ITC (https://www.trademap.org/Country_SelProduct_TS.aspx?nvpm=1%7c%7c48046%7c%7c%7cTOTAL%7c%7c%7c2%7c1%7c1%7c2%7c2%7c1%7c3%7c1%7c1%7c1)

In addition to worsened political relations, conflicts, and historical animosities, a significant impediment to deeper cooperation in the Black Sea region is the existence of competing regionalisms. These competing frameworks create a fundamental division between states aligning with the EU and those engaging with Russia's dominated Eurasian Economic Union (EAEU) (Vieira & Vasilyan, 2018). Bulgaria and Romania, as EU members since 2007, are fully integrated into the EU's internal market, while countries like Türkiye, Georgia, and Ukraine have entered into agreements with the EU, such as customs unions or Deep and Comprehensive Free Trade Agreements (DCFTAs). Meanwhile, the EAEU, operational since 2015, serves as Russia's integration project aimed at countering EU influence (Rotaru, 2018).

This division forces potential member states to make stark choices, as simultaneous participation in both the EU and EAEU is incompatible. For example, Armenia, prioritizing its security and economic ties with Russia, chose to join the EAEU, abandoning association agreement negotiations with the EU (Ter-Matevosyan et al., 2017). In contrast, Ukraine, despite geopolitical pressure, signed a DCFTA with the EU in 2014, aligning itself with a more advanced economic bloc (Zhelev & Garashchuk, 2019). Russia viewed Ukraine's decision as a direct threat to its geopolitical interests, contributing to its annexation of Crimea and subsequent invasion in eastern Ukraine.

Georgia has successfully balanced trade relations with both the EU and the EAEU. Following its 2008 conflict with Russia, a 2012 "normalization" dialogue restored bilateral travel and trade. With a DCFTA signed with the EU in 2014 and a Commonwealth of Independent States Free Trade Agreement in 2011, Georgia has maintained free trade agreements with countries from both blocs. However, after Russia's aggression in Ukraine, Georgia was granted EU candidate status in 2023. Full EU membership will require it to abandon its free trade agreement with the EAEU member states, highlighting the challenges of navigating competing regional frameworks.

These dynamics illustrate how contending regionalisms not only hinder economic cooperation within the Black Sea region but also exacerbate geopolitical tensions. While most Black Sea countries have sought closer economic ties with the EU, the fragmentation caused by overlapping and conflicting frameworks undermines efforts to build cohesive and stable regional trade relations.

5.2.3 *Regional Frameworks for Cooperation in the Black Sea*

Over the decades, the Black Sea region has witnessed the proliferation of frameworks aimed at fostering economic cooperation, addressing security challenges, and enhancing sustainable development. However, these efforts are often complicated by geopolitical rivalries, the lingering impacts of historical conflicts, and the diverse priorities of regional and external actors. Among the various stakeholders, the EU plays a central role, particularly through initiatives such as the Black Sea

Synergy. Bulgaria, as both an EU member and a littoral state, is uniquely positioned to act as a bridge between EU objectives and regional cooperation efforts.

The Black Sea Economic Cooperation (BSEC), established in 1992, is the region's most comprehensive multilateral framework, encompassing 13 member states, including EU and non-EU countries such as Ukraine, Türkiye, and Russia. Initially conceived as a mechanism to foster economic collaboration and trust, BSEC has achieved limited success due to several structural and geopolitical constraints. Its broad agenda—spanning trade, transport, energy, and environmental protection—has often been diluted by the divergent priorities of its members. Geopolitical tensions, particularly between Russia and Ukraine, have undermined BSEC's ability to implement cohesive policies. Moreover, the absence of strong enforcement mechanisms has reduced its effectiveness, relegating it to a largely symbolic platform for dialogue (Dungaciu & Dumitrescu, 2019; Yazgan, 2017). While Bulgaria remains an active participant, it has struggled to leverage BSEC to advance tangible regional outcomes, reflecting the framework's systemic weaknesses.

The EU's *Black Sea Synergy* (BSS), launched in 2007, represents a more focused effort to integrate the region into the EU's strategic framework. Unlike BSEC, which is a purely regional initiative, the BSS aligns with the EU's broader goals of governance reform, energy security, and environmental sustainability. Its strength lies in its ability to channel EU resources and expertise into regional projects. However, the BSS has been criticized for its limited scope and impact. The initiative has often been viewed as a top-down approach that struggles to accommodate the diverse needs and capacities of Black Sea states. Bulgaria, as an EU member, has actively supported the BSS, using it to advocate for projects that align with both regional and EU priorities. Despite these efforts, the BSS's progress has been stymied by the same geopolitical tensions that hinder BSEC, as well as by a lack of sustained political commitment from some member states (Yazgan, 2017).

The Common Maritime Agenda (CMA), adopted in 2019, offers a more targeted approach, focusing specifically on maritime issues such as the blue economy, environmental protection, and connectivity. Unlike BSEC and BSS, the CMA benefits from a narrower mandate, allowing for more focused interventions. Bulgaria has been a key proponent of the CMA, emphasizing its potential to address critical issues such as marine pollution and sustainable fisheries. The CMA also aligns closely with the EU's broader environmental and sustainability goals, including the European Green Deal. However, its success depends on sustained cooperation among Black Sea states, which remains a challenge given the region's fractured political landscape (Knudsen, 2015). The CMA's potential to drive meaningful change is further constrained by limited funding and a reliance on voluntary commitments from member states.

The Three Seas Initiative (3SI), though not exclusive to the Black Sea region, provides an important framework that enhances transcontinental connectivity. Founded in 2016, the 3SI includes 12 EU member states located between the Adriatic, Baltic, and Black Seas. Its focus on infrastructure development—spanning energy, transport, and digital connectivity—addresses historical gaps in Central and Eastern Europe, directly benefiting Black Sea states like Bulgaria and Romania.

The 3SI's emphasis on north-south connectivity contrasts with the traditional east-west orientation of Black Sea cooperation frameworks, offering a broader perspective on regional integration. For instance, projects like Via Carpathia and Rail Baltica aim to improve transport linkages, while energy initiatives, such as LNG terminals and pipelines, support diversification efforts that align with Black Sea energy security goals.

Since its inception in 2016, nine summits have been held, starting in Dubrovnik, Croatia, and most recently in Vilnius, Lithuania, in 2024. Bulgaria has been an active participant, hosting the 2021 summit in Sofia under the leadership of President Rumen Radev. He has proposed adding another priority to the existing ones—cooperation in innovation, science, and research—which will foster the sustainable transport, energy, and digital connectivity. Furthermore, Bulgaria advocates for a flexible 3SI, supporting the inclusion of strategic partners and like-minded countries in projects that add significant value. It highlights the need to connect the North-South Corridor to Greek Aegean ports and link it with Corridor VIII, connecting Bulgarian Black Sea ports to the Albanian Adriatic coast, enhancing regional connectivity (Three Seas Initiative, 2021).

Alongside the summits, a Business Forum has been held annually since 2018, fostering collaboration among private and public stakeholders. In the same year, a Letter of Intent was signed to establish the 3SI Investment Fund (3SIIF), operational since February 2020, to accelerate infrastructure projects. Bulgaria has contributed 20 million to the Fund through the Bulgarian Development Bank as a shareholder.

As of the end of 2024, the initiative encompasses 143 projects, estimated at €111 billion with 37% of the funding secured. Fifty-one percent of the projects focus on transport, 39% on energy, and 10% on digital infrastructure (Three Seas initiative, 2024). Bulgaria has proposed four major projects under the initiative, including the modernization of the Ruse-Varna railway line, construction of a tunnel under the Petrohan Pass, and expansion of the Chiren gas storage facility and the Black Sea Highway between Varna and Burgas (Ministry of Foreign Affairs of the Republic of Bulgaria, n.d.). All of these fall in the first two spheres, without projects related to digital connectivity. This gap limits the country's ability to fully capitalize on the initiative's potential to foster innovation and technological growth.

The 3SIIF made its inaugural investment in Bulgaria in 2022 by acquiring a significant stake in BMF Port Burgas, a leading Black Sea port operator. The infusion of capital from 3SIIF is expected to modernize port facilities, improve efficiency, and expand cargo handling capabilities. This development aligns with Bulgaria's vision to bolster its transport infrastructure, leveraging its strategic location to promote increased foreign investment sustainable growth.

The 3SI presents Bulgaria with significant opportunities to address persistent infrastructure gaps and strengthen regional in line with its national development priorities. However, the 3SI faces notable limitations. Its focus on EU member states excludes key Black Sea actors, reducing its effectiveness as a comprehensive framework for regional integration. Furthermore, its funding model relies heavily on member contributions and external support, raising concerns about its long-term sustainability. Bulgaria's contribution to the 3SIIF, while a step forward, is insufficient to cover the scope of its ambitious proposed projects, necessitating additional financial resources.

Implementation challenges further complicate Bulgaria's participation. Delays and bureaucratic hurdles, such as environmental and regulatory approvals, have slowed progress on critical projects like the Petrohan tunnel. Additionally, there are concerns that the initiative, rather than fostering inclusive economic development, might inadvertently deepen geopolitical divisions in the region (Ralchev, 2022). To fully capitalize on the 3SI, Bulgaria must address these challenges through strategic prioritization, enhanced project management, and a balanced approach to regional cooperation.

5.3 Bulgaria's Trade and Economic Relations in the Black Sea Region

The BSCs have long been vital trade and investment partners for Bulgaria, playing a significant role in its economic landscape. However, the period from 2014 to 2023 brought considerable changes, driven by evolving geopolitical tensions, sanctions, and shifting economic priorities. These developments have profoundly reshaped trade and investment ties, presenting both challenges and opportunities for Bulgaria.

5.3.1 Trade and Investment Dynamics

Among the BSCs, Russia was historically one of Bulgaria's most critical partners, but its influence has declined sharply over the last decade. This period saw escalation of the Russo-Ukrainian conflict into a full-fledged war, the imposition of sanctions and countersanctions, and Bulgaria's efforts to overcome its reliance on Russian energy imports. The compounded effects led to a significant disruption in trade. Bulgarian exports to Russia declined from 2.4% of total exports in 2014 to just 1.1% in 2023, signaling the near collapse of a once-substantial market (Table 5.2). On the import side, Bulgaria's reliance on Russian goods also diminished, with imports dropping from 15.2% of total imports in 2014 to 6.6% in 2023. This decline reflects Bulgaria's concerted effort to reduce its dependence on Russian energy resources, which historically dominated the trade relationship. The export/import (X/M) ratio remained critically low, fluctuating between 0.1 and 0.2, underscoring the persistent trade imbalance for Bulgaria.

Bulgaria's loss of the Russian market has accelerated its efforts to diversify trade relationships. Increased trade with other Black Sea countries, such as Romania, Türkiye, and Ukraine, has partially offset losses in the Russian market. Ukraine, in

Table 5.2 Shares of Black Sea countries (%) in Bulgarian exports and imports and Bulgaria's export/import ratios (2014–2023)

		2014	2015	2016	2017	2018	2019	2020	2021	2022	2023
Romania	Exports	7.9	8.1	8.6	7.8	8.4	8.7	9.1	10.0	10.1	9.2
	Imports	6.8	6.8	6.9	7.0	6.9	7.1	7.3	7.5	6.9	6.8
	X/M	*1.0*	*1.1*	*1.1*	*1.0*	*1.1*	*1.1*	*1.1*	*1.2*	*1.3*	*1.2*
Türkiye	Exports	9.4	8.6	7.8	8.9	7.8	7.3	6.4	6.1	5.9	5.8
	Imports	5.7	5.7	6.2	6.3	6.3	6.5	7.1	7.8	8.4	8.2
	X/M	*1.4*	*1.3*	*1.2*	*1.3*	*1.1*	*1.0*	*0.8*	*0.7*	*0.6*	*0.6*
Ukraine	Exports	0.9	0.8	0.6	0.5	0.7	1.1	0.8	1.2	2.4	1.9
	Imports	2.0	1.8	1.6	1.5	1.5	1.6	1.9	2.1	3.2	2.0
	X/M	*0.4*	*0.4*	*0.3*	*0.3*	*0.4*	*0.6*	*0.4*	*0.5*	*0.7*	*0.9*
Russia	Exports	2.4	1.7	1.6	2.7	1.4	1.8	1.5	1.2	1.0	1.1
	Imports	15.2	12.0	8.9	10.2	9.7	9.9	6.1	7.6	10.8	6.6
	X/M	*0.1*	*0.1*	*0.2*	*0.2*	*0.1*	*0.2*	*0.2*	*0.1*	*0.1*	*0.2*
Georgia	Exports	0.8	0.7	0.7	0.6	0.6	0.5	0.5	0.6	0.5	0.7
	Imports	0.8	0.9	0.5	1.0	1.0	1.0	1.5	0.9	0.9	0.6
	X/M	*0.9*	*0.7*	*1.2*	*0.6*	*0.5*	*0.4*	*0.3*	*0.5*	*0.5*	*1.0*

Source: ITC

particular, has emerged as an important export destination, with Bulgarian exports to Ukraine rising from 0.9% in 2014 to 1.9% in 2023.

Romania appeared to be Bulgaria's most consistent and stable trade partner among the BSCs. Bulgarian exports to Romania increased from 7.9% of total exports in 2014 to 10.1% in 2022 before stabilizing at 9.2% in 2023. Imports from Romania also maintained a steady share, ranging from 6.8% to 7.5% over the period. The X/M ratio improved to 1.2 in 2023, reflecting balanced trade flows. This growth highlights Romania's role as both a critical supplier and market for Bulgarian goods, facilitated by shared EU membership and integrated industrial supply chains.

The product structure of Bulgaria's trade with the Black Sea countries highlights the diversity of economic linkages (Table 5.3). Bulgaria's export composition to Romania shifted toward high-value products, with chemicals (17.2%) and machinery/electrical equipment (14.7%) dominating exports in 2023, reflecting increasing industrial integration within the EU. Imports from Romania also featured machinery (17.8%) and metals (12.8%), supporting Bulgaria's industrial supply chains.

Türkiye remained a crucial supplier of metals (23.6%) and machinery (14.9%) by 2023, while its importance as a market for Bulgarian mineral products diminished. Bulgaria's exports to Ukraine continued to be dominated by mineral products (45.2%), while imports increasingly consisted of agricultural goods like vegetable products (31.1%) and foodstuffs (12.1%), as Ukraine sought alternative export markets and routes. Trade with Russia was heavily skewed toward chemicals (60% of exports) and mineral products (95.5% of imports), reflecting its role as a supplier of raw materials. Georgia maintained a heavy reliance on mineral products for both exports (37.6%) and imports (87.7%), indicating limited diversification.

Table 5.3 Structure of Bulgarian trade with Black Sea countries according to top 3 product groups (2014 and 2023, %)

	Exports		Imports	
	2014	*2023*	*2014*	*2023*
Romania	Metals (16.9%)	Chemicals (17.2%)	Mineral products (22.4%)	Machinery/El. equipment (17.8%)
	Vegetable products (16.3%)	Machinery/El. equipment (14.7%)	Metals (14.3%)	Metals (12.8%)
	Machinery/El. equipment (16.2%)	Mineral products (12.1%)	Chemicals (11.7%)	Mineral products (12.1%)
Türkiye	Mineral products (31.1%)	Metals (29.4%)	Metals (19.7%)	Metals (23.6%)
	Metals (29.9%)	Machinery/El. equipment (20.8%)	Machinery/El. equipment (15.9%)	Mineral products (15.2%)
	Machinery/El. equipment (9.7%)	Animal products (8%)	Textiles (15.7%)	Machinery/El. equipment (14.9%)
Ukraine	Mineral products (42.2%)	Mineral products (45.2%)	Metals (59.5%)	Metals (43.4%)
	Chemicals (17.8%)	Chemicals (28%)	Mineral products (26.5%)	Vegetable products (31.1%)
	Machinery/El. equipment (14.3%)	Machinery/El. equipment (8.5%)	Chemicals (4.6%)	Foodstuffs (12.1%)
Russia	Chemicals (39.1%)	Chemicals (60%)	Mineral products (89%)	Mineral products (95.5%)
	Machinery/El. equipment (28.1%)	Foodstuffs (13.9%)	Metals (7.4%)	Metals (2.2%)
	Foodstuffs (8%)	Machinery/El. equipment (11.5%)	Machinery/El. equipment (1.2%)	Machinery/El. equipment (0.2%)
Georgia	Mineral products (62.1%)	Mineral products (37.6%)	Mineral products (89.2%)	Mineral products (87.7%)
	Chemicals (10.6%)	Transp. equipment (18.4%)	Chemicals (6%)	Chemicals (9.2%)
	Transp. equipment (8.1%)	Machinery/El. equipment (11.6%)	Metals (4.6%)	Textiles (1.5%)

Source: ITC

EU sanctions against Russia, implemented following the annexation of Crimea in 2014 and expanded after the 2022 invasion of Ukraine, significantly restricted not just trade but also Russian investment. These measures targeted key sectors, including energy, finance, and technology, effectively limiting Russia's access to the Bulgarian market. Russian FDI in Bulgaria declined from €1,957 million (5.2% of total FDI) in 2014 to €1,759 million (3.2%) in 2023 (Table 5.4). Taking into account the impact of sanctions and the degraded political relations, a further disinvestment is expected (Box 5.1).

Romania and Türkiye have emerged as Bulgaria's leading investment partners among the BSCs. Romanian FDI in Bulgaria grew by 70% to €490 million in 2023, while Bulgarian investment in Romania surged by 350% to €480 million. Similarly,

Table 5.4 FDI inward and outward stock between Bulgaria and the Black Sea countries (2014–2023, million euro and % of total)

	FDI inward stock					FDI outward stock				
	2014		2023		2014–2023 change	2014		2023		2014–2023 change
	€M	%	€M	%	%	€M	%	€M	%	%
Georgia	20.5	0.1	15.4	0.0	−25	0.9	0.1	27.0	0.7	2900
Türkiye	600.4	1.6	1265.9	2.3	111	44	2.9	53.6	1.3	21.8
Romania	288	0.8	489.8	0.9	70	106.6	7.0	480.1	11.7	350.4
Russia	1956.5	5.2	1758.9	3.2	−10	43.7	2.9	64.7	1.6	48.1
Ukraine	30.3	0.1	288.2	0.5	851	29.9	2.0	42.2	1.0	41.1

Source: BNB

Turkish FDI in Bulgaria doubled, reflecting strong bilateral ties in manufacturing and retail sectors. Despite an increase in absolute outward FDI stock to both Ukraine and Russia from 2014 to 2023, their shares as a percentage of Bulgaria's total outward FDI declined. Both countries' relative importance diminished as Bulgaria diversified its investments across broader international markets, reflecting cautious approach amidst geopolitical instability.

Box 5.1 LUKOIL Bulgaria—a giant facing market exit

LUKOIL Neftochim Burgas, Bulgaria's largest refinery and leading company by revenue, has long been a cornerstone of the country's energy sector. It plays a pivotal role in fuel production, distribution, and export, making it a vital contributor to Bulgaria's economy and trade within the Black Sea region. Despite its dominance, the company has faced significant criticism for years of avoiding corporate taxes through transfer pricing strategies, even with Bulgaria's corporate tax rate being one of the lowest in Europe at just 10%.

This tax avoidance, coupled with allegations of monopolistic practices, drew increasing political and public scrutiny. Recent geopolitical shifts, including sanctions on Russian entities, exacerbated these challenges, compelling LUKOIL to adapt. In 2023, the company ended its processing model for international subsidiaries, shifting profits back to Bulgaria as part of an agreement to secure an EU derogation permitting the export of its products. By 2024, LUKOIL transitioned to sourcing non-Russian crude, aligning with the EU's diversification objectives.

Amid these geopolitical and regulatory pressures, LUKOIL announced its intention to sell its Bulgarian assets, including the Burgas refinery, an extensive retail network, and key infrastructure. This sale presents an opportunity for strategic international investors to reshape Bulgaria's energy market by fostering greater competition and transparency, marking a significant shift in the country's trade and investment dynamics with Russia.

5.3.2 *Strategic Areas of Collaboration*

Bulgaria's Black Sea coastline offers unique opportunities to enhance its strategic importance in transport, energy, and the blue economy. As a coastal nation, Bulgaria can leverage regional collaboration to expand connectivity, diversify energy sources, and develop innovative maritime industries, strengthening its economic and geopolitical position.

Transport

Bulgaria's transport infrastructure plays a pivotal role in connecting the Black Sea region with broader European and Eurasian markets. As indicated by the Logistics Performance Index (LPI) scores, Bulgaria's infrastructure quality has improved moderately, reaching 3.1 in 2023, up from 2.9 in 2014. This reflects ongoing investments and alignment with EU transport policies, although there remains a significant gap compared to the regional leader, Germany, with a score of 4.3 (Fig. 5.1). Bulgaria's performance, however, surpasses that of some Black Sea neighbors, highlighting its potential to act as a regional transport hub.

Bulgaria has been actively involved in regional transport initiatives aimed at improving connectivity and facilitating trade. The Black Sea Ring Highway, a flagship project under the BSEC, seeks to establish a continuous road network around the Black Sea, enhancing regional trade and mobility. Similarly, Bulgaria's participation in the Trans-European Transport Network (TEN-T) corridors, particularly Corridor VIII, which links the Adriatic and Black Seas, demonstrates its dedication to integrating regional transport systems. These initiatives aim to reduce logistical bottlenecks, improve transit times, and foster economic cooperation within the Black Sea region.

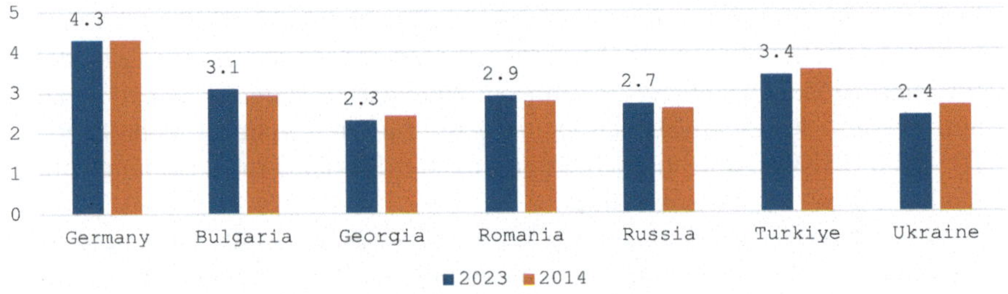

Fig. 5.1 Scores of BSCs and the best performer from the wider region, Germany, according to the Logistics Performance Index key dimension on quality of trade and transport infrastructure. (Note: scores range from 1 "very low" to 5 "very high". Source: World Bank Logistics Performance Index (https://lpi.worldbank.org/international/scorecard/column/C/BGR/2023/C+BGR+2014+C+GEO+2023+C+GEO+2014+C+UKR+2023+C+UKR+2014+C+RUS+2023+C+RUS+2014+C+TUR+2014+C+TUR+2023+C+ROU+2014+C+ROU+2023+C+FIN+2023+C+FIN+2014+C+DEU+2023+C+DEU+2014))

The modernization of Bulgaria's key ports, such as Varna and Burgas, complements these efforts by boosting maritime trade capacity and aligning with EU sustainability and digitalization goals. These ports serve as vital nodes for the TEN-T, facilitating multimodal transport solutions that enhance efficiency. The latest data shows that with 0.09% of GDP, Bulgaria ranks fourth after Iceland, New Zealand, and Lithuania, as top investor in its seaports infrastructure for 2018–2022 (ITF, 2024).

In addition to port modernization, initiatives like the Burgas-Istanbul ferry connection, proposed by a Turkish shipping company, highlight the potential for enhanced maritime connectivity in the Black Sea. Delayed since its conception in 2019 due to the COVID-19 pandemic, the project is now expected to launch in 2025, reflecting the strong demand for seamless links between major tourist and trade hubs in the region.

Regional cooperation under initiatives such as the Black Sea Synergy and the EU Strategy for the Danube Region can further enhance Bulgaria's role in facilitating seamless trade. Enhanced collaboration with neighboring countries on cross-border infrastructure projects, such as rail and road corridors, will strengthen interconnectivity and reduce logistical bottlenecks. By prioritizing these areas, Bulgaria can solidify its position as a vital link between Europe and the Black Sea, driving regional economic growth and integration.

Energy

Bulgaria's strategic geographical position at the crossroads of Europe and Asia positions it as a key player in enhancing regional energy security and fostering cooperation in the Black Sea and Southeast Europe. Central to its energy strategy is the development of the Balkan Gas Hub, a project aimed at diversifying energy sources, reducing dependence on Russian gas, and integrating Bulgaria into the broader European energy market (Assenova, 2018).

The Balkan Gas Hub is designed to leverage Bulgaria's geographic location and existing infrastructure to become a regional platform for gas transit and trade. Key to this vision is the Interconnector Greece-Bulgaria (IGB), which links Bulgaria to the Southern Gas Corridor (SGC) via the Trans Adriatic Pipeline (TAP). Operational since October 2022, the IGB provides Bulgaria with access to diversified gas sources, including Azerbaijani gas from the Shah Deniz II field and LNG from terminals in Greece and Türkiye. This pipeline, with an initial capacity of 3 billion cubic meters (bcm) annually and a potential expansion to 5 bcm, has significantly reduced Bulgaria's reliance on Russian gas and strengthened its integration into the European gas market.

The initial expectation was the IGB to be ready in 2014. Nonetheless, construction didn't start until 2019. It has faced several delays due to a combination of factors including securing funding from several sources, obtaining permits and meeting all regulations, opposition from local communities and environmental groups, technical and engineering challenges, and the impact of COVID-19, affecting funding, procurement, and construction.

Yet, this stands in stark contrast to the "Turkish Stream – Line 2," a 480-km pipeline constructed in just 1 year, which replaced Ukraine with Bulgaria as a gas corridor for Hungary and Serbia. The project has been highly controversial due to its geopolitical implications, undermining EU efforts to diversify energy supplies (Bowden, 2022). Although it enhances Bulgaria's role as a regional energy hub, it exposes the country to geopolitical risks and conflicts with EU energy diversification goals, highlighting the ongoing tension between national interests and EU policy priorities.

The EU has played a vital role in supporting Bulgaria's energy infrastructure projects. Through the Connecting Europe Facility (CEF), the EU has funded critical initiatives, including the IGB and the modernization of Bulgaria's gas transmission system. These projects align with the EU's Energy Union strategy, which prioritizes diversification, market integration, and the development of renewable energy infrastructure.

Bulgaria's participation in renewable energy projects, such as the High Voltage Direct Current (HVDC) submarine cable under the Black Sea, further exemplifies its commitment to sustainable energy solutions. This project, part of the Caspian-Black Sea Green Energy Corridor, aims to transmit renewable electricity from the South Caucasus to Europe, enhancing Bulgaria's role in the transition to a low-carbon energy future.

By capitalizing on its geographic advantage and leveraging EU support, Bulgaria can not only enhance its own energy security but also contribute significantly to the diversification and stability of Southeast Europe's energy market.

Blue Economy

The blue economy presents significant opportunities for Bulgaria and the other Black Sea coastal nations through enhanced regional cooperation. Bulgaria's blue economy sectors, such as tourism, fisheries, and maritime transport, contribute significantly to its GDP, with maritime tourism alone adding €995 million in gross value added (GVA) annually, representing 2% of the national GVA (World Bank, 2020). However, emerging industries like marine renewable energy and blue biotechnology such as food additives, animal feeds, pharmaceuticals, and cosmetics present untapped potential for diversification and innovation, which could be unlocked through enhanced regional cooperation (European Commission, 2022).

The Black Sea holds considerable promise for offshore wind energy, a key focus area under the EU's decarbonization strategy. Regional frameworks, such as the Common Maritime Agenda for the Black Sea, provide opportunities for Bulgaria to collaborate with neighboring countries on research, investment, and deployment of renewable energy technologies. By pursuing these joint initiatives, Bulgaria can position itself as a leader in sustainable energy production while contributing to regional energy transitions.

In fisheries and aquaculture, Bulgaria faces challenges related to overfishing and environmental pressures, which threaten the long-term sustainability of these sectors (European Commission, 2023). Collaborative efforts under the Black Sea Synergy framework can help address these issues by promoting shared policies for sustainable fisheries management and developing high-value aquaculture production. Such initiatives would enhance the resilience of marine ecosystems while improving the economic performance of fisheries across the region

Regional cooperation also plays a critical role in advancing sustainable marine practices and preserving the Black Sea's ecological balance. Cross-border efforts in marine spatial planning and pollution reduction, supported by the Strategic Research and Innovation Agenda for the Black Sea, are essential to mitigating environmental risks and ensuring the long-term viability of blue economy activities. By aligning with these initiatives, Bulgaria can drive innovation, promote sustainability, and strengthen its economic integration within the Black Sea region.

5.4 Conclusion

The Black Sea region is a dynamic and strategically significant area, offering both opportunities and challenges for regional and global stakeholders. As a vital crossroads between Europe, Asia, and the Middle East, its geoeconomic importance lies in trade, transportation, and energy flows. However, geopolitical rivalries, ongoing conflicts, and environmental concerns continue to shape its developmental trajectory.

A key finding of this study highlights the need for enhanced multilateral cooperation. While initiatives like the BSEC and regional EU strategies provide foundational frameworks, their effectiveness is often undermined by fragmented approaches and competing national interests. Strengthening governance, aligning regional objectives with broader European integration, and fostering sustainable development are crucial for building a resilient Black Sea region.

Energy security and environmental sustainability also remain critical. Diversifying energy routes, advancing renewable energy investments, and implementing robust environmental monitoring are vital steps to address resource dependency and ecological degradation.

The region's stability and progress will depend on proactive collaboration between local and external stakeholders. By fostering inclusive dialogue, promoting economic interdependence, and addressing security concerns through cooperative frameworks, the Black Sea can shift from a zone of competition to one of synergy. Achieving this transformation requires a shared commitment to tackling immediate challenges while building a long-term vision for a peaceful, prosperous, and integrated future.

References

Andreev, S. (2009). Sub-regional cooperation and the expanding EU: The Balkans and the Black Sea area in a comparative perspective. *Journal of Balkan and Near Eastern Studies, 11*(1), 83–106.

Assenova, M. (2018). *Bulgaria's ambitions for a Balkan Gas Hub: Challenges, opportunities and the role of a new offshore gas storage project*. The Jamestown Foundation: Washington D.C. https://jamestown.org/wp-content/uploads/2018/12/Bulgaria-Gas-Storage-full-web.pdf

Bowden, J. (2022). *South East Europe gas markets: Reconfiguring supply flows and replacing Russian gas*. OIES Paper: NG, No. 177. Oxford: The Oxford Institute for Energy Studies.

Commission on the Black Sea. (2010). A 2020 vision for the Black Sea region. Bertelsmann Stiftung, Gütersloh. www.bertelsmann-stiftung.de

Dungaciu, D., & Dumitrescu, L. (2019). Romania's strategic initiatives in the Black Sea area: From sub-regionalism to peripheral regionalism. *Southeast European and Black Sea Studies, 19*(2), 333–351.

Enderwick, P., & Buckley, P. (2020). Rising regionalization: Will the post-COVID-19 world see a retreat from globalization? *Transnational Corporations, 27*(2), 99–112.

European Commission. (2022). *The EU blue economy report 2022*. Publications Office of the European Union.

European Commission. (2023). *The EU blue economy report 2023*. Publications Office of the European Union.

ITF. (2024). Future transport infrastructure: Comparing national investments. Statistics Brief: June 2024. International Transport Forum. https://www.itf-oecd.org/future-infrastructure-comparing-national-investments

Knudsen, S. (2015). Marine governance in the Black Sea. In K. Kern (Ed.), *Governing Europe's marine environment: Europeanization of regional seas or regionalization of EU policies?* Routledge.

Manoli, P. (2016). *The dynamics of Black Sea subregionalism*. Routledge.

Ministry of Foreign Affairs of the Republic of Bulgaria. (n.d.). The three seas initiative. https://www.mfa.bg/bg/3109

Oğan, S. (2006). The Black Sea: New arena for global competition. *Transatlantic Policy Quarterly*. http://turkishpolicy.com/article/517/the-black-sea-new-arena-for-global-competition-summer-2006

Ralchev, P. (2022). Bulgaria: Sense, sensibility and wariness. In A. Sprūds & M. Vargulis (Eds.), *Three seas initiative: Mapping national perspectives*. Latvian Institute of International Affairs.

Rotaru, V. (2018). The Eurasian Economic Union – A sustainable alternative for the former Soviet space? *Journal of Contemporary European Studies, 26*(4), 425–442.

Stoilov, Y. (2023). Europe and the War in Ukraine: Support, degree of participation or neutrality. *Bulgarian Journal of International Economics and Politics, 3*(2), 128–130.

Ter-Matevosyan, V., Drnoian, A., Mkrtchyan, N., & Yepremyan, T. (2017). Armenia in the Eurasian Economic Union: Reasons for joining and its consequences. *Eurasian Geography and Economics, 58*(3), 340–360.

Three Seas Initiative. (2021). Bulgaria's vision. https://3seas.eu/about/bulgaria-s-vision

Three Seas Initiative. (2024). Status report of 2024. https://projects.3seas.eu/report

Toygar, A., & Yildirim, U. (2023). Examining the effects of the Russia-Ukraine conflict on global supply chains. In F. Özsungur (Ed.), *Handbook of research on war policies, strategies, and cyber wars* (pp. 184–199). IGI Global. https://doi.org/10.4018/978-1-6684-6741-1.ch010

Vieira, A., & Vasilyan, S. (2018). Armenia and Belarus: Caught between the EU's and Russia's conditionalities? *European Politics and Society, 19*(4), 471–489.

World Bank. (2020). *Bulgaria: Toward blue economy development*. The World Bank Group.

Yazgan, H. (2017). Black Sea synergy: Success or failure for the European Union? *Marmara University Journal of Political Science, 5*, 67–78.

Zhelev, P. (2021). *Building a closer Black Sea: Promoting trade and economic interdependence*. Middle East Institute.

Zhelev, P., & Garashchuk, A. (2019). Prospects for free trade between the Eurasian Economic Union and the European Union after the sanctions. *Studia Politica; Romanian Political Science Review, 19*(3/4), 345–556.

Chapter 6
Foreign Economic Relations of Bulgaria with Key Global Players

6.1 Introduction

For small, open economies like Bulgaria, foreign economic relations (FER) with major global players are pivotal in ensuring access to larger markets, advanced technologies, and essential capital for sustained development. Over the decades following the Cold War, Bulgaria's integration into the global economy has been primarily shaped by its relationship with the European Union (EU). As a key economic partner, the EU facilitated Bulgaria's transition to a market economy through economic agreements, development assistance, and stimulus for structural reforms that paved the way to Bulgaria's EU accession. This integration not only anchored the EU as Bulgaria's dominant trading partner, but since 2007, it has also established a regulatory framework for its foreign economic relations.

In addition to its deep integration within the EU, Bulgaria has cultivated significant economic ties with other global powers such as the USA and China. These relationships offer opportunities for diversification and growth but are nowadays unfolding against the backdrop of a rapidly eroding liberal economic order.

The era of hyperglobalization has given way to geoeconomic fragmentation, marked by economic decoupling, reconfigured supply chains, and rising geopolitical tensions—particularly the strategic competition between the USA and China (Aiyar et al., 2023). Numerous studies highlight that in recent years, international economic relations have become progressively fragmented along these geopolitical lines (Bosone & Stamato, 2024; Qiu et al., 2024; IMF, 2023). This means that global trade and investment patterns are reshaped, increasingly reflecting geopolitical priorities rather than economic efficiency. Accordingly, smaller states like Bulgaria are compelled to reassess their trade and investment strategies to navigate these shifts effectively (Mattlin et al., 2023).

Against this backdrop, analyzing the evolution of Bulgaria's trade and economic relations with the EU, the USA, and China is essential. This chapter adopts a

P. Zhelev, *Bulgaria in the Global Economy*, Societies and Political Orders in Transition, https://doi.org/10.1007/978-3-031-87923-4_6

comparative perspective, employing trade intensity indices, intra-industry trade evaluations, and sectoral analysis to uncover the importance and distinct characteristics of these economic partnerships, providing important insights for their future potential.

6.2 Bulgaria and the European Union: Evolution of Economic Partnership

We begin with an in-depth look at Bulgaria's economic relations with the EU, tracing the historical development of this partnership, the policy shifts that followed EU accession, and the current state of trade interactions within this framework, which not only anchors Bulgaria's economy but also shapes the terms of its exchanges with the other global actors.

6.2.1 Historical Overview of Bulgaria-EU Economic Relations

Bulgaria's relationship with the EU traces back to the end of the Cold War, when it sought to realign its economy and establish closer ties with Western Europe. Diplomatic relations with the European Economic Community (EEC), the EU's predecessor, were officially established on August 9, 1988, setting the stage for expanded economic cooperation. In May 1990, Bulgaria signed the Agreement on Trade, Commercial, and Economic Cooperation with the EEC, which came into effect later that year. This agreement established a formal framework for economic collaboration and extended most favored nation (MFN) status to both parties, granting each preferential treatment in trade.

Bulgaria's alignment with the EU gained momentum with its entry into the PHARE program in September 1990, a development initiative that provided crucial financial and technical assistance to support Bulgaria's economic restructuring. In December 1990, the 7th Grand National Assembly formalized Bulgaria's aspirations by declaring its intention to seek full EU membership. This commitment set the direction for Bulgaria's foreign economic policy and initiated a process of alignment with EU standards.

A significant milestone was reached in March 1993 with the signing of the Europe Agreement (also known as the Association Agreement), which provided a structured pathway for Bulgaria's eventual membership. Effective as of February 1, 1995, this agreement established a formal association framework, focusing on trade liberalization, economic cooperation, and regulatory alignment. Alongside the Association Agreement, an Interim Agreement on Trade and Trade-Related Matters took effect on December 31, 1993, enabling Bulgaria to benefit from early trade concessions while the full agreement awaited ratification. This arrangement allowed

Bulgaria to begin exporting industrial products to the EU with reduced tariffs, facilitating market access during its economic transition (Alexandrov & Petkov, 1997).

In December 1995, Bulgaria submitted its official application for EU membership, thereby committing to meet the Copenhagen Criteria—a set of standards requiring stable democratic governance, a functioning market economy, and alignment with the EU acquis communautaire (the body of EU law). Following Bulgaria's application, the EU developed the Accession Partnership in 1999, offering Bulgaria a targeted roadmap with clear reform priorities to guide its preparation for membership. To advance its candidacy, Bulgaria also made key concessions, including a 1999 memorandum on the decommissioning of Kozloduy Nuclear Power Plant units to meet EU environmental and safety requirements.

The path to accession progressed significantly after the Helsinki European Council's decision in December 1999 to formally open accession negotiations with Bulgaria in February 2000. This move recognized Bulgaria's ongoing reforms and marked a pivotal step toward membership. By October 2002, the European Commission formally recognized Bulgaria as a "functioning market economy," acknowledging the reforms Bulgaria had undertaken to create a stable economic environment (European Commission, 2002).

With all negotiation chapters closed by 2004, Bulgaria finalized its accession by signing the Treaty of Accession on April 25, 2005. This treaty confirmed Bulgaria's commitment to comply with EU standards across all policy areas, setting January 1, 2007, as the date for Bulgaria's official entry into the EU. Full membership in the EU marked the culmination of Bulgaria's integration efforts and solidified the EU as its primary trading partner.

6.2.2 Policy Shifts After EU Accession

Upon joining the European Union in 2007, Bulgaria relinquished its autonomy over trade policy, becoming subject to the EU's Common Commercial Policy, which is an exclusive responsibility of the EU. This shift meant that Bulgaria could no longer set its own tariffs, negotiate bilateral trade agreements, or implement national trade defense measures independently. Instead, all external trade policies, including tariffs and trade agreements with non-EU countries, are now determined collectively at the EU level. The Lisbon Treaty of 2009 further expanded this centralization to cover foreign direct investment, making investment policy an exclusive EU competence alongside trade. As a result, Bulgaria's role in shaping its foreign economic relations independently has significantly diminished.

However, Bulgaria retains the ability to promote its economic interests within the EU framework. Bulgarian authorities can still organize trade fairs, promote national exports, encourage inward investment, and provide targeted advice to businesses on importing and exporting to and from Bulgaria. Additionally, as an EU member state, Bulgaria participates in the EU's decision-making process on trade matters through representation in the Council of the EU and the European Parliament. Although it cannot unilaterally negotiate trade deals, Bulgaria can influence EU trade policy by aligning its interests with other member states and advocating for policies that benefit its economy.

The implications of these changes are substantial. Bulgaria's trade with other EU countries now flows freely without customs barriers, as intra-EU transactions are treated as domestic "dispatches" and "acquisitions," requiring only statistical reporting through the Intrastat system rather than traditional customs procedures. For trade with non-EU countries, Bulgaria adopted the Common Customs Tariff (CCT), leading to significant reductions in tariffs on goods. Pre-accession, Bulgarian tariffs averaged 19.2% on agricultural imports and 13% on industrial products. With the CCT in place, these rates fell to 9.7% for agricultural goods and 4.1% for industrial goods, exposing Bulgarian businesses to heightened competition from EU and international firms (World Bank, 2005).

Additionally, Bulgaria's existing regional trade agreements (RTAs) were abrogated, replaced by the EU's more extensive network of RTAs with countries worldwide, including Canada, Japan, South Korea, and Vietnam, among others. This transition broadened Bulgaria's access to global markets under preferential terms but also required adherence to the EU's collective approach. Furthermore, Bulgaria adopted the EU's Generalized System of Preferences (GSP), which provides lower tariffs on imports from developing countries, further aligning Bulgarian trade policy with the EU's broader commitments to global development.

Overall, EU membership has greatly increased the openness of Bulgaria's economy. By joining the EU's extensive trade and investment framework, Bulgaria gained access to new markets and investment flows. At the same time, the lower external tariffs and increased competition within the EU single market have pressured Bulgarian industries to modernize and become more competitive. While Bulgaria's trade policy autonomy is limited, its participation in the EU gives it access to the benefits of a unified trade strategy, making it an active, though integrated player in global trade.

6.2.3 Trade Relations of Bulgaria with the EU

Bulgaria's trade with the other member states of the EU has significantly expanded over the last decade, benefiting greatly from the unrestricted exchange within the single market. Between 2014 and 2023, Bulgaria's total exports to the EU grew from USD 22.4 billion to USD 28.6 billion, while imports rose to USD 31.9 billion, as shown in Table 6.1. Despite this growth, the country has consistently recorded a trade deficit in goods, peaking at USD 3.3 billion in 2023, with an export-to-import ratio declining to 0.90. This persistent deficit reflects Bulgaria's reliance on imports, particularly of higher-value manufactured goods, while primary commodities and lower-value products dominate its exports. However, the trade deficit in goods has been partially offset by a steady surplus in services trade, where exports increased

Table 6.1 Dynamics of Bulgaria's intra-EU exports, imports, and trade balance (2014–2023, million USD)

	Goods				Services				Total	
	Exports	*Imports*	*TB*	*X/M*	*Exports*	*Imports*	*TB*	*X/M*	*TB*	*X/M*
2014	17607	20747	−3140	0.85	4801	3346	1455	1.43	−1685	**0.93**
2015	15785	18172	−2387	0.87	4049	2411	1638	1.68	−748	**0.96**
2016	16779	18443	−1664	0.91	4590	2857	1733	1.61	69	**1.00**
2017	19056	21236	−2180	0.90	4817	3131	1686	1.54	−494	**0.98**
2018	21640	23361	−1721	0.93	5692	3150	2542	1.81	822	**1.03**
2019	21133	22951	−1818	0.92	5907	3182	2725	1.86	907	**1.03**
2020	20771	21266	−495	0.98	4394	2583	1811	1.70	1316	**1.06**
2021	27214	27926	−712	0.97	5741	3331	2410	1.72	1698	**1.05**
2022	31559	32109	−550	0.98						
2023	28613	31905	−3292	0.90						

Source: ITC

Table 6.2 exports and imports in 2007 and 2023 (million USD and % share)

	Exports				Imports			
Product group/year	*2007*		*2023*		*2007*		*2023*	
	mln. $	*%*	*mln. $*	*%*	*mln. $*	*%*	*mln. $*	*%*
All products	10660	100	29735	100	15983	100	32048	100
Primary commodities	3766	**35.3**	10674	**35.9**	2901	**18.2**	8138	**25.4**
All food items	928	8.7	4217	14.2	1283	8.0	4706	14.7
Agri. raw materials	218	2.0	215	0.7	200	1.3	342	1.1
Ores and metals	2021	19.0	4429	14.9	561	3.5	1212	3.8
Fuels	599	5.6	1799	6.1	855	5.3	1815	5.7
Manufactured goods	6893	**64.7**	19060	**64.1**	13082	**81.8**	23901	**74.6**
Chemicals	517	4.8	3093	10.4	2096	13.1	5134	16.0
Machinery and transp. equip.	1807	16.9	7596	25.5	6165	38.6	11738	36.6
Other manufactures	4570	42.9	8371	28.2	4821	30.2	7028	21.9

Source: UNCTAD (https://unctadstat.unctad.org/datacentre/dataviewer/my-report/4411)

from USD 4.8 billion in 2014 to USD 5.7 billion in 2021, ensuring an overall positive balance in the years after 2017.

The structure of Bulgaria's trade with the EU has evolved over the years, as indicated by Table 6.2. Manufactured goods remain the dominant component, accounting for 64.1% of exports and 74.6% of imports in 2023. Within this category, machinery and transport equipment have exhibited the strongest growth, increasing their share of exports from 16.9% in 2007 to 25.5% in 2023. This reflects Bulgaria's increasing integration into EU industrial supply chains, particularly in sectors such as automotive and electronics. Primary commodities, including food items and ores, have also grown significantly, with food exports quadrupling in value since 2007, underscoring the importance of the agri-food industry in Bulgaria's trade mix. Nevertheless, Bulgaria remains a net importer of higher-value goods, such as

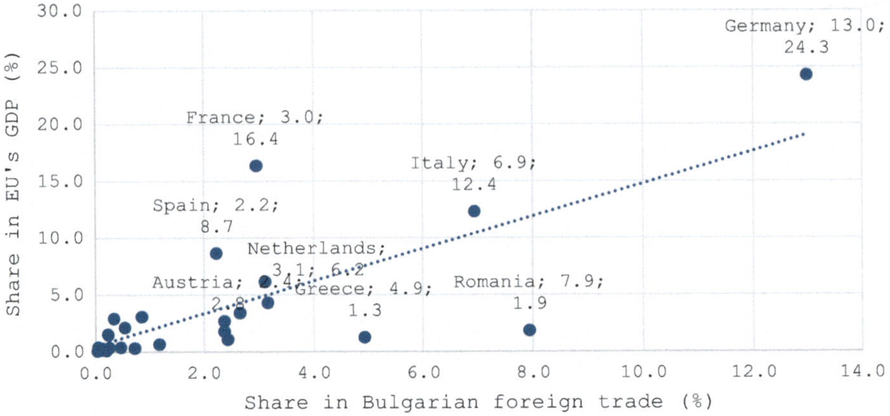

Fig. 6.1 Economic size and trade intensity of EU member states with Bulgaria in 2023. (Source: Based on Eurostat data)

chemicals and advanced machinery, highlighting the structural challenges of improving export competitiveness in these areas.

Figure 6.1 illustrates the major trade partners of Bulgaria within the EU, revealing a clear positive relationship between the economic size of a country, measured as its share of the EU's GDP, and its significance in Bulgaria's foreign trade. Germany stands out as Bulgaria's largest trade partner, accounting for 13% of Bulgaria's total trade share, while contributing 24.3% to the EU's GDP, reflecting its dominant position in EU trade networks and Bulgaria's integration into German supply chains.

Other large EU economies, such as Italy and France, also rank highly among Bulgaria's trade partners, driven by industrial complementarities and established investment relations. However, proximity plays an equally important role, as evidenced by the importance of Romania and Greece. Romania, Bulgaria's northern neighbor, accounts for 7.9% of Bulgaria's trade, facilitated by shared borders, infrastructure, and regional economic links. Similarly, Greece, despite its smaller economic size within the EU, features prominently due to geographical proximity and historical trade ties. This dual influence of economic size and geographical closeness shapes Bulgaria's trade dynamics within the EU, reinforced by sectoral complementarities, shared infrastructure, and historical and cultural ties.

6.3 Bulgaria's Foreign Economic Relations with the USA

6.3.1 Overview and Future Prospects

The diplomatic relationship between the USA and Bulgaria, established in 1903, has undergone significant transformation over the decades. Initially limited due to geopolitical constraints, particularly during Bulgaria's alignment with the Eastern Bloc, the partnership expanded dramatically after the Cold War. Bulgaria's transition to a market economy in the 1990s and its accession to NATO in 2004 and the EU in 2007 solidified its integration into Western political and economic structures, creating new opportunities for bilateral collaboration. Nowadays, the two nations regard each other as strategic partners, bound by shared commitments to democracy, security, and economic growth (U.S. Department of State, n.d.; Bulgarian Ministry of foreign Affairs, n.d.).

The legal framework underpinning US-Bulgaria relations has been strengthened through a series of agreements that promote economic, technical, and scientific cooperation. A pivotal moment in their economic partnership was the signing of the US-Bulgaria Bilateral Investment Treaty in 1992 (updated in 2007), ensuring investment protection and enabling US companies to operate in Bulgaria with confidence. The Agreement on Technical and Economic Assistance (1998) and the Scientific and Technological Cooperation Agreement (2008) advance capacity-building and innovation, while the Copyright Protection Agreement (1995) safeguards intellectual property rights. Furthermore, the Double Taxation Avoidance Agreement, signed in 2007 and effective from December 15, 2008, facilitates cross-border trade and economic activities (Bulgarian Ministry of Economy and Industry, n.d.). Together, these agreements create a strong foundation for collaboration across key sectors, fostering long-term bilateral growth and partnership.

The strategic partnership between the USA and Bulgaria extends beyond trade and investment, encompassing security, energy, and regional stability. The Defense Cooperation Agreement of 2006 facilitated joint military training and the use of Bulgarian bases by US forces, while the Ten-Year Defense Roadmap of 2020 emphasized military modernization, cybersecurity, and NATO interoperability. Complementing these efforts, energy diversification has become a cornerstone of the partnership, with the USA supporting Bulgaria's transition away from Russian energy dependency through projects involving liquefied natural gas (LNG), nuclear technology, and renewables (U.S. Embassy Sofia, 2024).

Educational and research collaboration is another key aspect of US-Bulgaria relations, with the Fulbright Program, established in 1993, at its core. The program facilitates academic exchanges, allowing Bulgarian students and scholars to study and research in the USA, while American academics contribute to Bulgaria's education system. Participants are required to return to Bulgaria for at least 2 years, ensuring that their expertise benefits local communities. This collaboration strengthens academic ties, promotes technological transfer, and prepares future leaders of Bulgaria.

American investment has been a cornerstone of US-Bulgaria bilateral relations. While BNB data does not rank the USA among the top 10 FDI sources, the Institute of Market Economics (2023) reveals that many US companies operate through European subsidiaries in Bulgaria, bringing actual American FDI to over BGN 5.5 billion by 2021—3.3 times higher than official figures. These investments support nearly 41,000 jobs with wages significantly above the national average, underscoring their critical role in Bulgaria's economic development (Institute for Market Economics, 2023).

Looking ahead, the future prospects for Bulgaria's economic partnership with the USA are promising but contingent on targeted collaboration in strategic sectors. Energy security is expected to remain a cornerstone of the relationship, with Bulgaria playing a key role in US-led efforts to diversify energy routes in Southeastern Europe through LNG imports and renewable energy projects. Innovation and digital transformation also present opportunities for enhanced cooperation, particularly in areas such as artificial intelligence, fintech, and cybersecurity, where Bulgaria's growing tech ecosystem aligns with US expertise and investment potential. Such efforts, coupled with deeper integration into US-EU transatlantic trade and technology initiatives, could further strengthen economic ties.

6.3.2 *Foreign Trade with the USA*

Foreign trade between Bulgaria and the USA has developed significantly but remains a relatively small component of Bulgaria's overall trade portfolio. Recent years have seen steady growth in trade volumes, driven by both goods and services.

Between 2014 and 2023, Bulgaria's total trade volume with the USA more than doubled, with goods exports increasing from USD 412 million in 2014 to USD 1.14 billion in 2023 (Table 6.3). The data reveals Bulgaria's consistent surplus in its trade

Table 6.3 Dynamics of Bulgaria's foreign trade with the USA (2014–2023, million USD)

	Goods				Services				Total	
	Exports	*Imports*	*TB*	*X/M*	*Exports*	*Imports*	*TB*	*X/M*	*TB*	*X/M*
2014	412	372	41	1.1	345	198	147	1.7	188	1.3
2015	421	268	153	1.6	385	221	164	1.7	317	1.6
2016	392	231	161	1.7	455	204	251	2.2	412	1.9
2017	462	263	199	1.8	433	169	263	2.6	462	2.1
2018	632	342	291	1.9	517	169	348	3.1	639	2.3
2019	634	361	273	1.8	554	182	372	3.0	645	2.2
2020	644	450	193	1.4	536	158	379	3.4	572	1.9
2021	1027	338	689	3.0	779	170	609	4.6	1299	3.6
2022	1091	852	238	1.3						
2023	1140	567	573	2.0						

Source: ITC

Table 6.4 Structure of Bulgaria's exports and imports to the USA in 2007 and 2023 (million USD and % share)

Product group/year	Exports				Imports			
	2007		*2023*		*2007*		*2023*	
	mln. $	*%*	*mln. $*	*%*	*mln. $*	*%*	*mln. $*	*%*
All products	452	100	1337	100	387	100	467	100
Primary commodities	211	**46.7**	291	**21.8**	122	**31.4**	129	**27.6**
All food items	68	15.1	176	13.2	25	6.4	32	6.8
Agri. raw materials	3	0.7	3	0.2	3	0.9	4	1.0
Ores and metals	8	1.9	65	4.9	6	1.5	10	2.2
Fuels	131	29.0	46	3.5	87	22.6	82	17.6
Manufactured goods	241	**53.3**	881	**65.9**	266	**68.5**	338	**72.4**
Chemicals	28	6.2	118	8.8	32	8.2	40	8.5
Machinery and transp. equip.	54	12.0	356	26.6	184	47.4	242	51.8
Other manufactures	159	35.1	407	30.4	50	13.0	57	12.1

Source: UNCTAD (https://unctadstat.unctad.org/datacentre/dataviewer/my-report/4411)

with the USA, both in goods and services, throughout the observed period. This surplus has been particularly prominent in services trade, where the export-to-import ratio reached a high of 4.6 in 2021. Service exports have been dominated by sectors such as information technology, tourism, and business process outsourcing, where Bulgaria's competitive advantages are evident (Institute for Market Economics, 2023).

The composition of trade has shifted significantly toward value-added products. Manufactured goods now dominate exports, rising from 53.3% in 2007 to 65.9% in 2023 (Table 6.4). Within this category, machinery and transport equipment experienced the highest growth, reflecting Bulgaria's increasing focus on high-tech and industrial goods. Meanwhile, primary commodities' share of exports has declined, indicating a shift toward more sophisticated trade profiles.

Despite these positive developments, the trade volume remains modest compared to Bulgaria's total foreign trade. Promoting diversification into sectors such as essential oils, precision instruments, and automotive components could further enhance Bulgaria's export competitiveness (Institute for Market Economics, 2020). Additionally, targeted policies to attract US investments in advanced manufacturing and R&D could strengthen bilateral economic ties.

6.4 Bulgaria's Foreign Economic Relations with China

6.4.1 Overview and Future Prospects

Bulgaria's relations with China date back to 1949 when Bulgaria became the second country to recognize the People's Republic of China after the Soviet Union. The bilateral ties were initially robust, with strong cooperation in the 1950s. However, the Cultural Revolution in China (1966–1976) and ideological disagreements between Beijing and Moscow caused a temporary cessation of interactions. Relations resumed in the early 1980s and have since been on an upward trajectory, marked by mutual respect and pragmatic cooperation (Sanders, 2021; Zhelev, 2018). In 2006, the establishment of the first Confucius Institute in Central and Eastern Europe in Sofia underscored the deepening ties between the two nations.

Over the years, Bulgaria and China have developed a solid legal and institutional framework to support their bilateral economic relations. The Bulgarian-Chinese Intergovernmental Joint Commission which has had 17 sessions so far discusses on a regular basis ways of deepening the collaboration in areas of common interest. Key intergovernmental agreements include the Treaty on Mutual Promotion and Protection of Investments (1989, amended 2007), the Double Taxation Avoidance Treaty (1989, amended 2002), and the Agreement on Economic Cooperation (2006) (Bulgarian Ministry of Economy and Industry (n.d.)). These agreements aim to promote investment, reduce fiscal barriers, and foster collaboration across sectors.

Bulgaria's participation in the China's grand strategy—the Belt and Road Initiative (BRI) and the "16+1" cooperation framework, established in 2012, which includes China and 16 Central and Eastern European countries—has further institutionalized collaboration. The BRI aims to enhance global trade and infrastructure connectivity, and Bulgaria's strategic location makes it a key participant in this initiative.

The "16+1" framework (now "14+1" after Greece joined in 2019, but Lithuania, Latvia, and Estonia withdrew in 2021 and 2022), closely aligned with the BRI, provides a structured platform for engaging with China, promoting high-level political dialogue. Under the framework, Bulgaria was designated to host the China-CEE Association for the Promotion of Agricultural Cooperation (established in 2014), a testament to its strategic importance in the agricultural sector. In 2018, Bulgaria hosted the 7th summit of the 16+1 format, while the next year, on the occasion of the 70th anniversary of the bilateral relations, President Radev and President Xi decided to upgrade them from a comprehensive friendly cooperative partnership to a strategic partnership (Habova, 2022).

Despite the intensified political relations and the alignment of the BRI's infrastructure and connectivity ambitions with Bulgaria's geographic positioning as a gateway between Europe and Asia, there have been no significant investment or China-supported infrastructure in Bulgaria so far. This gap reflects a combination of factors, including a reliance on EU funding that limits the scope for external partnerships, as well as concerns over governance, financial sustainability, and the need to align with EU regulations on foreign investments, which have made Bulgarian policymakers cautious. However, without a clear, long-term strategy that integrates national priorities with China's initiatives while respecting EU policy frameworks, Bulgaria risks missing critical opportunities to capitalize on its strategic location (Ganchev, 2023; Habova, 2022; Zhelev, 2018).

Bulgaria's foreign economic ties with China are strongly shaped by the broader dynamics of EU-China relations. As a member of the EU, Bulgaria is bound by EU policies that define China as a "strategic rival" while maintaining avenues for cooperation in trade, climate, and technology. The European Commission's "Strategic Outlook on China" has encouraged member states to align with EU-wide strategies, including greater scrutiny of Chinese investments under the EU's investment screening mechanism (European Commission, 2019). Unlike decoupling, the EU's current approach of "de-risking" focuses on reducing dependencies on China in critical sectors while maintaining selective engagement (European Commission, 2023). This framework will influence Bulgaria's future economic ties with China, with success conditioned on its ability to balance national interests with EU priorities and maintaining a cautious yet constructive engagement with China.

6.4.2 Foreign Trade with China

Bulgaria's trade with China has expanded significantly over the past decade but remains highly asymmetrical due to a persistent trade deficit. Between 2014 and 2023, Bulgaria's exports to China nearly doubled, rising from USD 709 million to USD 1.1 billion, while imports more than doubled, increasing from USD 1.1 billion to USD 2.9 billion (Table 6.5). This imbalance peaked in 2022 with a trade deficit of USD 2.5 billion, before narrowing slightly to USD 1.8 billion in 2023. The export-to-import ratio consistently ranges between 0.4 and 0.6, reflecting Bulgaria's dependence on Chinese imports, particularly manufactured goods. Additionally, it should be noted that trade statistics based on the country of destination may underestimate imports, as many Chinese goods enter Bulgaria through intermediaries in the EU.

Bulgaria's exports to China are dominated by primary commodities, which accounted for 73.9% of total exports in 2023 (Table 6.6). Within this category, food items have grown substantially, increasing from USD 3 million in 2007 to USD 573 million in 2023, driven by rising Chinese demand for high-quality

Table 6.5 Dynamics of Bulgaria's foreign trade with China (2014–2023, million USD)

	Goods				Services				Total	
	Exports	*Imports*	*TB*	*X/M*	*Exports*	*Imports*	*TB*	*X/M*	*TB*	*X/M*
2014	709	1147	−439	0.6	19.5	61.4	−41.9	0.3	−480	0.6
2015	611	1071	−460	0.6	18.1	37.0	−19.0	0.5	−479	0.6
2016	517	1151	−634	0.4	21.4	50.6	−29.2	0.4	−663	0.4
2017	769	1256	−487	0.6	26.0	45.0	−18.9	0.6	−506	0.6
2018	901	1556	−654	0.6	31.5	27.9	3.7	1.1	−651	0.6
2019	923	1703	−780	0.5	33.6	30.7	2.9	1.1	−777	0.6
2020	1052	1781	−729	0.6	18.1	25.9	−7.7	0.7	−737	0.6
2021	1329	2508	−1179	0.5	29.0	42.0	−13.0	0.7	−1192	0.5
2022	825	3360	−2535	0.2						
2023	1103	2880	−1776	0.4						

Source: ITC

agricultural goods. Exports of ores and metals, traditionally a key component, declined from 61.5% of total exports in 2007 to 30.2% in 2023, reflecting a gradual diversification. Manufactured goods, though still a smaller share at 26.1%, have shown growth, with other manufactures emerging as promising sectors.

In contrast, Bulgaria's imports from China are overwhelmingly composed of manufactured goods, which constituted 95.3% of total imports in 2023. Machinery and transport equipment represent over 50% of imports, followed by electronics, textiles, and chemicals. The growing complexity of imports highlights China's role as a primary supplier of advanced and consumer goods to Bulgaria.

These trends underscore both opportunities and challenges for Bulgaria's trade with China. While exports of food and agricultural products have grown impressively, they remain overshadowed by the sheer volume of Chinese manufactured imports, contributing to the large trade deficit. Leveraging Bulgaria's agricultural potential in wine, essential oils, and dairy products and attracting more Chinese investment in local manufacturing could support export capacity and promote a more balanced trade relationship.

Following the EU's imposition of antidumping tariffs of up to 45% on Chinese electric vehicles (EVs) in late 2024, there is a strategic opportunity for Bulgaria to attract Chinese FDI across the EV value chain. Establishing local production facilities could enable Chinese manufacturers to circumvent these tariffs and maintain competitiveness within the EU market. Such investments align with Bulgaria's economic objectives by creating high-value jobs and facilitating technology transfer.

Table 6.6 Structure of Bulgaria's exports and imports to China in 2007 and 2023 (million USD and % share)

Product group/year	Exports				Imports			
	2007		*2023*		*2007*		*2023*	
	mln. $	*%*	*mln. $*	*%*	*mln. $*	*%*	*mln. $*	*%*
All products	138	100	1339	100	1083	100	2762	100
Primary commodities	101	**72.9**	989	**73.9**	61	**5.6**	130	**4.7**
All food items	3	2.1	573	42.8	17	1.6	79	2.9
Agri. raw materials	1	0.8	2	0.1	13	1.2	27	1.0
Ores and metals	85	61.5	405	30.2	25	2.3	22	0.8
Fuels	12	8.5	10	0.7	5	0.5	1	0.0
Manufactured goods	37	**27.1**	350	**26.1**	1023	**94.4**	2632	**95.3**
Chemicals	3	2.3	46	3.5	46	4.3	253	9.2
Machinery and transp. equip.	24	17.7	183	13.7	560	51.7	1417	51.3
Other manufactures	10	7.1	121	9.0	416	38.4	962	34.8

Source: UNCTAD (https://unctadstat.unctad.org/datacentre/dataviewer/my-report/4411)

6.5 Comparative Analysis of Bulgaria's Economic Relations with Key Global Players

Bulgaria's economic relations with the EU, the USA, and China exhibit distinct patterns shaped by geography, regional integration, historical ties, and global trends. Comparing these relationships through key indicators provides valuable insights into their roles in Bulgaria's global economic engagement.

6.5.1 *Foreign Trade*

Figure 6.2 illustrates the export intensity of Bulgaria's trade with the EU, the USA, and China from 2014 to 2023. The export intensity index (EII) is calculated as follows:

$$EII = \frac{\left(\dfrac{BG\,\text{export to partner}}{\text{Total}\,BG\,\text{exports}}\right)}{\left(Partner'share\ in\ world\ imports\right)} \tag{6.1}$$

A value above 1 indicates stronger-than-average trade intensity, while values below 1 suggest underutilized potential.

The EU consistently dominates as Bulgaria's primary export destination, with an index averaging 2.2–2.3, slightly declining to 2.1 in 2023. This reflects Bulgaria's strong integration into the EU single market, supported by geographical proximity and regulatory alignment. In contrast, export intensity with China remains low, ranging between 0.15 and 0.28. Trade with the USA indicates even more modest relationship.

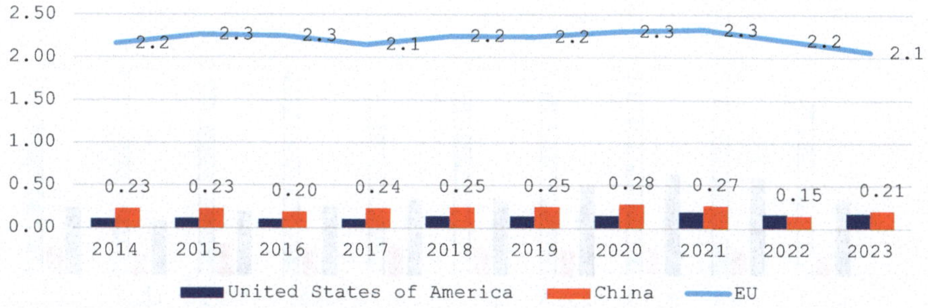

Fig. 6.2 Trends in export intensity of Bulgaria with the EU, the USA, and China (2014–2023). (Source: own calculations based on ITC data)

These trends underline the EU's critical role in Bulgaria's exports and highlight untapped potential for diversifying trade with the USA and China. Greater engagement with these partners could reduce Bulgaria's dependence on the EU and enhance its external trade resilience.

Further, to evaluate the trade patterns with the global players, we will use the Grubel-Lloyd (GL) index, which measures the degree of intra-industry trade (IIT).

$$GLi = \left(1 - \frac{\left[exports - imports\right]}{exports + imports}\right) * 100 \tag{6.2}$$

The index ranges from 0% (purely interindustry trade) to 100% (purely intra-industry trade), providing insights into the nature of trade relationships. IIT is considered a more advanced form of trade, often based on product differentiation, economies of scale, and integration into global value chains. It reflects economic maturity and specialization, where countries exchange similar products within the same industry. Conversely, interindustry trade involves the exchange of fundamentally different goods (e.g., agricultural exports for manufactured imports), typically reflecting comparative advantage in distinct sectors (Reinert, 2021).

Figure 6.3 illustrates the IIT patterns for Bulgaria with the EU, the US, and China. IIT with the EU is consistently high, exceeding 50% throughout the period and peaking at 54.1% in 2022. This reflects Bulgaria's robust integration into EU value chains, particularly in machinery and automotive components. In contrast, IIT with the USA remains moderate, between 15% and 20%. IIT with China is significantly lower, staying below 10%, reflecting a trade relationship based on dissimilar goods—primary commodities and agricultural products from Bulgaria versus manufactured goods from China. The trends in IIT highlight Bulgaria's strong industrial ties with the EU, while trade with the USA and especially with China remains primarily interindustry, with limited overlap.

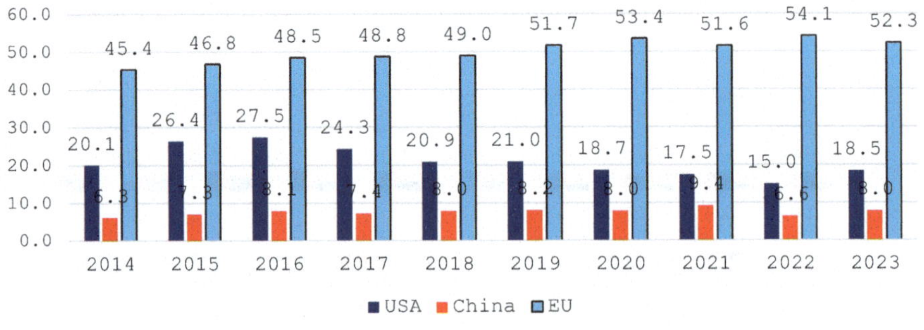

Fig. 6.3 Trends in intra-industry trade (Grubel-Lloyd Index, %, HS 4-digit level) of Bulgaria with the EU, the USA, and China (2014–2023). (Source: own calculations based on ITC data)

6.5.2 Investment Relations

FDI plays a crucial role in shaping Bulgaria's economic landscape, reflecting its integration into the global economy. Table 6.7 provides an overview of the sectoral composition of FDI in Bulgaria from the three biggest economic powers, highlighting significant differences in investment patterns.

The EU dominates Bulgaria's FDI landscape, accounting for over 74% of total FDI stock in 2023. EU investments are concentrated in key sectors such as manufacturing, finance, real estate, and services. The industrial sector alone captures 42.7% of EU-origin FDI, underscoring EU's role in forming Bulgaria's economic backbone. EU-driven FDI has contributed to economic development by facilitating technology transfer, supporting job creation, and enhancing productive capacity. However, this heavy reliance on EU investment raises concerns about overdependence, leaving Bulgaria vulnerable to regional economic fluctuations.

The USA accounted for €655 million of Bulgaria's FDI stock in 2023, a relatively small share but with significant strategic impact. US investments are concentrated in high-value, innovation-driven sectors such as information technology (26.1%), energy, and business process outsourcing. These sectors not only bolster Bulgaria's technological capabilities but also integrate the country into global knowledge networks. Prominent American companies, including IBM, Microsoft, Hewlett-Packard, and VMware, have established operations in Bulgaria, playing a pivotal role in developing its IT ecosystem. Their presence has driven the growth of skilled labor, innovation, and service exports, supporting Bulgaria's emergence as a regional technology hub.

China's investment footprint in Bulgaria remains modest compared to the EU and the USA. Despite being bolstered by the Belt and Road Initiative, Chinese FDI

Table 6.7 Sectoral composition of FDI stock in the nonfinancial enterprises in Bulgaria from major sending economies in 2023

	World	EU		USA		China	
Economic activities	*mln. EUR*	*mln. EUR*	%	*mln. EUR*	%	*mln. EUR*	%
All activities	32718	24384		655		88.4	
(A) **Agriculture**	86	64	0.3	–		–	
(B–E) **Industry**	13495	10424	42.7	176	26.8	..	
(F) **Construction**	455	314	1.3	..		..	
(G–I) **Trade and services**	7930	5744	23.6	153	23.4	19.4	21.9
(J) **Information and communication**	4012	3315	13.6	171	26.1	8.4	9.6
(L) **Real estate**	3873	2567	10.5	54	8.2	..	
(M–N) **Professional and admin.**	2661	1878	7.7	77	11.7	1.6	1.8
(O–Q) **Public services**	44	22	0.1	14	2.1	..	
(R–U) **Arts and recreation**	163	56	0.2	..		..	

Source: National Statistical Institute (2024, special enquiry, unpublished data)
Note: ".." confidential data; "–" no data recorded

has been sporadic, totaling just €88.4 million by the end of 2023. Table 6.7 highlights allocations in trade and services (€19.4 million, 21.9%) and information and communication (€8.4 million, 9.6%), led by companies like Huawei. However, confidentiality constraints ("..") in sectors such as industry suggest that these investments involve a limited number of investors, reflecting their small-scale impact. This fragmented investment pattern indicates that, despite diplomatic initiatives and participation in multilateral platforms, China's economic engagement in Bulgaria lacks a consistent focus and remains peripheral to the country's overall FDI landscape.

6.6 Conclusions

The analysis of Bulgaria's foreign economic relations demonstrates that the EU is by far its most significant trade and investment partner. This partnership not only drives Bulgaria's economic growth and technological adoption but also determines its trade and investment policy frameworks. The EU's role as a stabilizing force underscores its importance in safeguarding Bulgaria's economic security, especially amidst increasing global uncertainties. Strengthening this relationship should remain a central pillar of Bulgaria's foreign economic strategy, with an emphasis on fostering innovation, industrial upgrading, and deeper integration into European value chains.

In the context of heightened geopolitical tensions and geoeconomic rivalry, Bulgaria must adopt a balanced approach to its external partnerships. The USA offers opportunities for collaboration in strategic sectors such as energy, defense, and digital technologies, which can complement Bulgaria's economic ties with the EU. Similarly, China presents substantial opportunities for Bulgaria to diversify its export markets and attract investment, particularly through initiatives such as the Belt and Road. China's growing global economic footprint and demand for high-quality agricultural products align with Bulgaria's export potential, offering a platform to expand trade and foster bilateral cooperation in areas such as infrastructure and manufacturing.

Navigating these dynamics requires Bulgaria to carefully bridge its regional commitments with national interests. Policymakers should focus on diversifying partnerships while maintaining alignment with EU priorities. The country's ability to balance these relationships will determine its success in mitigating risks and capitalizing on emerging opportunities in the years ahead.

References

Aiyar, S., Chen, J., Ebeke, C., Garcia-Saltos, R., Gudmundsson, T., Ilyina, A., Kangur, A., Kunaratskul, T., Rodriguez, S., Ruta, M., Schulze, T., Soderberg, G., & Trevino, J. (2023). Geoeconomic fragmentation and the future of multilateralism. IMF Staff Discussion Note, SDN/2023/01.

Alexandrov, S., & Petkov, L. (1997). Paving the Way for Bulgaria's Accession to the European Union. *Fordham International Law Journal, 21*(3), 587–601.

Bosone, C., & Stamato, G. (2024). Beyond borders: How geopolitics is reshaping trade. European Central Bank Working Paper Series No. 2960. Frankfurt am Main: ECB. https://www.ecb.europa.eu/pub/pdf/scpwps/ecb.wp2960~6c3cc5e5b0.en.pdf

Bulgarian Ministry of Economy and Industry. (n.d.). Foreign economic and trade policy. https://www.mi.government.bg/foreign-economic-trade-policy/sasth/.

Bulgarian Ministry of Foreign Affairs. (n.d.). Bilateral relations: United States of America. https://www.mfa.bg/en/3165.

European Commission. (2002). Regular report on Bulgaria's progress towards accession. https://eur-lex.europa.eu

European Commission. (2019). EU-China – A strategic outlook. Joint Communication to the European Parliament, the European Council and the Council, JOIN(2019) 5, 12.03.2019. Strasbourg. https://commission.europa.eu/system/files/2019-03/communication-eu-china-a-strategic-outlook.pdf

European Commission. (2023). Speech by President von der Leyen on EU-China relations to the Mercator Institute for China Studies and the European Policy Centre. https://ec.europa.eu/commission/presscorner/detail/en/speech_23_2063

Ganchev, I. (2023). Making the case for a new coherent Bulgarian strategy towards China: A practitioner's analysis of bilateral political and economic relations (2015–2022). In A. Bogoni & B. F. G. Fabrègue (Eds.), *The dragon at the gates of Europe: Chinese presence in the Balkans and Central-Eastern Europe* (pp. 431–480). Blue Europe.

Habova, A. (2022). The role of China in Bulgaria. In A. Vangeli (Ed.), *The role of China in Southeast Europe* (pp. 22–27). Friedrich-Ebert-Stiftung.

Institute for Market Economics. (2020). *Potential export markets study: Bulgarian SMEs in selected sectors*. Executive Agency for Promotion of Small and Medium Enterprises.

Institute for Market Economics. (2023). *U.S.-Bulgaria economic partnership: Investments, jobs, and trade (1990–2022)*. American Chamber of Commerce in Bulgaria.

International Monetary Fund. (2023). Geoeconomic Fragmentation and foreign direct investment. In *IMF world economic outlook: A rocky recovery* (pp. 91–114).

Mattlin, M., Breslin, S., Sinkkonen, E., Kauppila, L., Cappelin, B., Söderström, I., & Ferchen, M. (2023). Enhancing small state preparedness: Risks of foreign ownership, supply disruptions and technological dependencies. FIIA Report 74. Helsinki: Finnish Institute of International Affairs.

Qiu, H., Xia, D., & Yetman, J. (2024). Deconstructing global trade: The Role of geopolitical alignment. *BIS Quarterly Review, September, 2024*, 35–50.

Reinert, K. (2021). *An introduction to international economics: New perspectives on the world economy*. Cambridge University Press.

Sanders, D. (2021). The Black Sea region caught between east and west. *Journal of Slavic Military Studies, 34*, 202–225.

U.S. Department of State. (n.d.). U.S. relations with Bulgaria. https://www.state.gov/u-s-relations-with-bulgaria/.

U.S. Embassy Sofia. (2024). Integrated country strategy: Bulgaria. https://www.state.gov/wp-content/uploads/2024/03/ICS_EUR_Bulgaria_29FEB2024_PUBLIC.pdf.

World Bank. (2005). Bulgaria: The road to successful EU integration – The Policy Agenda (Country Economic Memorandum). https://documents.worldbank.org

Zhelev, P. (2018). *Bulgarian-Chinese economic relations in the context of 16+1 cooperation*. China-CEE Institute Working Paper.

Chapter 7
Bulgaria's Foreign Trade in Goods

7.1 Introduction

Foreign trade has historically been a cornerstone of Bulgaria's economic development, with the exchange of goods significantly shaping the nation's growth trajectory. As a substantial contributor to the country's GDP and a vital source of employment across diverse sectors, the trade of goods serves as a barometer of Bulgaria's economic health and its integration into the global economy. It reflects not only the nation's comparative advantages and the effectiveness of its economic policies but also its ability to adapt to shifting global market trends. Moreover, the structure and complexity of the goods traded are crucial for understanding Bulgaria's position in the international division of labor and for anticipating its future economic prospects.

Since Bulgaria's accession to the EU in 2007, the country's foreign trade dynamics have undergone significant transformations. Integration into the EU single market has expanded Bulgaria's trading horizons, introduced new competitive pressures, and necessitated adjustments in domestic economic policies. These changes have had profound implications for the country's trade performance, influencing both the volume and the composition of exports and imports.

This chapter offers a comprehensive analysis of Bulgaria's foreign trade performance in the post-EU accession period, highlighting both progress and persistent challenges. It delves into the evolution of trade openness, the trajectory of Bulgaria's trade balance, and shifts in market shares. The analysis identifies the most competitive product sectors, outlines the country's principal trading partners, and examines the transformation in the structure of foreign trade over time. Furthermore, the chapter presents key institutions involved in promoting and upgrading Bulgaria's trade capabilities while addressing some of the issues they face. It also explores the role of industrial policy in supporting export development and structural transformation. By dissecting these dynamics, this chapter provides critical insights into

P. Zhelev, *Bulgaria in the Global Economy*, Societies and Political Orders in Transition, https://doi.org/10.1007/978-3-031-87923-4_7

Bulgaria's position within the global economy and the institutional landscape influencing export performance.

7.2 Conceptual Framework

Understanding Bulgaria's foreign trade dynamics requires a solid grasp of several key economic concepts. This section outlines the conceptual underpinnings relevant to the analysis of trade performance, including the importance of trade openness, trade balance and market position, trade diversification, comparative advantages, and economic complexity. These concepts are summarized in Table 7.1, providing a comprehensive framework for analyzing Bulgaria's foreign trade.

In the subsequent sections, we will apply this conceptual framework to examine Bulgaria's trade performance in detail, focusing on trade dynamics, the composition of exports and imports, and the evolution of trade patterns in recent years. This approach enables us to assess how effectively Bulgaria is integrating into the international division of labor and adapting to global economic shifts.

7.3 Dynamics and Role of Merchandise in Bulgaria's Foreign Trade

Bulgaria's merchandise trade is characterized by a very high level of openness, with the sum of exports and imports usually exceeding 100% of GDP (Fig. 7.1). This significant trade openness is shaped by several factors.

First, the volume of the internal market is small, making external trade essential for economies of scale and access to a broader range of products. Bulgaria cannot rely solely on domestic consumption for growth, making international trade crucial.

Next, the level of economic development also impacts trade openness. As an emerging economy, Bulgaria actively seeks access to advanced technologies, capital goods, and foreign investment, all of which help modernize its industries. Integration with the European Union has accelerated this process by providing a regulatory framework and market access, thereby boosting trade volumes.

The sectoral structure and diversification of Bulgaria's economy are additional factors influencing trade openness. Limited diversification means Bulgaria relies heavily on a few key industries that are embedded in European value chains. This results in high levels of both imports and exports, especially of intermediate goods, which underscores the country's role in the regional production network.

Resource endowments are also critical in understanding Bulgaria's trade. The country lacks significant natural resources, necessitating imports of raw materials and energy. This dependence drives high trade volumes.

Table 7.1 Key concepts for analyzing Bulgaria's foreign trade

Concept	Explanation	Relevance to the analysis of Bulgaria	References
Trade openness	The extent of a country's engagement in international trade relative to its GDP; measured by the trade-to-GDP ratio (sum of exports and imports divided by GDP)	Indicates countries' integration into the global economy. Higher openness drives growth, efficiency, and innovation but also increases vulnerability to global shocks, requiring adaptive policies	Krugman et al. (2018), World Bank (2024)
Trade balance and market position	Analyzes the overall performance of trade by assessing the surplus or deficit (trade balance) and evaluating the country's market share within the European and the global economy	Helps evaluate the sustainability of the country's foreign trade, revealing strengths or weaknesses in export competitiveness and positioning in global markets	Mikic and Gilbert (2007), IMF (2024)
Trade diversification	Expanding the variety of products exported and the range of trading partners; includes both product and market diversification	Highlights countries' resilience to shocks and its reliance on specific products or markets. A well-diversified portfolio mitigates risks associated with demand shocks or price volatility and opens new opportunities in emerging markets	IMF (2014), UNCTAD (2019)
Comparative advantage	The ability of a country to produce goods and services at a lower opportunity cost than others, guiding specialization and trade patterns; often measured using the Revealed Comparative Advantage (RCA) index	Identifies sectors where the country is most competitive (e.g., machinery, pharmaceuticals). Informs policy and investment decisions to focus on strengthening these sectors. Enhances gains from trade and economic efficiency	Balassa (1965), Porter (1990)
Economic complexity	A measure of the knowledge intensity and sophistication of a country's exports; higher complexity indicates advanced productive capabilities and specialized exports	Higher complexity is linked to greater income levels and growth prospects for the country. Reflects the ability to produce complex products, moving beyond low-tech goods. Supports competitiveness in global markets	Hausmann et al. (2013), Hidalgo and Hausmann (2009)

The very high trade openness of Bulgaria has accelerated growth, modernized key sectors through access to external markets, and introduced advanced technologies. However, high openness also exposes Bulgaria to global economic shocks. Such vulnerabilities were evident during significant disruptions like the 2008–2009 global financial and economic crisis and the COVID-19 pandemic, which

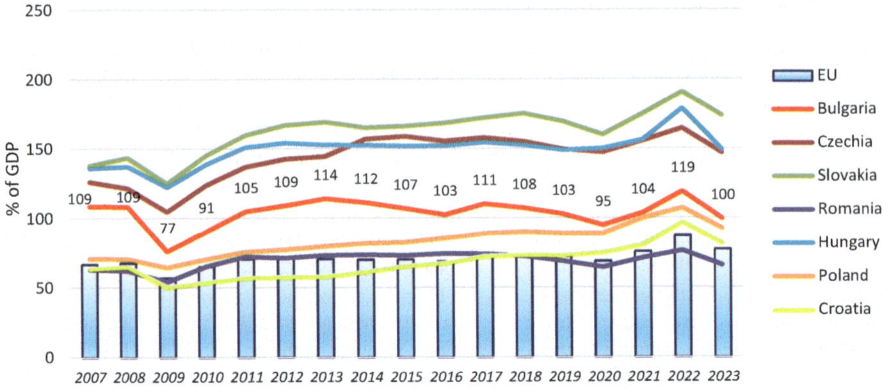

Fig. 7.1 Trade openness of Bulgaria and regional peers (2007–2023, % of GDP). (Source: World Bank Development Indicators (https://databank.worldbank.org/reports.aspx?source=2&series=TX.VAL.MRCH.CD.WT,TX.VAL.FOOD.ZS.UN,TX.VAL.AGRI.ZS.UN,TX.VAL.FUEL.ZS.UN,TX.VAL.MMTL.ZS.UN,TX.VAL.MANF.ZS.UN))

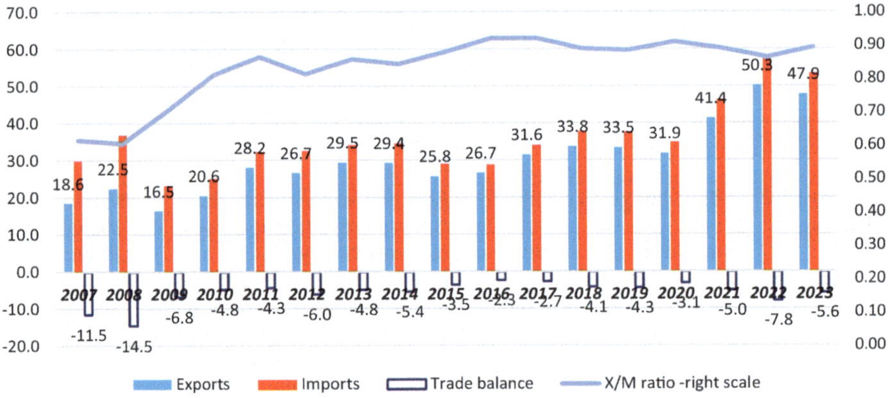

Fig. 7.2 Dynamics of Bulgarian merchandise trade (2007–2023, billion USD). (Source: ITC)

underscored the risks of a heavy reliance on external demand. The decline in trade openness in 2023 can be attributed to a combination of factors, including reduced external demand due to geopolitical tensions, supply chain disruptions, and inflationary pressures, which constrained both exports and imports.

Figure 7.2 illustrates the dynamics of Bulgaria's merchandise trade. In 2023, exports reached $47.9 billion, more than doubling from $18.6 billion in 2007, while imports increased from $30 billion to $53.5 billion over the same period. The notable trade flow expansions however were interrupted by external shocks. The 2008–2009 global financial and economic crisis led to a sharp contraction in trade, resulting in a trade openness level of only 77%—the lowest of the period (Fig. 7.1). Similarly, the COVID-19 pandemic caused disruptions that negatively affected

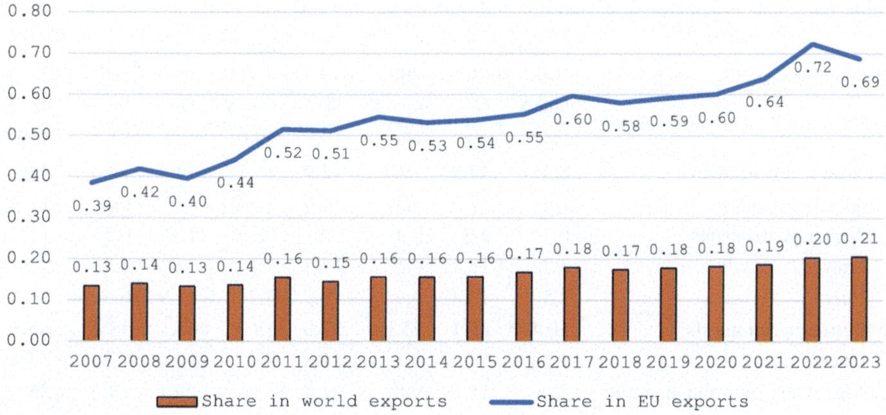

Fig. 7.3 Share of Bulgaria in the EU's and world export of goods (%, 2007–2023). (Source: own calculations based on data from ITC)

foreign trade due to supply chain bottlenecks. Another drop in trade flows occurred in 2023, mirroring earlier declines due to external pressures and global instability.

Bulgaria's trade balance in goods shows a consistent deficit, largely due to the composition of imports and exports. Imports have persistently exceeded exports in value as the latter consist of relatively lower value-added products. This ongoing trade deficit highlights Bulgaria's dependence on foreign goods to sustain domestic industries, particularly in manufacturing.

Despite these challenges, Bulgaria's market share within the EU has shown steady improvement since 2007. The importance of Bulgarian goods in EU markets has grown, driven by ongoing structural shifts and the gradual expansion of higher-technology sectors. In 2007, Bulgarian merchandise exports accounted for 0.39% of total EU exports, rising to nearly 0.7% in 2023 (Fig. 7.3). However, intense competition from countries with greater technological capacity has limited the pace of this growth. Globally, Bulgaria's share remains modest (0.21% in 2023), which underlines the need to enhance product complexity and boost export competitiveness through strategic policy measures.

7.4 Product and Geographical Structure of Bulgarian Foreign Trade in Goods

To provide a clearer picture of long-term trends and minimize the impact of annual fluctuations, the analysis of Bulgaria's trade structure focuses on 3-year averages for 2007–2009 and 2021–2023 (Table 7.2). This approach helps capture the underlying dynamics in the evolution of Bulgaria's foreign trade. Along with the growth in trade flows value, there was a significant change in the composition, especially in Bulgarian exports.

Table 7.2 Structure of Bulgaria's exports and imports in 2007 and 2023 (billion USD and % share)

Product group	Exports				Imports			
	2007–2009		*2021–2023*		*2007–2009*		*2021–2023*	
	bln. $	*%*	*bln. $*	*%*	*bln. $*	*%*	*bln. $*	*%*
All products	18.8	100	45.2	100	29.0	100	51.1	100
Primary commodities	8.4	**44.9**	19.4	**42.9**	10.1	**34.9**	17.6	**34.5**
All food items	2.4	12.9	7.5	16.6	2.3	8.0	6.1	11.9
Agri. raw materials	0.2	1.3	0.4	0.8	0.3	1.1	0.5	1.0
Ores and metals	3.2	17.1	6.6	14.5	2.3	7.9	4.7	9.2
Fuels	2.5	13.4	4.9	10.9	5.2	17.9	6.3	12.3
Manufactured goods	10.4	**55.1**	25.8	**57.0**	18.9	**65.1**	33.4	**65.5**
Chemicals	1.5	7.7	5.1	11.3	2.9	10.0	7.3	14.4
Machinery and transp. equip.	3.0	15.9	9.8	21.7	8.4	29.1	14.6	28.6
Other manufactures	5.9	31.5	10.9	24.0	7.5	26.0	11.5	22.5

Source: UNCTAD (https://unctadstat.unctad.org/datacentre/dataviewer/my-report/4411)

Primary commodities have seen a relative decrease in their share of total exports, from 44.9% in 2007–2009 to 42.9% in 2021–2023. Within primary commodities, food items increased their share of total exports, from 12.9% to 16.6%, indicating a growing competitive edge in the agri-food industry. Conversely, the share of fuels decreased from 13.4% to 10.9%, reflecting Bulgaria's shift toward higher value-added activities and decreasing reliance on energy exports.

Manufactured goods remain the dominant category in Bulgaria's exports, with a slight increase in their share from 55.1% in 2007–2009 to 57.0% in 2021–2023. Within this category, chemicals experienced significant growth, rising from 7.7% to 11.3% of total exports. This is indicative of the expanding role of the pharmaceutical and chemical sectors in Bulgaria's trade profile. Similarly, machinery and transport equipment grew substantially, reaching 21.7% of total exports by 2021–2023, suggesting deeper integration into European industrial supply chains.

On the import side, the product structure remained relatively stable. The share of fuels declined, from 17.9% in 2007–2009 to 12.3% in 2021–2023, highlighting both the rising share of manufactured imports and Bulgaria's efforts to diversify energy supply sources. Manufactured goods continued to dominate imports, with machinery and transport equipment accounting for 28.6% of total imports in 2021–2023, reflecting the ongoing need for industrial inputs and investment goods to support manufacturing and infrastructure development.

The analysis of Bulgaria's top export products over time (Table 7.3) reveals important insights into the content of the country's exports and level of product diversification. The data show that Bulgaria's export basket is still dominated by products of relatively low sophistication and limited processing. Refined petroleum oils were the leading export product in both 2007 and 2023, though their share decreased from 12.7% to 6.5%. This decline highlights a shift away from reliance on energy products, although their continued significance indicates that the Bulgarian export profile remains tied to primary and semi-processed goods. It is

Table 7.3 Top 10 products in Bulgarian exports (2007 and 2023, million USD and % share)

		2007			2023	
Rank	Product	mln. $	%	Product	mln. $	%
1	Refined petroleum oils	2366	**12.7**	Refined petroleum oils	2672	**6.5**
2	Unrefined copper	1039	**5.6**	Wheat and meslin	1682	**5.6**
3	Iron or steel products	754	**4.1**	Refined copper	1615	**3.5**
4	Women's clothing	405	**2.2**	Medicaments	1228	**3.4**
5	Men's clothing	350	**1.9**	Unrefined copper	963	**2.6**
6	Electrical energy	330	**1.8**	Sunflower oil	854	**2.0**
7	Unwrought zinc	328	**1.8**	Precious-metal ores	801	**1.8**
8	Refined copper	314	**1.7**	Sunflower seeds	754	**1.7**
9	Copper ores	254	**1.4**	Biodiesel and mixtures	749	**1.6**
10	Copper plates, sheets, strips	249	**1.3**	Insulated wire and cable	739	**1.6**

Source: ITC

important to note that Bulgaria does not possess crude oil resources; the refined petroleum products are produced from imported crude, which is largely processed at a single refinery. This highlights the import intensity associated with this export category and underscores the limited value-added locally.

Unrefined copper and wheat and meslin are other major exports, illustrating a dependence on basic commodities with minimal value-added processing. The growing presence of wheat and meslin, which rose to 5.6% of exports in 2023, signals the increasing importance of the agricultural sector, though this growth is still largely focused on bulk commodities rather than processed agricultural products.

The emergence of medicaments as a significant export product, with a share of 3.4% in 2023, points to some level of diversification and the development of more sophisticated manufactured goods. However, the rest of the top 10 products—such as sunflower oil, unrefined copper, biodiesel, and sunflower seeds—are still predominantly low-value-added goods that require minimal processing. This pattern reflects the limited structural change in Bulgaria's export profile over the past decade.

In terms of diversification, the share of the top 3 export products has decreased, yet they still represent a substantial portion of Bulgaria's total exports. In 2007, the top 3 products (refined petroleum oils, unrefined copper, and iron or steel products) made up approximately 22.4% of total exports. By 2023, the top 3 products (refined petroleum oils, wheat and meslin, and refined copper) accounted for around 15.6% of exports. This decline indicates some diversification, though the concentration in a few key commodities remains high, underscoring the need for further development of higher value-added industries to reduce vulnerability to price volatility in global commodity markets.

In terms of geographical diversification, the top 3 export partners (Germany, Romania, and Italy) accounted for 30.1% in 2023. The concentration in a few major partners remains relatively high as was in 2007, underscoring Bulgaria's continued reliance on key markets. Germany, which since 2014 emerged as the largest trading partner not just for exports but also for imports, plays a particularly crucial role, reflecting Bulgaria's integration into the EU's core industrial value chains. However, this strong dependence on Germany also poses risks, particularly regarding economic vulnerability to external shocks affecting Germany's economy. Any economic downturn or supply chain disruption in Germany could significantly impact Bulgaria's trade flows and overall economic stability. The relatively high share of top markets highlights the need for Bulgaria to expand its export base and explore new markets to mitigate these risks (Table 7.4).

Romania and Italy remained significant partners, maintaining stable shares in Bulgaria's exports over the years. Other key trading partners experienced notable changes. Türkiye, which was the largest export market in 2007 with 11.4%, saw its share decline significantly to 5.8% in 2023, indicating a relative reduction in importance. Greece also saw its share of Bulgarian exports decrease from 8.2% in 2007 to 5.5% in 2023, while France maintained a relatively stable presence, accounting for around 3.8% of exports in 2023.

On the import side, the share of the top 3 import partners has shifted significantly. In 2007, Russia, Germany, and Italy represented over 37% of total imports. By 2023, this concentration had decreased, with Germany, Türkiye, and Romania accounting for around 27.4% of imports, indicating a more diversified set of suppliers. Russia, which was the largest import partner until 2014, experienced a sharp decline in its importance for Bulgarian imports with its share dropping to 6.6% by 2023. China has steadily increased its importance, reaching 5.4% of Bulgaria's imports by 2023, reflecting growing demand for Chinese consumer and industrial goods. At the same time, the second biggest economy has not managed to position itself firmly among the top 10 export destinations for Bulgaria.

7.5 Structural Change and Economic Complexity of Bulgarian Merchandise Exports

To analyze Bulgaria's competitiveness in international goods trade and the structural shifts in its export composition, two key indicators are used: Revealed Comparative Advantage (RCA) and Relative Trade Balance (RTB). While RCA highlights Bulgaria's specialization in exporting certain goods, RTB indicates whether Bulgaria is a net exporter or net importer in those product categories.

RCA, known as the Balassa Index, measures how competitive Bulgaria is in exporting a particular product compared to the world average (Balassa, 1965). It is calculated as follows:

$$RCA_i = \frac{\left(X_{i,BG} / X_{total,BG}\right)}{\left(X_{i,world} / X_{total,world}\right)}$$

Table 7.4 Geographical structure of Bulgarian trade in goods according to top trading partners (2007 and 2023, %)

Rank	Exports						Imports					
	2007	%	2014	%	2023	%	2007	%	2014	%	2023	%
1	Türkiye	**11.4**	Germany	**12.0**	Germany	**13.7**	Russia	**17.1**	Russia	**15.2**	Germany	**12.4**
2	Italy	**10.3**	Türkiye	**9.4**	Romania	**9.2**	Germany	**11.5**	Germany	**12.2**	Türkiye	**8.2**
3	Germany	**10.1**	Italy	**9.0**	Italy	**7.2**	Italy	**8.6**	Italy	**7.0**	Romania	**6.8**
4	Greece	**8.2**	Romania	**7.9**	Türkiye	**5.8**	Türkiye	**6.9**	Romania	**6.8**	Italy	**6.7**
5	Belgium	**6.2**	Greece	**6.7**	Greece	**5.5**	China	**5.2**	Türkiye	**5.7**	Russia	**6.6**
6	Romania	**4.8**	France	**4.3**	France	**3.8**	Greece	**5.1**	Greece	**5.1**	China	**5.4**
7	Serbia	**4.3**	Belgium	**4.2**	Belgium	**3.3**	Romania	**3.9**	Spain	**4.9**	Greece	**4.4**
8	France	**4.0**	Singapore	**2.6**	Spain	**3.1**	France	**3.8**	Hungary	**3.4**	Netherlands	**4.1**
9	UK	**2.5**	China	**2.4**	Serbia	**2.6**	Austria	**2.5**	China	**3.3**	Poland	**3.9**
10	Russia	**2.4**	Russia	**2.4**	USA	**2.5**	Ukraine	**2.3**	France	**3.0**	Hungary	**3.5**

Source: ITC

where

$X_{i,BG}$ = Bulgaria's exports of product *i*
$X_{i,total}$ = Bulgaria's total goods exports
$X_{i,world}$ = global exports of product *i*
$X_{total, world}$ = total global goods exports

When $RCA_i > 1$, Bulgaria has a comparative advantage in exporting this product (its share in Bulgaria's exports is larger than its share in global exports). Reversely, when $RCA_i < 1$, Bulgaria has a comparative disadvantage, meaning it exports this product less intensively than the world on average.

RTB, suggested also by B. Balassa, measures whether Bulgaria is a net exporter or net importer in a given product category by comparing exports and imports (Balassa, 1986). It is calculated as follows:

$$RTB_i = \frac{\left(X_{i,BG} - M_{i,BG}\right)}{\left(X_{i,BG} + M_{i,BG}\right)}$$

where

$X_{i,BG}$ = Bulgaria's exports of product *i*
$M_{i,BG}$ = Bulgaria's imports of product *i*

Positive RTB_i, the closer to +1, means that the country is a strong net exporter (possessing significant trade surplus in this product). Negative RTB_i, the closer to −1, means it is a strong net importer (with significant trade deficit).

By using both RCA and RTB, we gain a comprehensive understanding of Bulgaria's position in global goods trade. RCA reveals which goods Bulgaria specializes in exporting, while RTB shows whether that specialization results in a trade surplus or dependence on imports. Together, these indicators help assess Bulgaria's industrial strengths and trade vulnerabilities, informing both policy decisions and business strategies. While Bulgaria has historically specialized in low-technology and resource-based exports (Zhelev & Tzanov, 2012), recent trends suggest gradual shifts in its trade profile, with some sectors gaining competitiveness and others facing increasing pressures.

Bulgarian primary products showed an upward trend in their comparative advantage, with RCA rising from 1.21 in 2007 to a peak of 1.66 in 2020, before falling slightly to 1.40 in 2023. This trend, accompanied by improved RTB, indicates that Bulgaria has maintained its specialization in primary commodities, reflecting limited structural change in the move away from raw materials. For resource-based manufactures, the comparative advantage was also maintained over the period. However, despite some fluctuations, the RTB figures for this category remained mostly negative, indicating a high import intensity. This implies that Bulgaria does not possess the necessary inputs, making the sector highly dependent on foreign supplies and less efficient (Table 7.5).

Table 7.5 Comparative advantages of Bulgarian products according to their factor intensity

	2007		2010		2015		2020		2023	
Products/index	RCA	RTB	RCA	RTB	RCA	RTB	RCA	RTB	RCA	RTB
Primary products	**1.21**	−0.23	**1.36**	−0.11	**1.56**	0.09	**1.66**	0.16	**1.40**	0.08
Resource-based manufactures: agro-based	**1.13**	−0.18	**1.34**	−0.06	**1.46**	0.02	**1.41**	−0.02	**1.41**	−0.06
Resource-based manufactures: other	**1.85**	0.01	**1.48**	−0.01	**1.40**	−0.05	**1.17**	−0.09	**1.13**	0.06
Low-technology manufactures: textile, garment, and footwear	**2.99**	0.17	**2.29**	0.17	**1.75**	0.17	**1.40**	0.10	**1.20**	0.01
Low-technology manufactures: other products	**1.34**	−0.18	**1.08**	−0.08	**1.07**	−0.02	**1.20**	−0.01	**1.17**	−0.03
Medium-technology manufactures: automotive	**0.10**	−0.88	**0.25**	−0.45	**0.26**	−0.55	**0.48**	−0.30	**0.38**	−0.44
Medium-technology manufactures: process	**0.87**	−0.43	**0.67**	−0.40	**0.74**	−0.40	**1.06**	−0.24	**1.06**	−0.20
Medium-technology manufactures: engineering	**0.75**	−0.37	**0.79**	−0.14	**1.02**	−0.04	**1.09**	0.00	**1.14**	0.00
High-technology manufactures: electronic and electrical	**0.30**	−0.46	**0.34**	−0.33	**0.32**	−0.29	**0.35**	−0.22	**0.41**	−0.29
High-technology manufactures: other	**0.51**	−0.29	**0.79**	−0.14	**0.72**	−0.16	**0.79**	−0.15	**0.69**	−0.20

Source: own calculations, based on UNCTAD (https://unctadstat.unctad.org/datacentre/)

On the other hand, the data reveals a gradual decline in Bulgaria's RCA for low-technology manufactures, particularly in textiles, garments, and footwear, which traditionally represented a significant strength for the country. In 2007, the RCA for this category was notably high at 2.99, signaling a strong specialization. However, by 2023, this figure had dropped to 1.20, accompanied by a declining RTB that suggests increasing competitive pressures and an erosion of Bulgaria's foothold in these industries. Despite this, these products still feature prominently in Bulgaria's export portfolio.

The most positive trend emerges in medium-technology manufactures, especially in the engineering subsector. This category saw a steady improvement in competitiveness, moving from a comparative disadvantage to comparative advantage over the analyzed period. RCA has grown from 0.75 in 2007 to 1.14 in 2023, with RTB gradually improving to reach parity by 2020. This trend reflects Bulgaria's gradual transition toward more sophisticated manufacturing capabilities, moving up the value chain and enhancing the technological content of exports. However, medium-technology automotive products continue to exhibit a low RCA and a negative RTB, indicating that Bulgaria still faces significant challenges in gaining a foothold in this competitive subsector. Moreover, high-technology manufactures, including electronics, remain an area of significant weakness, with an RCA of only 0.41 in 2023 (and RTB of −0.29), underscoring Bulgaria's struggle to compete in highly advanced industrial sectors.

These trends suggest that while Bulgaria has made incremental progress in diversifying its export base and moving toward higher value-added products, substantial challenges remain. The continued reliance on primary products and low-technology manufactures limits the country's capacity to enhance its competitiveness in global markets and underscores the need for targeted policy interventions to support technological upgrading and foster innovation.

Further insights into the broader structural transformation of the Bulgarian economy can be gained through examining the Economic Complexity Index (ECI), which measures the relative knowledge intensity of an economy by considering the complexity of its exports, where complexity is calculated based on both the diversity of a country's exports and how many other countries can produce those same goods. It essentially gauges how sophisticated and unique a country's productive capabilities are, with higher scores indicating that a country produces and exports more complex, less common products that require significant know-how and capabilities (Harvard Growth Lab, n.d.).

The trends in economic complexity, as illustrated in Fig. 7.4, offer further insight into the broader structural transformation of the Bulgarian economy. The Economic Complexity Index (ECI) for Bulgaria has shown a mixed trajectory over the years, reflecting some progress but most of the time stagnation. In comparison with selected CEE peers, Bulgaria's ECI has generally trailed behind, indicating that the complexity and sophistication of its export basket lag those of all the comparable regional counterparts.

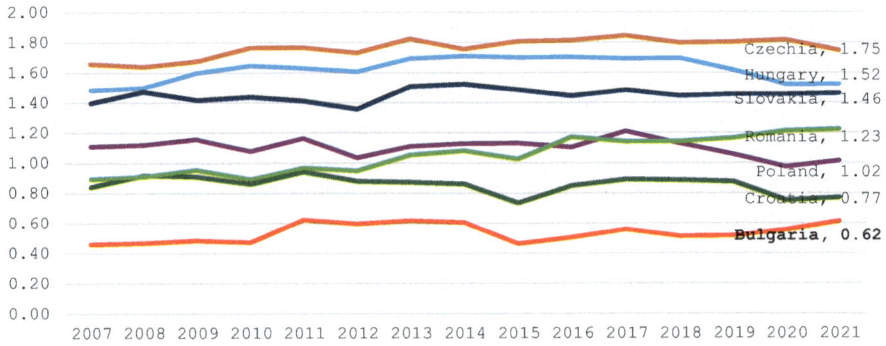

Fig. 7.4 Economic complexity index of Bulgaria and selected peers from CEE (2007–2021). (Source: Harvard growth Lab (https://atlas.cid.harvard.edu/rankings))

The comparative performance with other CEE countries highlights Bulgaria's challenges in keeping pace within the region, where other countries have significantly enhanced the complexity of their exports. Slovakia and Hungary, for example, have successfully leveraged foreign direct investments in the automotive and electronics sectors, which has boosted their ECI. In contrast, Bulgaria's progress in these high-value sectors has been more modest. A notable case is Romania, which has managed to surpass Croatia and Poland in economic complexity. Bulgaria's stagnating performance underscores the need for recalibrating industrial policies, with a particular focus on R&D investments and fostering stronger linkages between domestic firms and global value chains.

7.6 Institutional Support for the Development of Bulgarian Foreign Trade

For small, open economies like Bulgaria, exports are a pivotal driver of economic growth, employment, and technological advancement. Limited domestic markets compel such economies to rely on international trade, enabling firms to attain economies of scale, diversify revenue streams, and enhance productivity through global competition (Melitz, 2003). To optimize these advantages, policymakers often adopt two types of policies: *export promotion*, which prioritizes market access, risk mitigation, and financial/logistical assistance for exporters, and *export upgrading*, which focuses on enhancing the quality, complexity, and value-added composition of exports through targeted industrial policies. The latter is essential to avoid the "middle-income trap" and facilitate a transition from low-value-added production to innovation-intensive activities and integration into global value chains. However, export upgrading remains contentious, as it necessitates proactive state intervention—such as provision of financial support, tax incentives, import restrictions, and sector-specific infrastructure investments—which often sparks debate over market distortions and resource allocation efficiency. Nevertheless, recent years have seen a resurgence of interest in strategic industrial policy frameworks worldwide, particularly amid global supply chain disruptions, geopolitical shifts, and the pursuit of green and digital transitions (Millot & Rawdanowicz, 2024).

7.6.1 Export Promotion: Institutions Facilitating Bulgaria's International Trade

In Bulgaria, the Ministry of Economy is the principal institution responsible for shaping and implementing foreign economic policy, within the limits imposed by the EU's Common Commercial Policy. As an EU member, Bulgaria adheres to the trade agreements, tariff structures, and external trade regulations set at the supranational level. However, within this framework, the Ministry actively develops national policies to strengthen Bulgaria's export sector, enhance industrial competitiveness, and support internationalization. Its efforts are implemented through a network of specialized agencies and trade representatives abroad.

An integral part of Bulgaria's foreign trade support system is the network of Commercial Representative Offices (STIVs). These offices play a key role in promoting Bulgaria's economic interests abroad by facilitating foreign direct investment, supporting domestic businesses in accessing international markets, and fostering bilateral trade relationships. Currently, Bulgaria has 45 trade representatives stationed in 37 countries (Ministry of Economy and Industry, n.d.). By providing on-the-ground insights, establishing business connections, and advocating for Bulgarian enterprises, STIVs serve as crucial instruments in enhancing the country's global economic presence.

However, the strategic potential of STIVs is often constrained by systemic inefficiencies and inconsistent governance. A recent case illustrates these challenges: in 2023, the Ministry of Economy and Industry initiated a merit-based selection process for trade representatives, emphasizing qualifications, language proficiency, and expertise in international economic relations (Varbanova & Veselinova, 2024). While the process aimed to enhance professionalism, its abrupt annulment by a caretaker government on contested procedural grounds raises questions about either the robustness of the original framework or the influence of political considerations in the reversal. Regardless of the underlying reasons, the outcome reflects a broader issue of institutional instability that hampers the consistent functioning of Bulgaria's foreign trade representation. A notable consequence is that Bulgaria has been without trade representatives in the USA—one of its key economic partners—for over a year, leaving posts in Washington, Chicago, and Los Angeles vacant. Such gaps limit Bulgaria's ability to fully leverage STIVs as instruments for advancing its long-term economic objectives abroad.

The core of Bulgaria's export promotion infrastructure consists of three key institutions: the Bulgarian Small and Medium Enterprises Promotion Agency (BSMEPA), the Bulgarian Development Bank (BDB), and the Bulgarian Export Insurance Agency (BAEZ) (see Table 7.6). Each of these entities plays a distinct role in supporting Bulgarian exporters. BSMEPA focuses on assisting businesses in internationalization through trade fairs, matchmaking events, and capacity-building programs. BDB provides financial instruments, including pre-export and post-export financing, to ensure businesses have the necessary working capital. Meanwhile, BAEZ helps mitigate commercial and political risks by offering export credit insurance and guarantees.

While these institutions play key roles in supporting exporters, their effectiveness has been uneven due to governance and strategic focus issues. This is particularly evident in the case of the BDB, which has faced criticism for straying from its core mission of supporting SMEs and fostering export-led growth. Instead, BDB has extended substantial loans to companies in sectors like retail (e.g., 150 million BGN to Technomarket), construction (e.g., 148.5 million BGN to Roadway Construction),

Table 7.6 Specialized institutions in support of Bulgarian foreign trade

Institution	Year	Aim	Role/function	Programs/measures
Bulgarian Small and Medium Enterprises Promotion Agency (BSMEPA)	2004	To support the development and internationalization of Bulgarian SMEs by improving their competitiveness and access to global markets	Implements government policies for SME growth, provides market intelligence, organizes trade missions, and facilitates participation in international trade events	National Export Portal, SME capacity-building programs, international trade fairs, B2B matchmaking events, administration of the National Innovation Fund
Bulgarian Development Bank (BDB)	1999	To promote sustainable economic development by providing financial support to SMEs, exporters, and key economic sectors	Provides financial instruments such as loans, guarantees, and credit lines to businesses, particularly in export-oriented sectors	Pre-export and post-export financing, investment loans, working capital financing, sectoral support programs, SME financing schemes
Bulgarian Export Insurance Agency (BAEZ)	1998	To facilitate Bulgarian exports by offering risk mitigation solutions, ensuring financial stability, and improving the competitiveness of exporters	Offers export credit insurance, guarantees, and risk management solutions to protect exporters from commercial and political risks	Export credit insurance, pre-shipment and post-shipment financing insurance, factoring, risk coverage for exporters, insurance-backed financing option

Source: BSMEPA (n.d.), BDB (n.d.), BAEZ (n.d.)

and debt collection (e.g., 75 million BGN to S.G. Group)—industries with limited connection to technological modernization, innovation, or exports. Collectively, these loans to a handful of large companies accounted for over one-third of BDB's credit portfolio, diverting significant resources away from SMEs and export-oriented sectors (Stoyanov, 2020). This concentration of lending has raised concerns about political favoritism and the misallocation of public funds, undermining the bank's ability to support strategic export development and international market engagement (Minasyan, 2021).

The above challenges highlight wider systemic issues within Bulgaria's specialized export support framework. Institutional overlap, fragmented responsibilities, governance inefficiencies, and political interference have hindered the ability of these institutions to effectively promote exports and support economic modernization. Addressing these structural weaknesses will be essential for ensuring that Bulgaria's export promotion infrastructure can fully contribute to the country's long-term competitiveness and integration into global markets.

7.6.2 Export Upgrading: Policies for Structural Transformation

In the initial phase of its transition to a market economy, Bulgaria decisively refrained from pursuing any form of industrial policy, viewing it as a vestige of its centralized, planned economic past. This aversion was further reinforced by the EU's conditionality, which emphasized horizontal, nondiscriminatory policies over targeted sectoral interventions. Consequently, Bulgaria's policy framework during its EU integration period resulted in a passive policy that lacked the strategic depth necessary to fundamentally alter the structure of the economy (Zhelev, 2012).

However, as global dynamics evolved—marked by the rise of China, environmental crises, technological advancements, and geopolitical tensions—the EU's stance on industrial policy dramatically shifted. These changes underscored the need for a more proactive approach to maintaining competitiveness. Long before the formulation of the EU's current Industrial Plan, various strategies and initiatives encouraged member states to reinvigorate their industrial policies. Notably, the concept of Smart Specialization emerged as a pivotal element, becoming a prerequisite for accessing structural funds. Smart Specialization is a strategic approach to development based on the identification of regions' areas of competitive advantage, fostering innovation and economic growth through targeted support (Gianelle et. al., 2016).

Bulgaria responded by crafting its Smart Specialization Strategies for 2014–2020 and subsequently for 2021–2027. In contrast to the previous horizontal approach, these strategies focused on identifying specific areas of competitive advantage to guide state support measures and align business strategies with national and regional strengths. The priorities include *clean technology*; *circular and low carbon economy*; *industry for healthy living, bioeconomy, and biotechnology*; *informatics and ICT*; *mechatronics and microelectronics*; and *new technologies in the creative and recreational industries* (Ministry of Innovation and Growth, 2022).

While EU membership restricts Bulgaria's use of traditional trade policy instruments, it offers substantial access to EU Structural Funds, which support national development goals. This, in turn, enables the alignment of regional and innovation policies with broader industrial objectives, setting the stage for a coherent industrial policy framework. Table 7.7 illustrates how Bulgaria's industrial policy framework is supported by the existence of a combination of innovation and regional policy tools, which if coordinated properly can serve the broader objectives of industrial policy.

The mere existence of policy tools is not sufficient for achieving structural transformation; what truly matters is how effectively these tools are implemented. Drawing from international experiences, several preconditions for effective policy implementation can be identified:

- *Institutional environment*: Robust legal frameworks and governance structures are essential for policy success (Tian, 2020).

Table 7.7 Key instruments and funding mechanisms in Bulgaria's industrial policy

	Industrial policy	
Category	Innovation policy tools	Regional policy tools
Horizontal policy instruments	Green and digital transition measures Business environment and e-governance Human capital policy and migration policy	
Targeted policy instruments	Support for research, development, and innovation	Tax incentives for projects in underdeveloped areas
	Creation of venture capital funds	FDI attraction mechanisms
	Technology parks (e.g., Sofia Tech Park)	Development of industrial zones and infrastructure
Funding mechanisms	EU Structural Funds (innovation programs)	EU Structural Funds (regional development programs)
	Recovery and Resilience Plan (innovation support measures)	Recovery and Resilience Plan (regional development measures)
	Bulgarian Development Bank (SME modernization and start-ups financing)	Bulgarian Development Bank (SME financing in high- unemployment regions)
	National Innovation Fund and National Research Fund	

- *Political will and high-level support*: Sustained political commitment is crucial to drive and maintain industrial policy initiatives (Rodrik, 2004; Robinson, 2010).
- *Sector-specific strategies*: Policies must align with Bulgaria's latent comparative advantages, focusing on sectors where the country has the potential to excel (Lin, 2014).
- *Accountability, transparency, and flexibility*: Transparent processes and adaptable strategies enhance policy effectiveness and public trust (Terzi et al., 2022; Rodrik, 2004).

Despite the strategic frameworks and available instruments, Bulgaria's industrial policy faces significant challenges in meeting the preconditions for success. While there have been efforts to strengthen the institutional environment through legal reforms and alignment with EU standards, governance structures continue to suffer from inefficiencies and allegations of corruption, leading to low public trust. Political instability in recent years has further hindered the formation of stable governments, undermining the continuity and predictability necessary for long-term policy implementation. Although sector-specific strategies have been developed, such as the Smart Specialization Strategies, they often fall short of effectively harnessing and stimulating Bulgaria's latent comparative advantages. Additionally, accountability and transparency mechanisms are weak, limiting flexibility and responsiveness in policy execution. Without addressing these shortcomings, the potential for effective export upgrading and structural transformation remains limited.

7.7 Conclusions

Bulgaria's foreign trade trajectory since EU accession reflects a dual narrative of integration-driven progress and entrenched structural vulnerabilities. By capitalizing on EU membership, the country has expanded market access, deepened participation in European value chains, and diversified its export portfolio—evidenced by rising trade openness and a gradual shift toward higher value-added sectors such as machinery and chemicals. These advancements underscore Bulgaria's potential to evolve into a competitive player within the EU's economic landscape.

Yet, persistent challenges threaten this momentum. A chronic trade deficit, rooted in reliance on low-technology exports and primary commodities, highlights the fragility of Bulgaria's trade model. While sectors like engineering and certain medium-technology manufactures demonstrate emerging competitiveness, the economy lags behind regional peers such as Slovakia and Hungary in technological sophistication and economic complexity. Institutional inefficiencies and political instability further undermine the potential of state support mechanisms designed to foster export growth and structural transformation.

Bulgaria possesses the instruments and funding for a successful industrial policy aimed at export upgrading and structural transformation. However, realizing this potential demands more than ad hoc measures; it requires a cohesive strategy underpinned by transparent governance, long-term political consensus, and sustained political commitment.

References

BAEZ. (n.d.). Bulgaria Export Insurance Agency. https://baez.bg/en

Balassa, B. (1965). Trade liberalisation and "revealed" comparative advantage. *The Manchester School of Economic and Social Studies, 33*(2), 92–123.

Balassa, B. (1986). Comparative advantage in manufactured goods: A reappraisal. *The Review of Economics and Statistics, 68*(2), 315–319.

BDB. (n.d.). Bulgarian Development Bank website. https://bbr.bg/en/

BSMEPA. (n.d.). Bulgarian small and medium enterprises promotion agency website. https://www.b2bconnect.bg/

Gianelle, C., Kyriakou, D., Cohen, C., & Przeor, M. (2016). Implementing smart specialisation: A handbook. Brussels: European Commission.

Harvard Growth Lab. (n.d.) The Atlas of economic complexity. https://atlas.hks.harvard.edu/

Hausmann, R., Hidalgo, C., Bustos, S., Coscia, M., Simoes, A., & Yıldırım, M. (2013). *The Atlas of economic complexity – mapping paths to prosperity*. MIT Press.

Hidalgo, C. A., & Hausmann, R. (2009). The building blocks of economic complexity. *Proceedings of the National Academy of Sciences, 106*(26), 10570–10575.

IMF. (2014). *Economic diversification in low-income countries: Stylized facts and macroeconomic implications*. International Monetary Fund.

IMF. (2024). *Direction of trade statistics*. International Monetary Fund. https://data.imf.org/?sk=9d6028d4-f14a-464c-a2f2-59b2cd424b85

Krugman, P. R., Obstfeld, M., & Melitz, M. J. (2018). *International economics: Theory and policy* (11th ed.). Pearson.

Lin, J. (2014). Industrial policy revisited: A new structural economics perspective. *Revue d'Economie du Development, 22*(01), 51–70.
Melitz, M. (2003). The impact of trade on intra-industry reallocations and aggregate industry productivity. *Econometrica, 71*(6), 1695–1725.
Mikic, M., & Gilbert, J. (2007). *Trade statistics in policymaking: A handbook of commonly used trade indices and indicators*. United Nations.
Millot, V., & Rawdanowicz L. (2024). The return of industrial policies: Policy considerations in the current context, OECD Economic Policy Papers, No. 34, OECD Publishing, Paris. https://doi.org/10.1787/051ce36d-en
Minasyan, G. (2021). Problem: Balgarska banka za razvitie [Problem: Bulgarian Development Bank]. Ikonomicheski zhivot, June 3. https://ikj.bg/glasove-mneniya/problem-balgarska-banka-za-razvitie/
Ministry of Economy and Industry. (n.d.) Commercial services Abroad. https://www.mi.government.bg/en/policies-and-strategies/foreign-economic-and-trade-policy/commercial-services-abroad/
Ministry of Innovation and Growth. (2022). Innovation strategy for smart specialisation of the Republic of Bulgaria (ISIS. https://www.strategy.bg/StrategicDocuments/View.aspx?lang=bg-BG&Id=1569
Porter, M. E. (1990). *The competitive advantage of nations*. Free Press.
Robinson, J. (2010). Politique industrielle et dévelоppement: Analyse en termes d'économie politique [Industrial policy and development: A political economy perspective]. *Revue d'Economie du Developpement, 24*(4), 21–45.
Rodrik, D. (2004). Industrial policy for the 21st century. https://drodrik.scholar.harvard.edu/files/dani-rodrik/files/industrial-policy-twenty-first-century.pdf
Stoyanov, V. (2020, April 9). Dezinfektsiya v BBR [Disinfection at BBR]. *Capital Daily*. https://www.capital.bg/biznes/finansi/2020/04/09/4052300_dezinfekciia_v_bbr/
Terzi, A., Singh, A., & Sherwood, M. (2022). *Industrial policy for the 21st century: Lessons from the Past*. Discussion Paper 157, Luxembourg: Publications Office of the European Union.
Tian, G. (2020). From industrial policy to competition policy: A discussion based on two debates. *China Economic Review, 62*, 101505.
UNCTAD. (2019). Trade and development report 2019: Financing a global green new deal. In *United Nations Conference on Trade and Development*
Varbanova, M., & Veselinova, M. (2024, May 16). Sluzhebnata gavra s targovskite atasheta, in Bulgarian [The official joke with the trade attaches]. *Capital Daily*. https://www.capital.bg/politika_i_ikonomika/bulgaria/2024/05/16/4626249_slujebnata_gavra_s_turgovskite_atasheta/
World Bank. (2024). *World development indicators*. The World Bank Group. https://data.worldbank.org
Zhelev, P. (2012). Industrial policy under conditions of EU membership – the case of Bulgaria, evolution of international trading system: Prospects and challenges. In *Conference proceedings, St. Petersburg State University*, 2012, pp. 259–276
Zhelev, P., & Tzanov, T. (2012). Bulgaria's export competitiveness before and after EU accession. *East-West Journal of Economics and Business, XV*(1&2), 107–128.

Chapter 8
Bulgaria's Foreign Trade in Services

8.1 Introduction

In the contemporary global economy, the service sector stands as a pivotal force, representing over two-thirds of global GDP, employing the majority of the workforce, and driving the creation of new jobs, notably among women and younger employees. Furthermore, the trade in services has emerged as a critical element in strategies for economic growth, establishing itself as the most dynamic aspect of global trade in recent years and generating jobs with higher added value (World Bank & WTO, 2023). This sector encompasses a wide array of activities—from financial and business services to tourism and digital technologies—each playing a crucial role in the economic frameworks of both developed and developing nations. Within the European Union, the service sector plays a particularly significant role, not only supporting the internal market and fostering economic integration among member states but also constituting a growing share of the economy, increasingly interwoven with the manufacturing sector and serving as a crucial pillar of the digital economy and a catalyst for innovation (Sunesen & Thelle, 2018). For Bulgaria, a member state since 2007, the service sector has become the cornerstone of its economy contributing 71.3% to national GDP (Eurostat, 2024) and dominating employment and export growth. This reflects Bulgaria's radical transformation since its transition to a market economy in the 1990s (Mihov, 2002).

Despite its centrality, academic research on Bulgaria's service trade remains fragmented. Existing studies disproportionately focus on manufacturing export competitiveness (Bierut & Kuziemska-Pawlak, 2017) or structural changes in merchandise trade (Rangelova & Bilyanski, 2020), leaving Bulgaria's service trade largely unexplored. Recent analyses, such as Ditsiou et al. (2023), highlight Bulgaria's strong intra-EU trade performance, while Dimanov (2023) identifies key comparative advantages in ICT, travel, and business services. However, gaps persist in understanding how these advantages align with Bulgaria's post-2020 economic

P. Zhelev, *Bulgaria in the Global Economy*, Societies and Political Orders in Transition, https://doi.org/10.1007/978-3-031-87923-4_8

trajectory, particularly amid digitalization and external shocks like geopolitical instability and economic downturns.

This chapter aims to address this gap by providing an in-depth examination of Bulgaria's service trade over the period 2007–2022. Specifically, it will analyze the trade dynamics, product structure, and the comparative advantages that define Bulgaria's specialization in the global service market. Through this analysis, the chapter will illuminate the strategic sectors driving Bulgaria's trade successes and identify potential areas for policy enhancement for sustaining growth in an era of digital and geopolitical disruption.

8.2 Services: Some Conceptual Issues

Services, in the context of international trade, encompass intangible economic activities exchanged between producers and consumers that are residents of different countries, typically resulting in the satisfaction of human wants or needs. Unlike goods, which are tangible and can be stored, services are often consumed simultaneously with their production, making them inherently different in nature. The World Trade Organization defines trade in services as "the supply of a service from the territory of one Member to the territory of any other Member" (WTO, n.d.).

Services possess several distinguishing characteristics (Findlay & Roelfsema, 2021; Lim & de Meester, 2014; Doh & Pearce, 2004):

- Intangibility: Services are intangible and cannot be touched or felt in the same manner as goods, which makes their quality assessment prior to consumption challenging.
- Inseparability: Services are often produced and consumed simultaneously, meaning that production and consumption cannot be separated and require direct interaction between the provider and the consumer.
- Heterogeneity: Services are variable and can differ from one provider to another or even from one instance to another.
- Perishability: Services cannot be stored or inventoried like goods; they must be consumed at the time of production.

The production of both goods and services utilizes various production factors like labor and capital. However, while goods such as automobiles encapsulate the value of these services, making them storable and tradable over time, services like haircuts or live concerts are consumed instantly and depend heavily on the real-time presence of both the provider and the consumer. This non-storability is a key differentiator in how services are perceived and traded.

Given the differences, an interesting question is whether traditional trade theories, originally formulated to explain goods trade, can adequately apply to the increasingly significant sector of service trade. Classical trade theory suggests that nations engage in trade to leverage their comparative advantages, thereby enhancing economic welfare through specialization. This principle, though rooted in goods trade, extends to services, implying that the core rationale—nations trading to capitalize on their respective strengths—remains intact (Römisch, 2001). New trade theories that incorporate technological advantages and economies of scale and scope are also generally applicable to services. However, Banga (2005) highlights that for services, the integrated world market is unlikely to result in uniform prices across different national markets due to the involvement of local and imported production factors and the necessity to conform to local regulatory systems, which affect costs. Consequently, while the foundational principles of trade theories can be adapted to services, recognizing the specific attributes of services is crucial for a comprehensive understanding of their trade patterns.

Services can be classified into various categories based on their nature and function. The United Nations' Central Product Classification (CPC) provides a framework for the classification of services based on their economic activity. The CPC divides services into several broad categories, each containing more specific subcategories. These categories cover various sectors such as maintenance and repair, transportation; accommodation and food services; information services; financial and insurance activities; real estate, professional, scientific, and technical services; administrative and support services; and public administration and defense, education, as well as health and social work services (UNSD, n.d.). This system is pivotal for statistical analysis, helping to precisely identify and analyze the economic contributions of different service sectors, facilitate international comparisons, and support economic policy formulation.

Service trade is facilitated in several modes, reflecting the diverse nature of service delivery. In the General Agreement on Trade in Services (GATS), the only comprehensive multilateral agreement promoting trade in services through progressive liberalization, the channels through which it occurs are defined as follows:

- Cross-border supply (Mode 1): Services are provided from one country to another, often via digital means, such as in the cases of financial and professional services.
- Consumption abroad (Mode 2): Consumers travel to another country to receive the service, common in tourism, healthcare, and education.
- Commercial presence (Mode 3): A service provider establishes a presence in a foreign country through foreign direct investment (FDI), allowing for the local provision of services.
- Presence of natural persons (Mode 4): Service providers travel to another country to deliver services directly, applicable in areas like engineering and consulting. (WTO, n.d.)

Following these definitions, trade in services is traditionally measured through the Balance of Payments (BoP) statistics, capturing three of these modes: cross-border supply, consumption abroad, and the presence of natural persons. However, this measurement overlooks services delivered under commercial presence (Mode 3), where a foreign service provider's local operations in another country are not captured in standard BoP metrics. This gap highlights a significant aspect of global service trade that remains largely undetected, underestimating the international service market dynamics and their economic impacts.

Historically, services were considered non-tradables due to their non-storability, which demands significant mobility—either from the producer or the consumer or through a well-developed communications network. Until the early 1970s, these mobility and communication capabilities were limited, preventing services from significantly impacting global trade. Additionally, higher barriers such as regulatory restrictions, licensing requirements, and varying standards across jurisdictions further impeded the tradability of services. Cultural and linguistic differences also posed substantial challenges, complicating the delivery of services across borders.

Over the subsequent decades, however, the situation began to evolve. Technological advancements in transportation and communications significantly expanded, enhancing the mobility of both service providers and consumers. The advent of the Internet and digital communication tools dramatically transformed the landscape, enabling services to be delivered electronically and reducing the necessity for physical presence. Concurrently, many countries began to liberalize their service markets, especially within services regional trade agreements, reducing regulatory barriers and harmonizing standards to facilitate easier cross-border exchange (Benz et al., 2022). This gradual shift has led to an increasingly integrated global service market, where services such as finance, education, and information technology have become some of the most dynamically traded sectors of the global economy.

This transformation has overturned the traditional view of services as largely non-tradable and less critical to economic development compared to manufacturing. Driven by technological advancements, enhancements in tradability and scalability have increased the storability, flexibility, and global access of services (World Bank, 2024). Consequently, services are now recognized as key contributors to productivity, competitiveness, and living standards. Reflecting this evolution, the World Bank and the WTO (2023) highlight that expanding service trade is essential for future economic transformation.

8.3 Dynamics and Role of Services in Bulgaria's Foreign Trade

The service sector has been a cornerstone of Bulgaria's economic transformation since its transition from a centrally planned economy to a market-driven system. Under socialist governance, producer-oriented services such as banking, insurance, telecommunications, and IT were stifled by state monopolies, technological stagnation, and isolation from global markets (Römisch, 2001). Post-1989 reforms dismantled these constraints, catalyzing structural shifts toward privatization, FDI, and regulatory harmonization with EU standards. The accession to the European Union further accelerated this transformation, as it opened up new markets and brought about the free movement of services, aligning Bulgaria's service industries more closely with European norms.

This evolution marked a significant shift in Bulgaria's economic landscape, turning the service sector into a pivotal component of the country's foreign trade. The liberalization and expansion of services not only diversified Bulgaria's economic activities but also integrated its economy more deeply into the global market.

Between 2007 and 2022, Bulgaria's service exports grew by 50.6%, rising from €8.3 billion to €12.5 billion, while imports expanded by 19.0%, increasing from €5.8 billion to €6.9 billion (Fig. 8.1). This divergence resulted in a widening trade surplus, which increased from €2.5 billion in 2007 to €5.6 billion by 2022. The export-import (X/M) ratio—a key measure of trade competitiveness—rose from 1.4 in 2007 to 1.8 in 2022, highlighting Bulgaria's increasing specialization in services production.

Notably, the sector has played a crucial role in stabilizing Bulgaria's external accounts. Services have consistently offset the chronic trade deficit in goods, acting as a buffer against external imbalances. Furthermore, the sector demonstrated remarkable stability during crises: even in 2020, at the height of global pandemic disruptions, exports dipped only modestly before rebounding sharply, highlighting services' role as an anchor of economic stability.

Despite this impressive absolute growth, Bulgaria's relative position in global and EU markets presents a more complex picture. The country's share of global service exports declined from 0.23% in 2007 to 0.18% in 2022, while its share of EU service exports fell from 0.57% to 0.45% (Fig. 8.2). This discrepancy—rising absolute exports but a shrinking market share—suggests Bulgaria's growth, while impressive, lagged behind the explosive expansion of global service trade post-2008.

Two key insights emerge. First, EU accession provided access to 450 million consumers, catalyzing export growth, but at the same time Bulgaria faced intense competition from larger EU economies, constraining its ability to expand intra-EU market share. Second, the constantly positive trade balance and rising X/M ratio reflect Bulgaria's success in developing high-margin services such as IT and

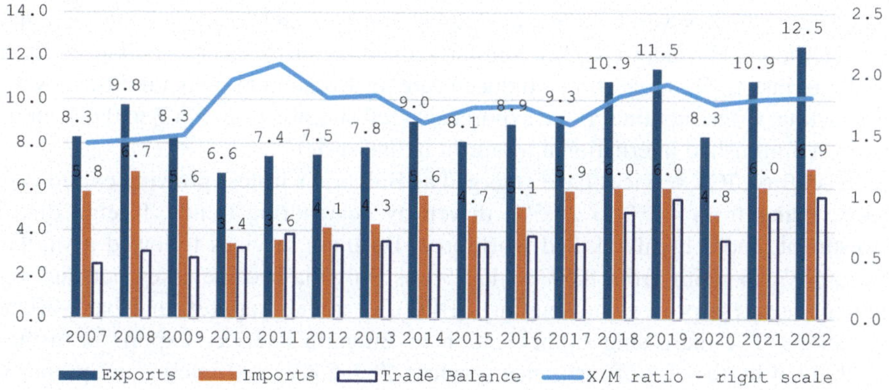

Fig. 8.1 Dynamics of Bulgaria's trade in services (billion USD, 2007–2022). (Source: ITC)

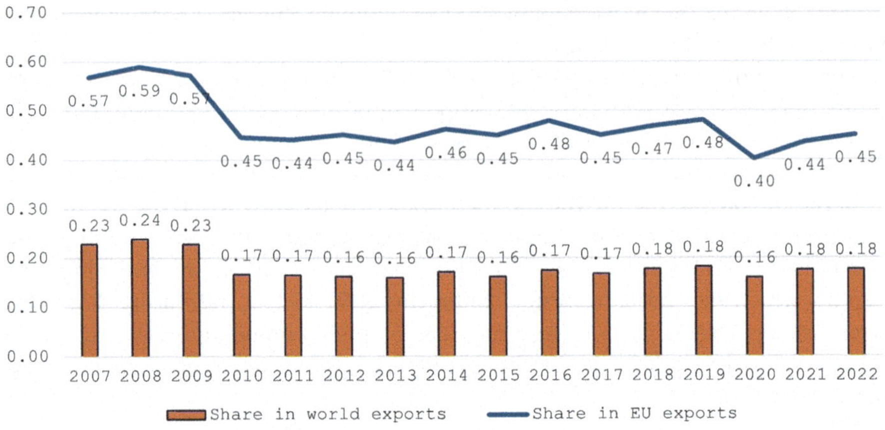

Fig. 8.2 Share of Bulgaria in the EU's and world export of services (%, 2007–2022). (Source: ITC)

business process outsourcing (BPO), which require minimal imported inputs, allowing for greater value retention.

8.4 Key Trends in the Product and Geographical Structure of Bulgarian Foreign Trade in Services

Bulgaria's service trade composition has undergone substantial changes, reflecting both the rise of knowledge-intensive sectors and shifts in global economic conditions. While traditional strengths in tourism and transport persist, ICT services, business outsourcing, and professional services have expanded significantly.

The most notable transformation in Bulgaria's service exports is the decline in travel services, which accounted for 42.7% of total exports in 2007–2009 but fell to 23.5% in 2020–2022 (Fig. 8.3). This decline was exacerbated by the COVID-19 pandemic, which severely impacted global tourism and restricted international travel (Ando & Hayakawa, 2022). Similarly, manufacturing services collapsed from 20.9% to just 1.9%, suggesting a reduced role for Bulgaria in global industrial subcontracting. Construction service exports also fell sharply, from 3.6% to 0.6%, indicating a diminished international footprint in this sector.

In contrast, ICT services have emerged as Bulgaria's fastest-growing export category, rising from 4.1% to 24.5%, driven by nearshoring trends, foreign direct investment, and a highly skilled workforce. Business services followed a similar trajectory, expanding from 8.5% to 17.2%, as Bulgaria became a key outsourcing hub for business process outsourcing (BPO), customer support, and back-office operations. The increasing sophistication of Bulgaria's service exports is further highlighted by the rise of insurance services (0.9–5.8%) and intellectual property charges (0.1–2.1%).

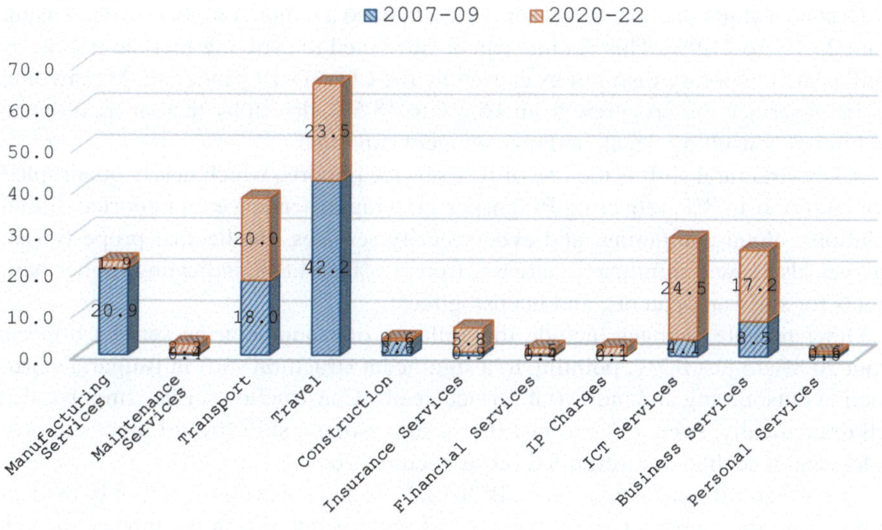

Fig. 8.3 Structure of Bulgaria's exports of services (%, 2007–2009 and 2020–2022) (Source: ITC)

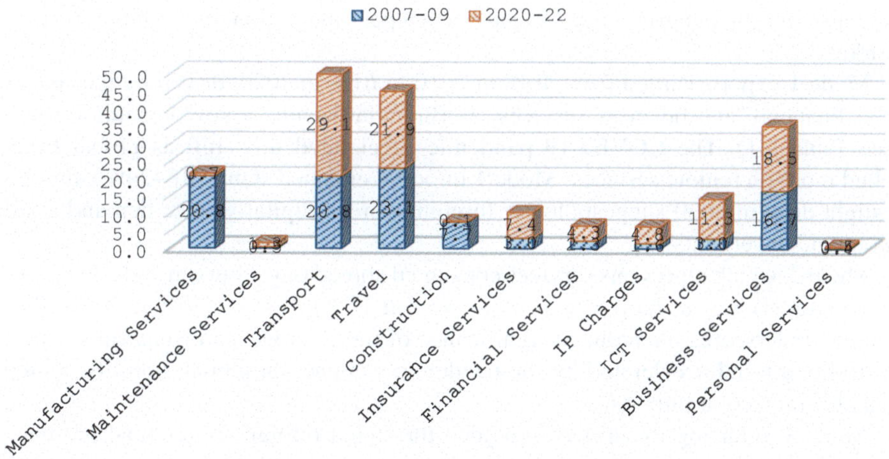

Fig. 8.4 Structure of Bulgaria's imports of services (%, 2007–2009 and 2020–2022). (Source: ITC)

Transport services have maintained a strong position, increasing slightly from 18.0% to 20.0%, reinforcing Bulgaria's role as a regional logistics hub. Meanwhile, maintenance service exports expanded from 0.4% to 2.3%, indicating increasing demand for Bulgarian technical expertise in engineering and repair services.

On the import side, transport services emerged as the largest category, increasing from 20.8% in 2007–2009 to 29.1% in 2020–2022 (Fig. 8.4). This reflects Bulgaria's deepening integration into regional and global supply chains, with rising demand for logistics, freight, and passenger transport services.

Despite a slight decline, travel services remained a major component, decreasing from 23.1% to 21.9%. This decline can be attributed to evolving tourism trends, as well as the temporary disruptions caused by the COVID-19 pandemic. Meanwhile, business service imports grew from 16.7% to 18.5%, driven by increasing reliance on foreign consulting, legal, and management expertise.

A key structural shift is the rise of ICT service imports, which nearly quadrupled from 3.0% to 11.3%, reflecting Bulgaria's growing dependence on imported digital solutions, cloud computing, and cybersecurity services. Intellectual property (IP) charges also saw a significant increase, from 1.6% to 4.8%, indicating higher payments for software, patents, and licensing fees.

Other notable changes include the collapse of manufacturing service imports from 20.8% to just 0.7%, pointing to a significant structural shift in Bulgaria's production outsourcing and industrial service needs. Construction service imports also fell dramatically, from 7.7% to just 0.1%, suggesting a shift toward domestic providers and a decline in foreign-led infrastructure projects.

The structural transformation of Bulgaria's trade in services is not only evident in the changing composition of exports and imports but also in the modes through which these services are delivered internationally. The evolution of service delivery methods between 2010 and 2020 reflects the increasing digitalization of trade, shifts in consumption patterns, and Bulgaria's deeper integration into global service markets.

Mode 1 exports surged from 40% in 2010 to 61% in 2020, driven by the rise of ICT, financial, and business services, as Bulgaria became a key outsourcing hub (see Table 8.1). The COVID-19 pandemic accelerated this shift as global firms relied more on remote services. Mode 1 imports remained stable (18–24%), though a slight drop in 2020 suggests lower foreign-sourced digital service demand amid economic uncertainty.

Mode 2, which represents services consumed abroad (e.g., tourism and education-related travel), saw a sharp drop in exports from 47% in 2010 to 19% in 2020. This decline underscores the reduced significance of travel services in Bulgaria's export portfolio, a trend accelerated by the pandemic's impact on global mobility, which had also impact on imports.

Mode 3, referring to services provided through a foreign commercial presence (e.g., subsidiaries and foreign-owned companies operating in Bulgaria), remained a

Table 8.1 Structure of Bulgarian trade in services according to modes of delivery (2010, 2014, 2017, 2020, %)

	Export				Import			
Mode	*2010*	*2014*	*2017*	*2020*	*2010*	*2014*	*2017*	*2020*
M1	40	46	43	61	18	24	24	18
M2	47	37	36	19	5	6	7	3
M3	10	12	16	13	75	68	68	78
M4	3	5	5	7	2	2	1	1

Source: WTO Tismos database and Eurostat

dominant feature of Bulgaria's service imports, accounting for 75% in 2010 and increasing to 78% in 2020. This stability indicates the continued importance of foreign firms in Bulgaria's service sector, particularly in finance, insurance, and telecommunications.

For exports, Mode 3 saw moderate growth, rising from 10% to 13%, reflecting a modest expansion of Bulgarian service firms establishing operations abroad. However, this mode remains a relatively small share of total service exports, suggesting that Bulgarian companies are not yet significant global investors in service sectors.

Mode 4, which covers temporary movement of Bulgarian service professionals abroad, remained minor but showed a slight increase in exports (from 3% to 7%). This may be linked to increased labor mobility within the EU, particularly in specialized service sectors like IT, engineering, and consulting. On the import side, Mode 4 stayed very low at 1%, indicating limited foreign labor inflows for service provision in Bulgaria.

As Bulgaria moves beyond its traditional reliance on tourism and transport services, its trade relationships are also shifting. The country's service trade is becoming more globally diversified, with declining ties to nearby regional partners like Russia and Greece and growing integration with Western European and Anglo-American markets.

Germany remained Bulgaria's top export market (14.0% in 2010 to 13.4% in 2021), reflecting deep economic linkages in ICT, business, and transport services (see Table 8.2). At the same time, Russia's share dropped sharply (from 9.2% to 3.5%), largely due to geopolitical tensions and a decline in Russian tourism demand.

In contrast, the UK (9.0–9.4%) and especially the USA (3.0–7.2%) gained importance, signaling Bulgaria's increasing reliance on high-value digital service markets. Meanwhile, Türkiye (4.3%) and France (4.2%) strengthened their roles,

Table 8.2 Geographical structure of Bulgarian trade in services according to top trading partners (2010 and 2021, %)

	Exports				Imports			
Rank	2010	%	2021	%	2010	%	2021	%
1	Germany	14.0	Germany	13.4	Germany	16.0	Germany	12.7
2	Russia	9.2	UK	9.4	Greece	8.2	UK	5.4
3	UK	9.0	USA	7.2	UK	7.1	Türkiye	4.6
4	Greece	7.3	Türkiye	4.3	Liberia	5.7	Greece	3.8
5	Türkiye	6.1	France	4.2	Türkiye	5.6	Austria	3.8
6	Italy	4.7	Netherlands	3.9	Austria	5.1	Switzerland	3.5
7	France	4.3	Romania	3.6	USA	4.5	Italy	3.4
8	Romania	4.2	Russia	3.5	Italy	4.2	France	3.3
9	Austria	3.1	Ireland	3.1	Hungary	3.3	Netherlands	3.0
10	USA	3.0	Belgium	3.1	Romania	2.9	Belgium	2.9

Source: ITC

and the rise of Ireland (3.1%) and Belgium (3.1%) suggests expanding trade in business services.

Germany remained the largest source of service imports, though its share declined (from 16.0% to 12.7%) as Bulgaria diversified its service providers. The UK (5.4%) and Türkiye (4.6%) grew in importance, while Greece's share dropped sharply (8.2% to 3.8%), reflecting reduced demand of Greek tourism during the pandemic.

A structural shift is also evident in the decline of Liberia (5.7% in 2010) as a major import partner, historically linked to maritime services, while Austria (3.8%) and Switzerland (3.5%) gained ground, particularly in finance and consulting.

These evolving trade patterns highlight Bulgaria's pivot toward Western European and North American markets while reducing the importance of some regional partners.

8.5 Comparative Advantages of Bulgaria in Services

Bulgaria's shifting sectoral composition and evolving trade partnerships signal deeper structural changes in its global service market competitiveness. While the country has strengthened its presence in certain service sectors, the extent to which it holds a comparative advantage remains essential for understanding its long-term positioning in an increasingly digital and competitive economy.

A closer look at Revealed Comparative Advantage (RCA) and Relative Trade Balance (RTB) indices reveals which service industries Bulgaria excels in, where it faces competitive pressures, and how its specialization has evolved. Table 8.3 presents data on the competitive performance of the Bulgarian services in world trade.

A striking trend is the collapse of Bulgaria's RCA in manufacturing services on physical inputs owned by others, from 14.8 in 2007 to just 0.2 in 2022. This once-dominant sector, linked to Bulgaria's role as a subcontracting hub for EU industries, has gradually lost relevance due to global supply chain restructuring, automation, and increased competition from lower-cost economies. Despite this, the RTB remained positive (0.2–0.6), suggesting that while the sector has shrunk, Bulgaria still exports more than it imports in this category.

Similarly, construction services experienced a dramatic decline, with RCA plummeting from 1.9 in 2007 to near-zero in 2010 and only modestly recovering to 0.5 in 2022. However, the RTB shifted from negative (−0.3 in 2007) to strongly positive (0.9 in 2022), implying that while Bulgaria no longer specializes in exporting construction services, it has significantly reduced its reliance on imported foreign contractors.

Travel services have remained one of Bulgaria's strongest sectors, with RCA fluctuating between 1.6 and 2.1. The RTB peaked in 2010 at 0.6 but fell to 0.2 in 2020 before rebounding to 0.4 in 2022, indicating a decline in Bulgaria's net surplus during the pandemic but partial recovery thereafter. This suggests

Table 8.3 Comparative (dis)advantages of Bulgaria in trade with services (2007–2022)

	2007		2010		2015		2020		2022	
	RCA	RTB	RCA	RTB	RCA	RTB	RCA	RTB	RCA	RTB
Manufacturing services on physical inputs owned by others	**14.8**	0.2	**4.7**	0.7	**2.2**	0.8	**1.6**	0.7	**0.2**	0.6
Maintenance and repair services n.i.e.	**0.5**	0.1	**0.4**	0.1	**0.8**	0.2	**1.6**	0.6	**1.5**	0.5
Transport	**1.0**	0.1	**1.0**	0.2	**1.2**	0.2	**1.2**	0.2	**0.9**	0.0
Travel	**1.8**	0.4	**2.1**	0.6	**1.6**	0.5	**1.9**	0.2	**1.7**	0.4
Construction	**1.9**	−0.3	**0.0**	−0.9	**0.2**	−0.2	**0.3**	0.7	**0.5**	0.9
Insurance and pension services	**0.3**	−0.5	**0.6**	0.1	**2.6**	0.3	**2.6**	0.3	**1.7**	0.1
Financial services	**0.0**	−0.6	**0.0**	−0.4	**0.2**	−0.4	**0.1**	−0.3	**0.2**	−0.2
Charges for the use of intellectual property n.i.e.	**0.0**	−0.8	**0.0**	−0.7	**0.1**	−0.6	**0.2**	−0.3	**0.4**	0.0
Telecommunications, computer, and information services	**0.6**	0.2	**1.1**	0.3	**1.1**	0.4	**1.6**	0.5	**1.8**	0.6
Other business services	**0.5**	−0.2	**0.4**	−0.2	**0.6**	0.0	**0.6**	0.2	**0.7**	0.2
Personal, cultural, and recreational services	**0.9**	0.5	**0.9**	0.2	**1.0**	0.4	**0.4**	0.3	**0.4**	0.3

Source: own calculations based on ITC data

increasing outbound tourism and stronger competition from regional rivals such as Greece and Türkiye, which have capitalized on diversified offerings and stronger branding.

At the same time, as Holleran (2020) highlights, Bulgaria's tourism model has relied heavily on rapid coastal urbanization, leading to overdevelopment, environmental strain, and economic vulnerabilities. Bulgaria ranks 40th out of 119 economies in the Travel & Tourism Development Index 2024, reflecting both its established tourism sector and persistent structural challenges. While the country excels in health and hygiene (6th rank), it lags in cultural resource promotion (47th), tourist service and infrastructure (43rd), and demand sustainability (89th) (World Economic Forum, 2024). These shortcomings weaken its ability to compete with top-tier destinations and fully leverage its cultural and natural assets, while weak regulatory oversight and speculative real estate expansion over time have undermined long-term sustainability.

Transport services, another key Bulgarian sector, have shown relative stability in RCA (1.0–1.2 between 2007 and 2020) but declined to 0.9 in 2022, indicating growing competition in logistics and freight transport. The RTB remained weak (0.0–0.2), reflecting a low trade surplus, suggesting that import dependence offsets Bulgaria's export gains in this sector. Despite Bulgaria's strategic location as a transit hub for Europe-Asia trade, deficiencies in transport infrastructure limit its full potential, reducing efficiency in the Trans-European transport network and constraining export growth (Cebeci & Yankova, 2013). Moreover, heavy reliance on road freight has environmental costs, prompting a push for multimodal transport solutions to enhance sustainability and competitiveness (Yotsov et al., 2017).

A positive trend is observed in other business services, where RCA improved from 0.5 to 0.7 and RTB turned positive, rising from −0.2 in 2007 to 0.2 in 2022. This suggests Bulgaria has enhanced its role in consulting, legal, and professional services, though it still lags behind more established outsourcing hubs in Central Europe.

Despite the rise in knowledge-intensive sectors, financial services remain an area of persistent weakness, with RCA never exceeding 0.2 and RTB staying negative throughout (−0.6 in 2007, improving to −0.2 in 2022). This indicates continued reliance on foreign financial institutions and a lack of internationally competitive banking or investment services.

Similarly, charges for the use of intellectual property (IP) exhibit low RCA (0.0 to 0.4) and mostly negative RTB until 2022 (0.0). This suggests Bulgaria remains a net importer of patents, copyrights, and licensing rights, with limited domestic innovation capacity in high-value intellectual property services.

Bulgaria's most remarkable transformation is in telecommunications, computer, and information services (ICT), where RCA more than tripled from 0.6 in 2007 to 1.8 in 2022, shifting from a comparative disadvantage to comparative advantage. The RTB steadily increased from 0.2 to 0.6, confirming that Bulgaria is now a competitive net exporter of ICT services. This reflects the country's growing role as a regional outsourcing hub, attracting foreign investment in software development, cybersecurity, and business process outsourcing (BPO).

While Bulgaria's overall comparative advantage in ICT services has strengthened, a closer look at its two main subsectors—computer services and information services—reveals distinct growth patterns (Fig. 8.5). The bifurcation in their trajectories suggests that Bulgaria's ICT specialization is evolving unevenly, with information services driving the bulk of the sector's rapid expansion.

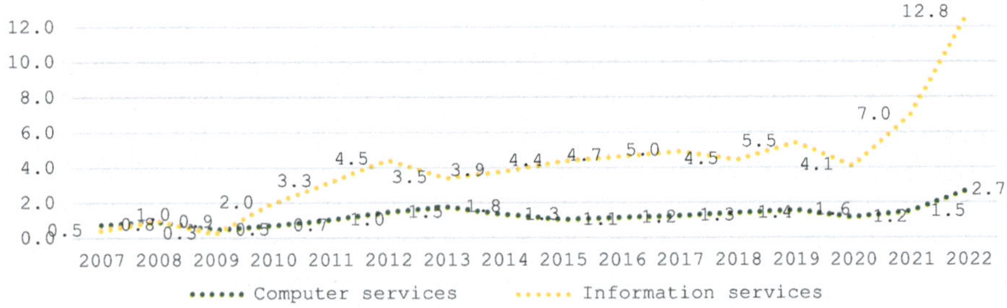

Fig. 8.5 Dynamics of the RCA index of the Bulgarian ICT services (2007–2022). (Source: own calculations based on ITC data)

Box 8.1 Can Bulgaria become a European Silicon Valley?

Bulgaria's emergence as a competitive ICT exporter and a thriving start-up ecosystem has sparked debates about its potential to evolve into a "European Silicon Valley." While the comparison is aspirational, Bulgaria's trajectory reveals both promise and structural limitations.

The case for

- Low costs and skilled workforce: Bulgaria offers lower operational costs than Western Europe and a highly skilled IT workforce, attracting tech firms and R&D centers. A flat 10% corporate tax rate, among the lowest in the EU, further boosts its appeal for digital businesses.
- Niche specialization: The country's hypergrowth in cloud services, SaaS, and blockchain (evidenced by RCA > 12 in information services) mirrors Silicon Valley's early dominance in scalable digital solutions. Start-ups such as Gtmhub (OKR software) and Payhawk (fintech unicorn) highlight this potential.
- EU integration: Bulgaria's access to the single market and EU digital funding enhances its tech infrastructure and regulatory alignment, providing a strong platform for scaling technology businesses. Government-backed initiatives further support smart cities, IoT expansion, and digital transformation across industries.

The challenges

- Scale limitations: Bulgaria's ICT workforce (~126,000) is dwarfed by Germany's 2.1 million[1] or Estonia's per capita tech density. Tripling STEM graduates by 2030 is necessary but unlikely under current policies.
- Innovation ecosystem gaps: Venture capital remains nascent—2022 VC investment attracted $77M vs. Estonia's $1.3B,[2] and R&D spending lags at 0.8% of GDP, while the EU average is 2.3%,[3] limiting high-tech innovation.
- Brain drain: Many Bulgarian IT professionals work remotely for foreign firms, diverting talent away from domestic start-up creation.

Pathways to success

Bulgaria's best hope lies in becoming a "Silicon Valley for Southeast Europe" rather than a global rival. Key steps include the following:

(continued)

[1] Eurostat, Employed ICT specialists, Retrieved from: https://ec.europa.eu/eurostat/databrowser/view/isoc_sks_itspt/default/table?lang=en

[2] Statista (n.d.) Venture capital transaction value in Central and Eastern Europe in 2022, Retrieved from: https://www.statista.com/statistics/1423508/cee-vc-transaction-value-by-country/

[3] Eurostat, Gross domestic expenditure on R&D by sector, Retrieved from: https://ec.europa.eu/eurostat/databrowser/view/sdg_09_10__custom_13090092/default/table

- Leverage niche strengths: Double down on cybersecurity, AI-driven SaaS, and blockchain—sectors where Bulgaria already outperforms some of its regional peers.
- Policy incentives: Introduce tax incentives for R&D expenditures and adopt Estonia's e-residency model to attract digital nomads.
- Education-industry synergy: Integrate AI/ML training into university curricula, and expand partnerships with tech firms to mitigate skill mismatches.

Information services have experienced exponential growth, particularly after 2020, with RCA surging from 5.5 in 2019 to 12.8 in 2022. This dramatic increase points to a significant structural shift, likely fueled by the expansion of cloud computing, data analytics, and software-as-a-service (SaaS) platforms. The post-pandemic acceleration suggests that Bulgaria has successfully capitalized on rising global demand for scalable digital solutions, securing a stronger position in high-value ICT exports.

In contrast, computer services have followed a more gradual upward trend, with RCA rising from 0.5 in 2007 to 2.7 in 2022. While this indicates a steady improvement in competitiveness, the slower pace suggests that Bulgaria remains constrained by competition from other IT outsourcing destinations, particularly in traditional IT support, system integration, and infrastructure services. Unlike the highly scalable nature of information services, computer services are more dependent on workforce expansion, which may limit their growth potential in the absence of productivity-driven efficiency gains.

These diverging trends indicate that Bulgaria's ICT transformation is increasingly driven by high-value digital exports, rather than traditional IT outsourcing. The shift toward cloud-based and data-driven services aligns with global trends favoring automation, AI integration, and digital platforms over conventional IT labor outsourcing. The challenge moving forward will be to sustain growth in both subsectors while fostering innovation and upskilling the workforce to support higher-value service exports.

8.6 Conclusion

Since EU integration, Bulgaria's foreign trade in services has undergone a profound transformation, marked by the decline of low-value-added activities and the rise of knowledge-intensive sectors. The gradual withdrawal from outward processing activities in manufacturing services reflects broader economic shifts—as incomes rise and labor costs increase, these activities have lost competitiveness. In their place, ICT and business services have become the primary engines of growth, driving Bulgaria's repositioning within global service markets.

While this shift represents clear progress, it also raises critical challenges about long-term sustainability. ICT, particularly information services, has expanded rapidly, generating strong export surpluses and competitive advantages. However, it is highly skill-intensive and does not generate jobs on a mass scale or across regions. Moreover, it lacks deep integration with other sectors, limiting its broader economic impact. Without strong forward and backward linkages to domestic industries, finance, and R&D, ICT risks becoming an enclave of high-value activity disconnected from the wider economy, reducing its potential for spillover structural upgrading across sectors.

This challenge is compounded by weaknesses in foundational high-value sectors—financial services, intellectual property, and R&D-intensive industries—where persistent deficits and low competitiveness highlight systemic gaps in innovation capacity and capital markets.

Equally critical is the evolution of traditional service sectors. Tourism remains one of Bulgaria's largest service exports, but its heavy reliance on low-cost, seasonal visitors limits its growth potential. Moving toward higher-value, experience-based tourism, improving infrastructure, and expanding into premium market segments will be essential to overcoming cyclical volatility and regional competition. Similarly, transport and logistics must embrace digitalization and efficiency improvements to maintain their role in Bulgaria's service trade portfolio.

Looking ahead, Bulgaria's competitiveness hinges on transcending cost-driven outsourcing. A proactive state role is vital: fostering digital infrastructure, aligning education with emerging skill demands, and bridging ICT with high-productivity industries like advanced manufacturing or green energy. By anchoring growth in innovation and integration, Bulgaria can ensure its service economy evolves beyond isolated success stories into a resilient, diversified engine of long-term development.

In sum, the structural shift toward knowledge-intensive services marks a pivotal step in Bulgaria's economic maturation. Yet, sustaining this momentum demands a holistic vision—one that weaves digital excellence into the fabric of a broader, innovation-driven economy.

References

Ando, M., & Hayakawa, K. (2022). Impact of COVID-19 on trade in services. *Japan & The World Economy, 62*, 1–17.

Banga, R. (2005). Trade in services: A review. *Global Economy Journal, 5*(2). https://doi.org/10.2202/1524-5861.1068

Benz, S., Jaax, A., & Yotov, Y. (2022). *Shedding Light on the drivers of services tradability over two decades*. OECD Trade Policy Paper No. 264.

Bierut, B. K., & Kuziemska-Pawlak, K. (2017). Competitiveness and export performance of CEE countries. *Eastern European Economics, 55*(6), 522–542. https://doi.org/10.1080/00128775.2017.1382378

Cebeci, C., & Yankova, M. (2013). Analysis of the Logistics Systems in Bulgaria under the Requirements of the European Union. *Research Journal of Applied Sciences, Engineering and Technology, 6*(14), 2526–2534. https://doi.org/10.19026/rjaset.6.3733

Dimanov, D. K. (2023). Comparative Advantages of Bulgaria in International Trade in Services for the Period 2011–2020. *Knowledge – International Journal, 49*(1), 207–213.

Ditsiou, A., Siskos, E., & Darvidou, K. (2023). Efficiency of the intra-EU trade in goods and services: Geographical and product structure analysis. *Problems and Perspectives in Management, 21*(2), 653–666. https://doi.org/10.21511/ppm.21(2).2023.59

Doh, J., & Pearce, J. (2004). Revising our understanding and expectations of the international trade in services. *Journal of Transnational Management Development, 9*(1), 59–78. https://doi.org/10.1300/J130v09n01_05

Eurostat. (2024). National accounts aggregates by industry. https://ec.europa.eu/eurostat/databrowser/view/nama_10_a64__custom_11048194/default/table

Findlay, C., & Roelfsema, H. (2021). Services. In F. Kimura, M. Pangestu, S. Thangavelu, & C. Findlay (Eds.), *Handbook on East Asian economic integration* (pp. 137–155). Edward Elgar Publishing Ltd.

Holleran, M. (2020). Coasts of aspiration: Climbing the tourism 'ladder'. In *Tourism, urbanization, and the evolving periphery of the European Union*. Palgrave Pivot. https://doi.org/10.1007/978-981-15-0218-7_3

Lim, A., & de Meester, B. (2014). An introduction to domestic regulation and GATS. In A. Lim & B. De Meester (Eds.), *WTO domestic regulation and services trade: Putting principles into practice* (pp. 1–22). Cambridge University Press.

Mihov, I. (2002). The economic transition in Bulgaria (1989–1999). In *Transition: The first decade* (pp. 401–439). MIT Press.

Rangelova, R., & Bilyanski, V. (2020). Structural changes in the foreign trade and economic growth of Bulgaria and Romania in the years of EU membership. *Economic Thought Journal, 2*, 3–24.

Römisch, R. (2001). Trade in services in the Central and East European Countries. WIIW Research Report No. 274. The Vienna Institute for International Economic Studies.

Sunesen, E., & Thelle, M. (2018). Making EU trade in services work for all: Enhancing innovation and competitiveness throughout the European Economy. Copenhagen Economics. https://copenhageneconomics.com/wp-content/uploads/2021/12/final-report-on-single-market-for-services-15nov2018_v2.pdf

United Nations Statistics Division. (n.d.). Central product classification (CPC) Version 2.1. https://unstats.un.org/unsd/classifications/Econ/cpc

World Bank. (2024). Digital progress and trends report 2023. Washington D.C. https://doi.org/10.1596/978-1-4648-2049-6

World Bank & World Trade Organization. (2023). Trade in services for development - fostering sustainable growth and economic diversification. https://www.wto.org/english/res_e/booksp_e/trade_in_services_and_development_e.pdf

World Economic Forum. (2024). Travel and tourism development index 2024 edition. https://www.weforum.org/publications/travel-tourism-development-index-2024/interactive-data-and-economy-profiles-afaa00a59c/

World Trade Organization. (n.d.). General agreement on trade in services. https://www.wto.org/english/docs_e/legal_e/26-gats_01_e.htm

Yotsov, I., Dimitrakiev, D., Zaburtov, A., & Koritarov, T. (2017). Analysis of the logistics transport corridors in the black sea region based on the short sea shipping concept. In *8th Annual General Assembly of the International Association of Maritime Universities - Global Perspectives in MET: Towards Sustainable, Green and Integrated Maritime Transport*, IAMU 2017, 1, 502–512.

Chapter 9
The Role of Bulgaria in the Global Value Chains

9.1 Introduction

Global value chains (GVCs) have become an integral part of the global economy, reshaping patterns of production, trade, and investment. As countries seek to maximize their economic potential, understanding their participation in GVCs has become increasingly important. Research has shown that a higher level of integration into GVCs can have a positive impact on a country's export position. Entities involved in GVCs often exhibit higher labor productivity and a greater propensity to export. This is due to their efficiency and innovation, which enables them to compete effectively in international markets. By participating in these chains, countries can leverage their unique strengths and resources to specialize in specific stages of production, thereby boosting their productivity and enhancing their overall competitiveness in the global marketplace (OECD, 2013). For Bulgaria, actively participating in GVCs can be a strategic approach to drive economic growth, create employment opportunities, and enhance its position in the global economy.

This chapter aims to investigate the characteristics of Bulgaria's participation in GVCs, both at the overall economy level and within specific industrial sectors. By examining various indicators as well as comparing Bulgaria's participation to that of other Central and Eastern European countries (CEECs), we seek to shed light on the extent and dynamics of Bulgaria's integration into GVCs against its regional counterparts. Thus, shifts in the country's GVC involvement and additional context and understanding of Bulgaria's position within the global economy are provided.

P. Zhelev, *Bulgaria in the Global Economy*, Societies and Political Orders in Transition, https://doi.org/10.1007/978-3-031-87923-4_9

9.2 The Concept of GVCs and Determinants of Participation

In recent decades, there has been a significant transformation in the nature of international trade, characterized by the increasing interdependence of production processes across multiple countries. This phenomenon is referred to by various terms in the economics literature, including "global supply chains," "global value chains," "international production networks," "vertical specialization," "multistage production," "internationalization of production," "unbundling of production," "offshore outsourcing," "international production networks," "global production sharing," "trade in tasks," and "international production fragmentation" (WTO, 2013; Cigna et al., 2022). The concept highlights the specialization of countries in specific stages of production within a global context.[1]

In the past, companies predominantly concentrated their manufacturing activities within a single country. However, the landscape has significantly evolved. The traditional concept of associating a product with a specific country through the label "Made in …" has become increasingly outdated. In the current global context, the notion of a product being exclusively tied to a single country is no longer applicable. The intricate nature of modern production processes, particularly within GVCs, means that a finished product can no longer be attributed solely to one country's manufacturing or assembly. Instead, it is the collaborative efforts across multiple countries that contribute to the creation of the final product. As Antras (2020) states, nowadays most goods are "Made in the World."

International fragmentation of production is an extension of the international division of labor concept that was first introduced by Adam Smith in the eighteenth century. Unlike Smith's famous example with the pin factory where the production process is divided into different stages in one location, in GVCs, production is dispersed geographically across borders allowing finer division of labor. Value is incrementally added to the end product across several countries, resulting in a far more complex outcome than a pin. In contrast to conventional international trade that typically involves transactions between two countries, where one country exports and the other imports, trade within GVCs encompasses multiple border crossings.

GVCs, as defined broadly by the World Bank, are the sequential phases of production and delivery of a product or service to consumers, where value is added at each stage, with the condition that a minimum of two stages occur in different countries. Thus countries, sectors, or companies participate in a GVC if they are engaged in (at least) one stage in a GVC (IBRD, 2020). Similar is the definition provided by Gereffi and Stark (2016)—the full range of activities such as design, production, marketing, distribution, and support to the final consumer, carried out in interfirm networks on a global scale. A more specific definition of GVC trade is presented by Borin and Mancini (2015) where trade flows cross a minimum of two national

[1] While acknowledging that internationalized value chains may often exhibit a regional rather than purely global nature, we adopt the traditional term GVCs.

borders, distinguishing it from direct trade within gross trade that only involves a single border crossing.

Let's explore a particular GVC using the example of bicycles. Country A imports raw materials such as steel, aluminum, rubber, and plastic components worth $200 from various countries, including Country B. These materials serve as the building blocks for bicycle production. Country A's manufacturers assemble the components, including the frame, wheels, brakes, gears, and other parts, to create the intermediate product—bicycle frames and subassemblies. They also add finishing touches and conduct quality control checks. Country A exports these bicycle frames and subassemblies to Country C, generating $500 in export value. Country C specializes in bicycle assembly and manufacturing. They receive the bicycle frames and subassemblies from Country A and integrate them with additional components such as handlebars, seats, pedals, and chains to create fully functional bicycles. Country C exports the finished bicycles to Country D, resulting in a total export value of $800. In this example, Country A focuses on sourcing raw materials from country B and manufacturing intermediate bicycle components, while Country C specializes in bicycle assembly and final manufacturing. By participating in this GVC, all countries contribute to the overall value creation of bicycles, from raw materials to the complete product.

GVC integration enables countries to allocate their resources efficiently by focusing on tasks where they possess a comparative advantage, without the need to establish an entire value chain independently. Specialization is not in whole industries but rather in certain segments of the GVC. This is achieved through the importation of intermediate goods from other countries. By adding value to these imported intermediates, countries can subsequently sell the final products in their domestic markets or reexport them (Jouanjean et al., 2017). This approach allows countries to leverage the expertise and capabilities of other nations while optimizing their own strengths, facilitating economic specialization, and enhancing overall competitiveness.

Given the significant opportunities that GVCs offer to the emerging economies, it is important to determine which factors drive the participation in them. This would provide important insights to policymakers in prioritizing efforts to enhance attractiveness for boosting GVC engagement.

A dedicated econometric study has found out that while structural factors, such as market size, level of development, and geographical location, are key determinants of GVC participation, enhancing trade and investment policies, along with improving logistics and customs operations, intellectual property rights protection, infrastructure development, and institutional frameworks, can actively contribute to fostering increased participation in global value chains (Kowalski et al., 2015). Based on a modified factor-content methodology, Pathikonda and Farole (2017) confirm that efficient institutions, quality logistics, and closeness to markets are among the most important underlying factors driving participation in GVCs. Furthermore, on the example of Southern African Customs Union countries, the authors exhibit that minimizing policy-related disparities can enhance a country's competitiveness and enable it to effectively engage in GVCs.

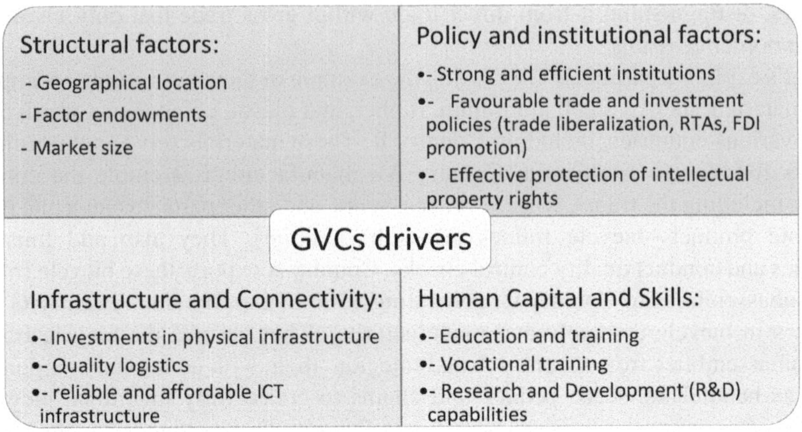

Fig. 9.1 Drivers of countries' participation in GVCs

The World Bank in its flagship World Development Report 2020 makes similar conclusions. Participation in GVCs is primarily influenced by fundamental factors such as resource availability, market size, geographic location, and institutional frameworks. However, it is important to note that these fundamentals do not necessarily determine the outcome. By adopting appropriate policies and reforms, countries have the ability to shape and influence each of these fundamental factors, ultimately affecting their participation in GVCs (IBRD, 2020). Figure 9.1 provides a summary of the underlying factors that drive participation in GVCs as established in the theoretical and empirical literature.

9.3 Measurements of Countries' Integration into the GVCs

Measuring countries' integration into GVCs poses challenges due to the limitations of customs data, which only provides information on the origin and destination of goods/services, without details on production processes or usage. The emergence of GVCs has challenged traditional trade statistics (recorded in gross value terms), as gross exports can lead to double-counting and misrepresent countries' roles. To rectify this, the concept of trade in value added has gained traction, breaking down exports by origin and destination of value added. To do that, researchers combine customs data with input-output tables, constructing global input-output databases like WIOD, OECD TiVA, and Eora. These databases trace value-added trade flows across borders, revealing the contributions of different nations to GVCs.

The most comprehensive framework for decomposing value-added exports is developed by Koopman et al. (2011). This framework divides exports into domestic value added (DVA), returned domestic value added, and foreign value added. Domestic value added is further split between the DVA in the exports of final goods absorbed by the direct importer, the DVA exports of intermediate goods absorbed by the direct importer, and the DVA in intermediate goods reexported by the direct importer to other foreign countries (indirect value-added exports). The latter can serve as a proxy of how two countries involved in bilateral trade participate in a GVC. It includes the value added by the exporter that passes through the direct importer during one or more stages of production before eventually being incorporated into intermediate or final goods exported to third countries. The indirect value-added export (also referred to as forward GVC participation) is one of the two major components in the indicators commonly used for analyzing a country's role in GVCs (Dell'Agostino, 2017).

Countries engage in GVCs in two basic ways—through backward and/or forward linkages. Backward participation involves the proportion of foreign value added included in a country's overall gross exports. On the other hand, forward participation refers to the proportion of domestically produced value added that is embedded in a country's exports and subsequently reexported by the destination nation. Figure 9.2 uses the example of international production of bicycle presented above to illustrate in a simplified way how Country A is engaged in the GVC of that good.

Country A's backward participation encompasses sourcing and incorporating raw materials worth \$200 into the production process. Its forward participation involves creating and supplying intermediate goods for further processing, generating indirect value-added exports of \$300. The traditional trade measurement depicted in this illustration shows exports among the four countries amounting to \$1500. However, it is important to note that only a value-added of \$800 has actually been generated.

Table 9.1 provides information about the key indicators traditionally used for measuring countries and sectors' involvement and position in GVC. Both indicators (GVC participation index and GVC position index) are derived from the indices of backward and forward GVC participation. The GVC participation index, which serves as a measure of a country's overall engagement in GVCs, is a sum of the two

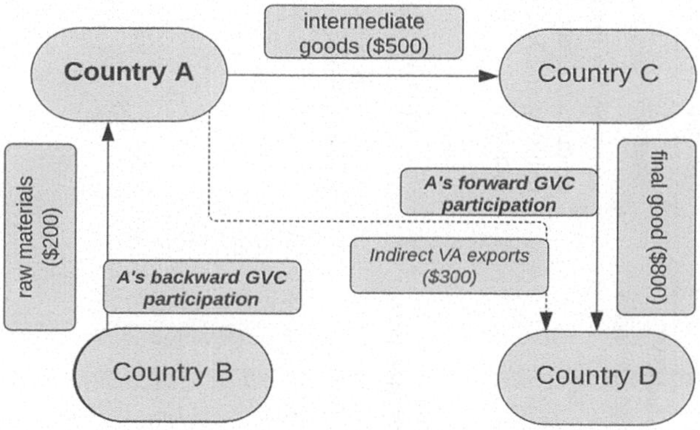

Fig. 9.2 Country A's participation in GVCs

Table 9.1 Key indices for measuring country and sector participation in GVCs

Index	Formula	Meaning
Backward GVC participation index	$Backward\,GVC_{participation} = {FVA}/{X}$, where FVA is the value of imported intermediate products, included in the export of a particular industry, and X is the gross exports in that industry	Backward GVC participation reflects the buyer perspective or the sourcing side in GVCs, where an economy buys imported intermediates (foreign value-added) to produce its exports. It is also referred as vertical specialization
Forward GVC participation index	$Forward\,GVC_{participation} = {DVX}/{X}$, where DVX is the domestic value-added exported to third countries for further exportation	Forward GVC participation reflects the supply side or the seller perspective, capturing the domestic value-added contained in inputs sent to third economies for further processing and export through supply chains
GVC participation index	$GVC_{participation} = \frac{DVX + FVA}{X}$	GVC participation is defined as a country's percentage of exports that are part of a multistage trade process. It is determined by dividing the total of FVA and DVX by gross exports. The bigger the percentage, the greater the extent of a country's engagement in GVCs
GVC position index	$GVC_{position} = \ln\left(1 + \frac{DVX}{X}\right) - \ln\left(1 + \frac{FVA}{X}\right)$	The GVC position index defines a country's overall position in GVCs on an aggregate basis. A positive number implies that a nation adds more value to other countries' exports than other countries add to its own (i.e., a country moves **upstream** in GVCs). A negative number implies that a country sources more foreign value-added inputs for its own exports than it sells domestic inputs to the exports of other countries (i.e., a country takes a **downstream** position in GVCs)

Source: Compiled by the author based on OECD Trade in Value-Added (TiVA) database

indices. The higher the value, the more intensive is the involvement. The GVC position index is calculated as a difference between the logarithms of country's forward and backward participation. A positive value indicates that the country in question exports more intermediate goods than it imports from abroad, obtaining a higher stage of development in the GVCs. If the index has a negative value, the country is more a buyer than a seller of intermediate goods and has a lower status in the GVCs.

Furthermore, the World Bank offers a useful classification that allows a systematic approach to understand the diverse ways in which countries engage in GVCs. The framework categorizes countries based on the nature of their economic engagement within GVCs, size, and level of GVC participation, in four taxonomy groups:

1. *Commodities*: This group includes economies with a lower share of manufacturing in their total domestic value-added exports (less than 60%) and backward linkages in manufacturing of less than 20%, 10%, and 7.5%, respectively, for small countries (population less than 20 million people), medium-size countries, and large countries (population over 1 billion). In addition, the group is divided into three subcategories based on the share of primary goods' domestic value added in exports: low participation (< 20%), limited commodities (20% ≤ share < 40%), and high commodities (≥ 40%).
2. *Innovative activities*: It is for countries not falling into the previous categories and depends on size—intellectual property receipts equal to or above 0.15 % of GDP and R&D intensity equal to or above 1.5% for small countries, while for the rest, ≥0.1% and ≥1% accordingly.
3. *Advanced manufacturing and services*: The share of manufacturing and business services in total domestic value added in exports should be ≥80%, while backward manufacturing is no less than 30%, 20%, and 15% for small, medium-size, and large countries, respectively.
4. *Limited manufacturing:* Encompasses the remaining countries (IBRD, 2020).

9.4 Bulgaria's Input in the GVCs

By utilizing the input-output methodological approach and the OECD TiVA database, it becomes possible to methodically analyze the value added of Bulgarian export goods. This involves breaking down the value-added components within the output, determining the proportion of each component, and conducting a comprehensive examination of Bulgaria's export levels. Our analysis will encompass the period 1995–2018 as this is, at the time of writing, the most comprehensive and up-to-date available data.

Over the analyzed period, Bulgaria's reliance on domestic value added in exports, as indicated by the DVA/X percentage, gradually decreased from 82.3% in 1995 to 67.3% in 2005 and then to 63.2% in 2018 (see Table 9.2). This suggests a diminishing role of domestic production in the country's export activities. Conversely, the FVA/X percentage, representing the share of foreign value added in exports,

Table 9.2 Domestic and foreign value added in Bulgarian exports from 1995 to 2018 (in million USD and %)

Year	Gross exports (X) (Million USD)	DVA (Million USD)	FVA (Million USD)	DVA/X (%)	FVA/X (%)
1995	5789	4765	1024	82.3	17.7
1996	5459	3859	1600	70.7	29.3
1997	5278	3885	1393	73.6	26.4
1998	6022	4486	1536	74.5	25.5
1999	5585	3740	1845	67.0	33.0
2000	4647	3345	1302	72.0	28.0
2001	4724	3390	1334	71.8	28.2
2002	5281	3939	1343	74.6	25.4
2003	7002	5104	1898	72.9	27.1
2004	10,271	7152	3119	69.6	30.4
2005	12,263	8256	4007	67.3	32.7
2006	15,432	9921	5510	64.3	35.7
2007	22,056	13,144	8912	59.6	40.4
2008	26,947	15,727	11,220	58.4	41.6
2009	20,795	13,993	6803	67.3	32.7
2010	23,899	15,955	7944	66.8	33.2
2011	32,010	20,265	11,746	63.3	36.7
2012	30,764	19,020	11,744	61.8	38.2
2013	33,490	20,646	12,843	61.7	38.3
2014	34,267	21,270	12,997	62.1	37.9
2015	30,019	18,897	11,122	63.0	37.0
2016	31,635	20,728	10,907	65.5	34.5
2017	36,328	23,253	13,075	64.0	36.0
2018	39,437	24,926	14,511	63.2	36.8

Source: Calculated by the author, based on OECD TiVA database 2021

exhibited an upward trend, rising from 17.7% in 1995 to 32.7% in 2005 and 36.8% in 2018. This long-term trend indicates an increasing dependence on foreign inputs and integration into international production networks. It also shows lower self-reliance, typical for a small open economy, and that the potential advantages of higher exports documented in conventional trade statistics may be inflated (Bjelić et al., 2020).

While a decreasing DVA share may indicate a reduced direct contribution of domestic production to exports, it does not necessarily imply declining efficiency from the country's participation in the international division of labor. It is important to note that the decreasing share of DVA is a relative measure that reflects the changing composition of the country's export sector. When analyzing the process of upgrading in GVCs, the focus should not solely be on the proportion of domestic value-added exports. Rather, the crucial factor lies in how a country effectively utilizes foreign inputs and engages in GVC participation to increase the overall level

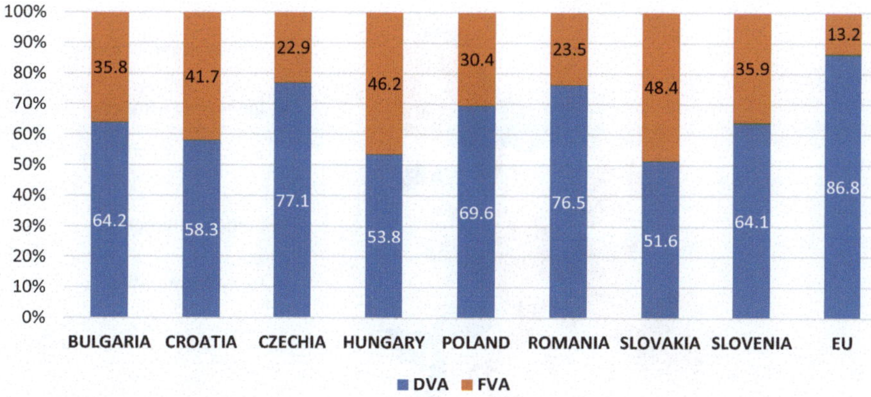

Fig. 9.3 Domestic and foreign value added in the exports of selected CEECs for 2016–2018 av., %. (Source: OECD TiVA database 2021)

of its economic activity (i.e., the total amount of DVA in aggregate) (Jouanjean et al., 2017).

When looking at the data, it is evident that DVA and FVA in Bulgaria exhibit an extremely strong linear relationship between them (corr. = 0.99). The positive correlation between DVA and FVA indicates that as Bulgaria integrates further into GVCs and relies more on foreign inputs, it also experiences an increase in the domestic value added. Though the highly positive association between the two variables does not necessarily entail a cause-and-effect relationship, it suggests that the utilization of foreign inputs and participation in GVCs contribute to expanding the overall economic activity and value added in Bulgaria's export-oriented industries.

Comparing Bulgaria to other CEECs (Fig. 9.3), it is evident that the country shares a similar pattern of having a higher share of FVA in its exports, indicating a significant reliance on foreign inputs. This aligns with the broader trend observed in the region, where the new EU member states have embraced integration into GVCs and utilized foreign value added to enhance their export-oriented industries. The highest share of DVA in the exports on average for the last 3 years with available data is registered by Czechia (77%), while the lowest by Slovakia (51.6%). Bulgaria is at par with Slovenia (64%). However, when compared with the EU (86.8%), all the countries from the sample are far below in terms of the DVA contribution in the gross exports. The significant difference between the EU and the CEECs in terms of DVA and FVA distribution implies distinct trade and economic structures within the old and the new member states. The higher reliance on DVA in the EU reflects a more established and self-sustained domestic production base, emphasizing the importance of domestic industries and value chains.

The East-West divide in the EU is very well illustrated in Fig. 9.4, which depicts the different types of GVC participation. All of the Western EU nations (with the exception of Portugal) are specialized in innovative activities. This indicates their strength in high-value-added activities, emphasizing innovation, research and

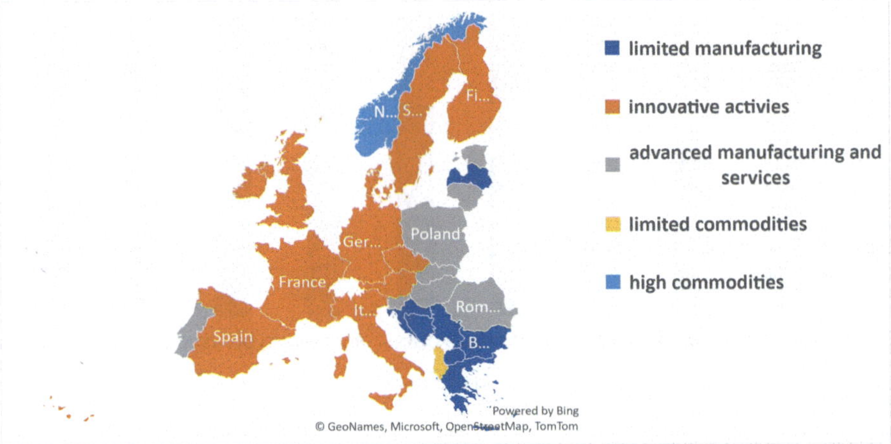

Fig. 9.4 Taxonomy of GVC participation of European countries, 2015. (Source: IBRD, 2020)

development, and knowledge-intensive processes within the global value chains. The only CEE country that has managed to upgrade its role in the GVCs is Czechia. Its success can be attributed to its focus on skill building, innovation, increased Internet usage, a growing share of high-skilled workers, and an increase in R&D expenditure, ranking the country among the top innovators globally (IBRD, 2020).

Additionally, there is a further division among the CEECs, as some of them being categorized as specialized in advanced manufacturing and services while others (including Bulgaria) in limited manufacturing. The presence of limited manufacturing specialization among some CEECs (mostly on the Balkans) suggests that these countries focus more on lower value-added manufacturing processes, indicative of a lower degree of technological advancement, limited innovation capacity, and a concentration on industries that rely on lower-skilled labor and cost competitiveness.

Continuing with the analysis, we see that over the period 1995–2018, Bulgaria has significantly increased its integration into the GVCs. The GVC participation index has risen from 33.2% in 1995 to 47.7% in 2005 and reached its peak of 54.1% in the end of the period (Fig. 9.5). This confirms that the Bulgarian economy has been progressively becoming more open over the last three decades.

However, the primary catalyst for this increased integration into GVCs is the growth of backward linkage. Between 1995 and 2018, Bulgaria experienced a more than twofold increase in the extent of backward linkage, with the backward participation indicator rising from 17.7% to 36.8%. On the other hand, the forward participation in GVCs experienced a comparatively smaller increase. Starting at 15.5% in 1995, it saw a gradual rise to 17.3% in 2018, an increase of less than 2 percentage points. These findings align with the previous analysis, emphasizing the growing importance of importing intermediate inputs for producing Bulgarian exports. Overall, Bulgaria's GVC participation index, considering both the intensity and

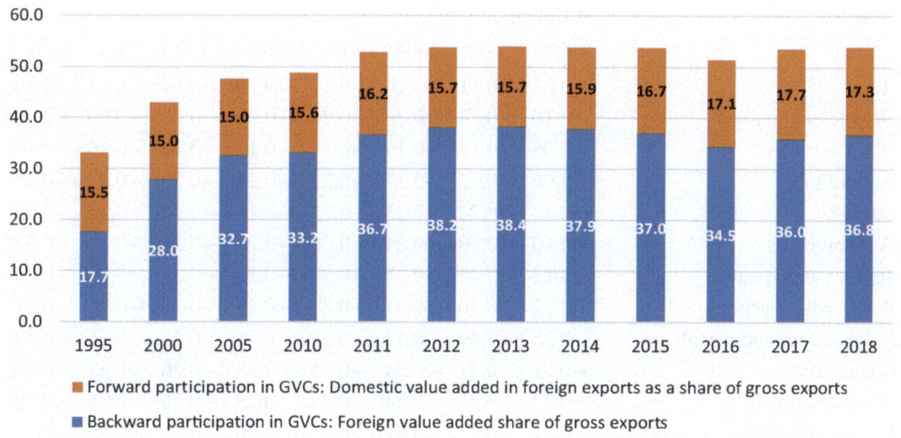

Fig. 9.5 Indicators of Bulgaria's participation in GVCs (%). (Source: OECD TiVA database 2021)

Table 9.3 GVC position indices of selected CEECs

	1995	2000	2005	2010	2015	2016	2017	2018
Bulgaria	−0.02	−0.11	−0.14	−0.14	−0.16	−0.14	−0.14	−0.15
Croatia	−0.08	−0.08	−0.11	−0.08	−0.08	−0.07	−0.08	−0.09
Czechia	−0.07	−0.09	−0.14	−0.17	−0.17	−0.17	−0.17	−0.17
Hungary	−0.12	−0.27	−0.25	−0.27	−0.23	−0.23	−0.22	−0.22
Poland	0.00	−0.02	−0.04	−0.07	−0.05	−0.05	−0.06	−0.07
Romania	−0.03	0.02	0.00	−0.01	0.00	0.00	0.00	−0.01
Slovakia	−0.12	−0.12	−0.17	−0.20	−0.21	−0.22	−0.22	−0.22
Slovenia	−0.14	−0.14	−0.16	−0.14	−0.11	−0.11	−0.12	−0.13
EU	0.05	0.05	0.05	0.02	0.02	0.02	0.01	0.01

Source: Calculated by the author, based on OECD TiVA database 2021

structure of its participation (with a prevalent emphasis on backward participation), closely resembles that of the other CEECs (BNB, 2016).

The dominant backward participation in GVCs of Bulgaria is reflected in its GVC position index. It shows a negative trend throughout the years (Table 9.3). The index started at −0.02 in 1995 and reached its lowest point at −0.16 in 2015. It remained relatively stable around −0.14 to −0.15 from 2016 to 2018. The dynamics of the GVC position index indicates growing specialization of the country in the downstream or later stages of production within global value chains. It emphasizes that Bulgaria's participation in the earlier stages, such as producing intermediate goods and services for other countries' exports, is relatively limited. Instead, Bulgaria's focus is increasingly centered on activities that add value in the downstream stages, such as assembly, processing, or distribution. The significant dependence on foreign value-added components to finalize the production process within GVCs is a common characteristic among all the remaining CEECs that recorded negative GVC position indices in 2018. This pattern contrasts with the average

Table 9.4 GVC position indices of Bulgaria by sectors

	1995	2000	2005	2010	2015	2016	2017	2018
Total	−0.02	−0.11	−0.14	−0.14	−0.16	−0.14	−0.14	−0.15
Total manufactures	−0.10	−0.22	−0.26	−0.26	−0.28	−0.26	−0.26	−0.28
Total services	−0.08	−0.17	−0.19	−0.15	−0.17	−0.16	−0.16	−0.16
Agriculture	−0.06	−0.12	−0.17	−0.23	−0.24	−0.22	−0.23	−0.25
Mining	−0.13	−0.22	−0.23	−0.18	−0.18	−0.16	−0.17	−0.19
Food products	−0.10	−0.19	−0.21	−0.26	−0.29	−0.29	−0.31	−0.32
Textiles and apparel	−0.12	−0.22	−0.27	−0.28	−0.36	−0.33	−0.35	−0.35
Wood, paper, printing	−0.22	−0.30	−0.31	−0.27	−0.29	−0.29	−0.30	−0.31
Coke and refined petroleum	−0.38	−0.49	−0.52	−0.59	−0.58	−0.54	−0.56	−0.59
Chemicals	−0.21	−0.31	−0.34	−0.35	−0.38	−0.36	−0.37	−0.40
Pharmaceuticals	−0.22	−0.31	−0.34	−0.23	−0.28	−0.26	−0.28	−0.29
Rubber and plastics products	−0.27	−0.35	−0.41	−0.42	−0.40	−0.38	−0.40	−0.39
Other nonmetallic mineral products	−0.19	−0.30	−0.31	−0.31	−0.39	−0.37	−0.38	−0.39
Basic metals	−0.18	−0.30	−0.37	−0.35	−0.44	−0.42	−0.42	−0.44
Fabricated metal products	−0.16	−0.26	−0.32	−0.30	−0.33	−0.29	−0.28	−0.29
Computer, electronic, and optical products	−0.29	−0.36	−0.37	−0.39	−0.34	−0.33	−0.34	−0.31
Electrical equipment	−0.15	−0.28	−0.34	−0.32	−0.40	−0.38	−0.37	−0.38
Machinery	−0.13	−0.26	−0.33	−0.30	−0.32	−0.30	−0.31	−0.31
Motor vehicles	−0.24	−0.33	−0.38	−0.29	−0.34	−0.32	−0.33	−0.34
Other transport	−0.16	−0.26	−0.35	−0.29	−0.40	−0.39	−0.39	−0.39
Utilities	−0.15	−0.23	−0.27	−0.34	−0.34	−0.33	−0.33	−0.36
Construction	−0.13	−0.23	−0.31	−0.26	−0.32	−0.29	−0.30	−0.31
Wholesale and retail	−0.06	−0.15	−0.19	−0.16	−0.19	−0.18	−0.17	−0.17
Transportation and storage	−0.15	−0.25	−0.27	−0.23	−0.27	−0.25	−0.26	−0.26
Accommodation and food	−0.06	−0.14	−0.18	−0.16	−0.18	−0.18	−0.18	−0.18
Information and comms	−0.12	−0.21	−0.19	−0.14	−0.16	−0.13	−0.13	−0.12
Finance and insurance	−0.04	−0.15	−0.10	−0.04	−0.06	−0.06	−0.07	−0.07
Other business sector services	−0.06	−0.16	−0.22	−0.15	−0.17	−0.16	−0.16	−0.15
Other services	−0.07	−0.16	−0.18	−0.13	−0.13	−0.13	−0.13	−0.13

Source: Calculated by the author, based on OECD TiVA database 2021

performance of the EU, as the old member states tend to exhibit a greater presence in the upstream stages in GVCs. Their positioning upstream suggests a higher degree of value addition and a lesser dependence on imported inputs.

Finally, we look at Bulgaria's GVC position index on a sectoral level. Table 9.4 demonstrates that Bulgaria holds a solid downstream position with negative GVC position indices across all branches of the economy, which are all net buyers of value added in intermediates. The sectors where Bulgaria is most downstream are Coke and refined petroleum, basic metals, chemicals, rubber and plastics products, and other transport equipment. As a rule, services are less dependent on foreign inputs, and finance and insurance, information and communications, other services, accommodation and food service activities, and wholesale and retail trade exhibit higher (less negative) GVC position indices, suggesting that Bulgaria is relatively less downstream there.

The sectoral analysis reveals Bulgaria's growing concentration in downstream activities within GVCs. This emphasizes the importance of strategic initiatives aimed at enhancing value addition and improving Bulgaria's positioning in the earlier stages of production within GVCs.

9.5 Conclusions

This chapter has examined Bulgaria's participation in GVCs through various indicators and comparative analysis. The findings provide valuable insights into the extent and dynamics of Bulgaria's integration into GVCs, highlighting areas for improvement and strategic initiatives.

The analysis demonstrates that Bulgaria has progressively increased its participation in GVCs over time, particularly driven by a growing emphasis on backward linkages. The country has shown a tendency to specialize in downstream activities within GVCs, relying heavily on imported inputs and foreign value-added components. This downstream positioning is evident across all sectors, which are all net buyers of value added in intermediates.

Comparing Bulgaria's GVC participation with other CEECs, we note that the country's performance aligns closely with its regional counterparts. The analysis suggests that the high reliance on foreign value-added inputs to complete the production process within GVCs is a common characteristic among the CEECs with negative GVC position indices. In contrast, the old EU member states tend to be positioned more upstream in GVCs, contributing relatively more to the creation of intermediate goods and services for other countries' exports. The East-West divide within the EU highlights the need for policies and strategies to promote economic convergence and support the development of advanced industries and innovation capacity in the Eastern EU nations. This need is more pronounced in Bulgaria, which, along with some other Southeastern European countries, has been specialized in limited manufacturing activities in the GVCs.

To fully leverage participation in GVCs, Bulgaria should focus on strategic initiatives aimed at increasing value addition and repositioning itself in the earlier stages of production within GVCs. This entails a shift toward higher value-added activities, such as research and development, innovation, and the production of intermediate goods and services.

By promoting domestic industries that can contribute more value-added components and reducing reliance on imported inputs, Bulgaria can strengthen its competitiveness and capture a larger share of the value created within GVCs. This requires ensuring strong institutions, fostering a favorable business environment, attracting foreign direct investment that brings advanced technology and knowledge, and investing in education and skills development to enhance the capabilities of the workforce. Furthermore, improving infrastructure, connectivity, and logistics networks will facilitate the efficient flow of goods, services, and information within GVCs. This will enable Bulgaria to better integrate into global value chains and enhance its position as a preferred location for higher value-added activities.

In summary, while Bulgaria has made significant progress in its embeddedness into GVCs, strategic initiatives aimed at enhancing value addition and repositioning in the earlier stages of production are crucial to fully capitalize on the benefits of this integration. By implementing these measures, Bulgaria can further strengthen its position within GVCs, drive sustainable economic growth, and secure competitiveness in the global economy.

References

Antràs, P. (2020). Conceptual aspects of global value chains. *The World Bank Economic Review, 34*(3), 551–574. Washington, DC: The World Bank Group.

Bjelić, P., Petrović, I., Zorić, A., & Kastratović, R. (2020). Serbia in global value chains. In X. Xin (Ed.), *CEE countries in Europe: Toward center or periphery in global value chains*.

Borin, A., & Mancini, M. (2015). *Follow the value added: Bilateral gross export accounting*. Working Paper Series No. 1026. Banca d'Italia.

Bulgarian National Bank. (2016). Economic review, No. 3/2016. BNB.

Cigna, S., Gunnella, V., & Quaglietti, L. (2022). *Global value chains: Measurement, trends and drivers*. ECB Occasional Paper No. 289/2022. https://ssrn.com/abstract=4007756

Dell'Agostino, L. (2017). *Italy's participation in international supply and production networks using value added trade data*. Dipartimento di Economia, Università degli Studi Roma Tre, Working Paper No. 228.

Gereffi, G., & Stark, K. (2016). *Global value chain analysis: A primer* (2nd ed.). The Duke Center on Globalization.

International Bank for Reconstruction and Development / The World Bank. (2020). *World Development Report 2020: Trading for development in the age of global value chains*. The World Bank Group.

Jouanjean, M., Gourdon, J., & Korinek, J. (2017). *GVC participation and economic transformation: Lessons from three sectors*. OECD Trade Policy Papers No. 207. Paris: OECD Publishing. https://doi.org/10.1787/617d7a19-en

Koopman, R., Powers, W., Wang, Z., & Wei, S. (2011). *Give credit where credit is due: Tracing value added in global production chains*. NBER Working Paper No. 16426.

Kowalski, P., Gonzales, J., Ragoussis, A., & Ugarte, C. (2015). *Participation of developing countries in global value chains: Implications for trade and trade-related policies*. OECD Trade Policy Papers No. 179. Paris: OECD Publishing. https://doi.org/10.1787/5js33lfw0xxn-en

OECD. (2013). *Interconnected economies: Benefiting from global value chains*. OECD Publishing. https://doi.org/10.1787/9789264189560-en

Pathikonda, V., & Farole, T. (2017). The capabilities driving participation in global value chains. *Journal of International Commerce, Economics and Policy, 8*(1) www.worldscientific.com/doi/abs/10.1142/S1793993317500065

World Trade Organization. (2013). *World Trade Report 2013: Factors shaping the future of World Trade*. WTO.

Chapter 10
Foreign Direct Investment in Bulgaria

10.1 Introduction

Foreign direct investment (FDI),[1] an important form of international capital flow, serves as a crucial conduit of globalization, fostering stable ties and development across countries. It has been a cornerstone in the economic transformation of Central and Eastern European countries (CEECs), facilitating their transition from centrally planned to market economies (Günther & Kristalova, 2016). As these countries opened their markets and reformed their economic structures, FDI emerged as a critical driver of growth, modernization, and regional integration. The ability of CEECs to attract and effectively utilize FDI has varied significantly, resulting in different levels of economic prosperity across the region (Sohinger, 2005). This chapter explores the role and impact of FDI in Bulgaria, which, like the other CEECs, relied on FDI to trigger its development but whose experience differs from some of its more advanced counterparts.

The benefits of FDI—such as faster economic growth, increased labor productivity, technological advancement, job creation, and improved export performance (Lungu, 2024; Marinova & Marinov, 2019; Mehic et al., 2013; Geenhuizen, 2014)—make it a highly sought-after resource for emerging economies. Consequently, countries worldwide, including those in the CEE region, actively compete to attract FDI. This competition is expected to intensify amid the ongoing disruptions in global FDI flows caused by rising geopolitical and trade tensions. At the same time, the ensuing trends of nearshoring and friendshoring present new opportunities for

[1] Unlike portfolio investment, FDI involves a more substantial and long-term commitment to a foreign economy. According to the OECD definition, FDI reflects the objective of establishing a lasting interest by a resident enterprise in one economy (direct investor) in an enterprise (direct investment enterprise) that is resident in an economy other than that of the direct investor. This lasting interest indicates a long-term relationship and significant management influence, usually involving ownership of 10% or more of the voting power (OECD, 2009, p. 48).

P. Zhelev, *Bulgaria in the Global Economy*, Societies and Political Orders in Transition, https://doi.org/10.1007/978-3-031-87923-4_10

Bulgaria. As companies seek to relocate their supply chains closer to home or to politically stable and allied countries, Bulgaria's strategic location and EU membership make it an attractive destination for such investments (Zavarská, 2022).

Nevertheless, the geopolitical confrontation and rising protectionism have added layers of complexity and risk to inward FDI. Host countries, including Bulgaria, must navigate these challenges while ensuring that FDI contributes positively to their economic development. The recent paradigm shift recognizes that while FDI can be beneficial, it also brings potential risks, necessitating a balanced approach to openness and protection through screening mechanisms.

Furthermore, it is widely recognized that despite its potential, FDI is not a silver bullet for economic development. The positive effects of FDI are contingent upon the host country's ability to absorb and utilize the benefits. Effective policies and a conducive regulatory environment are crucial for maximizing the advantages of FDI while mitigating its potential downsides, such as economic dependence on foreign capital, market monopolization, intensive profit repatriation, and contribution to increased regional disparities (Rodionova et al., 2019; Pavlinek, 2004).

The goal of this chapter is to provide a comprehensive understanding of the role of FDI in Bulgaria's economy. It delves into FDI patterns and trends, examining the main source countries and sectors that have attracted investment. Additionally, the chapter discusses Bulgaria's business environment, including positive and negative aspects as well as regulatory frameworks and investment policies designed to attract foreign investors.

10.2 Bulgaria as a Destination for FDI

Bulgaria's transformation into an open, market-driven economy has made it an increasingly attractive FDI destination in CEE. However, alongside its strengths, structural challenges persist, shaping the dynamics of FDI inflows. This section explores the strategic advantages driving Bulgaria's appeal to investors and the key risks that may affect its long-term competitiveness.

10.2.1 Strategic Advantages of Bulgaria

Locational (competitive) advantages of host countries of FDI, as known from the eclectic paradigm of Dunning, consist of two main elements—*economic determinants* such as market size or relative labor costs and *policy-related determinants* such as the business environment or investment promotion (Kalotay, 2008, p. 7). While investment promotion mechanisms will be explored in detail later, this section highlights Bulgaria's broader institutional, economic, and geographic strengths that position it as a competitive hub for foreign capital. Drawing on data from the

Invest Bulgaria Agency (IBA) and independent sources, the analysis underscores key factors driving the country's appeal.

Institutional Stability and Fiscal Discipline

Bulgaria's integration into supranational frameworks, including its accession to the EU in 2007 and NATO in 2004, has reinforced its political credibility and regulatory alignment with European standards. A cornerstone of its economic stability is the currency board regime, implemented in 1997, which pegs the Bulgarian lev (BGN) rigidly to the euro (1 EUR = 1.95583 BGN). This policy has curtailed exchange rate fluctuations, fostering predictability for cross-border investors. Complementing this stability is the nation's fiscal conservatism: with government debt at 23.1% of GDP in 2023, Bulgaria maintains one of the EU's lowest debt-to-GDP ratios, trailing only Estonia and Luxembourg (Eurostat, n.d.).

Cost-efficient Business Environment

Bulgaria's tax regime is a focal point for cost-conscious enterprises. The flat 10% corporate tax rate—unchanged since 2007—is among the most competitive in the EU, contrasting sharply with averages exceeding 21% in Western Europe (Enache, 2024). Operational affordability extends beyond taxation: office rents in Sofia, for instance, average €10–€15.50/m^2, significantly below regional peers like Bucharest (€14–€19/m^2) or Bratislava (€14.5–€17.5/m^2) (Colliers, 2023). Energy costs further amplify this advantage. Despite global price volatility, Bulgaria's diversified energy mix—including nuclear, renewable, and coal sources—has ensured stable electricity supply at rates significantly below the EU average (Eurostat, 2024).

Strategic Market Connectivity

Bulgaria's geographic and trade policy positioning enhances its role as a gateway to diverse markets. As a member of the EU, the country benefits from duty-free access to over 1.3 billion consumers through 45 free trade agreements (IBA, n.d.). Its transportation infrastructure, anchored by five Pan-European corridors, facilitates seamless logistics to the EU/EFTA bloc, Black Sea economies, and Türkiye—a critical node for Middle Eastern trade. This connectivity is bolstered by ongoing investments in the fields of transport, energy, and digital services under the EU's Connecting Europe Facility (European Commission, n.d.).

Skilled Human Capital

Bulgaria's workforce combines technical proficiency with linguistic versatility. The country ranks third globally in IT specialists per capita, and over 50% of the population speaks at least one foreign language, with English, German, and Russian proficiency prevalent among professionals (IBA, n.d.).

10.2.2 Challenges and Risks

While Bulgaria's low-tax model attracts investment, some analysts caution that reliance on fiscal incentives may divert attention from structural challenges. For example, the OECD (2023) notes that underinvestment in public infrastructure—partly linked to low tax revenues—could strain long-term competitiveness. To present a balanced view of Bulgaria as an investment destination, it is important to also consider the potential challenges that investors may face. While Bulgaria offers numerous advantages, there are certain barriers to FDI that warrant attention:

Rule of Law Concerns and Recent Political Crisis

Frequent political changes, with six parliamentary elections between 2021 and 2024, have led to governance instability and uncertainty. Investors have raised concerns about the consistency and reliability of Bulgaria's legal and regulatory environment.

Corruption and Judicial Inefficiency

Corruption and inefficiencies in the legal system pose significant challenges, making it difficult to secure necessary permits and enforce judicial decisions, which complicates business operations (US Department of State, 2023).

Decreasing Population and Labor Shortages

A rapidly shrinking and aging population is leading to labor shortages, particularly in skilled sectors, potentially driving up wage costs and hindering business growth (Molnar et al., 2023).

Infrastructural and Bureaucratic Challenges

Bulgaria's transport and logistics networks, especially in peripheral areas, face limitations. Despite improvements in digital connectivity, bureaucratic hurdles and slow administrative processes continue to complicate business operations (Moraliyska, 2023).

A recent real-world example that illustrates the difficulties of Bulgaria's business environment, particularly related to its shrinking population and the implications for host economies of FDI dependency, is presented in Box 10.1.

Box 10.1 The Exit of Leoni from Bulgaria
FDI carries significant risks for host economies, particularly when transnational corporations (TNCs) decide to scale down or withdraw their operations. A recent example is Leoni Bordnetz-Systeme GmbH, a global supplier of automotive cable systems, which announced in July 2024 that it would cease production at its Pleven plant in Bulgaria by the end of the year.

Leoni's withdrawal reflects the vulnerability of host economies to the strategic decisions of TNCs. The move was influenced by several factors, including broader industry shifts and market volatility but most importantly rising labor costs exacerbated by significant inflation and a lack of available workforce in the Pleven region. These challenges, coupled with the labor-intensive nature of cable production, rendered the Pleven plant uncompetitive within the company's global operations. Pleven, a district facing industrial decline and significant outward migration, struggled to provide the labor necessary to sustain Leoni's production processes. As a result, the low-cost environment that initially attracted Leoni became unsustainable.

The loss of such a major employer can have severe economic and social impacts on the local community as 1300 jobs will be lost. This case underscores the importance of diversifying the economic base and developing strategies that go beyond low-cost labor to sustain long-term competitiveness.

10.3 Dynamics of FDI in Bulgaria

10.3.1 Chronological Overview

In the socialist period, Bulgaria had very little foreign capital as the rigid central planning system created significant obstacles for foreign investments. The changes that began in the early 1990s, with the transition to a market economy, made it possible for Bulgaria to attract FDI. Still, other critical reforms and conditions were necessary to create a conducive environment for foreign investors (Koparanova, 1998).

Bulgaria's experience with FDI has evolved significantly over the years, influenced by both internal dynamics and external economic conditions. Figure 10.1 illustrates the initial low levels of incoming FDI during the 1990s, a significant surge leading up to EU membership, a sharp decline following the global financial crisis, and a subsequent stabilization and modest recovery in the following years.

The following periodization offers a clear framework for understanding the shifts in Bulgaria's investment landscape over the years, identifying five distinct periods, with a focus on both historical trends and emerging developments:

- *Early transition and instability* (1990–1997)
- *Stabilization, reforms, and EU integration* (1998–2007)
- *Global financial crisis and market adjustment* (2008–2014)
- *Postcrisis recovery and resilience* (2015–2022)
- *Taking advantage of green and digital transition and reshoring trends* (2023 onward)

The first period, from 1990 to 1997, is characterized by significant economic and political instability as Bulgaria transformed its economy. The hyperinflation and political turmoil of this time discouraged foreign investment, as reflected in the very low FDI inflows of just $1093 million USD, representing only 1.5% of the total FDI received by the country up to 2022 (Table 10.1). The figure shows this period as one of minimal and fluctuating FDI, underscoring the high-risk environment that deterred investors.

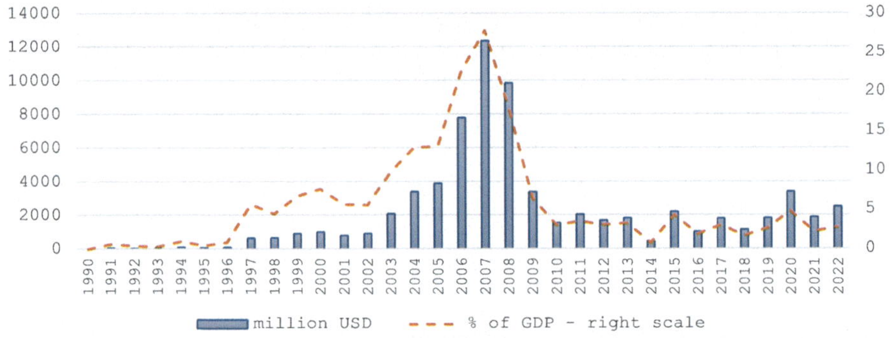

Fig. 10.1 Inward FDI flows to Bulgaria (1990–2022, in million USD and % of GDP). (Source: UNCTAD, date accessed: 01.08.2024)

Table 10.1 FDI inflows in Bulgaria by periods

	1990–1997	1998–2007	2008–2014	2015–2022	Total
FDI inflows (million USD)	1093	33947	20838	15843	71721
Share in the total, %	1.5	47.3	29.1	22.1	100

Source: Own calculations based on UNCTAD, date accessed: 01.08.2024

The second period, from 1998 to 2007, marks a significant turnaround in Bulgaria's FDI landscape. Following the introduction of a currency board in 1997, Bulgaria experienced macroeconomic stabilization and implemented key structural reforms, which restored investor confidence. This period also saw intensified privatization efforts and a surge in FDI, particularly in anticipation of EU accession. FDI inflows during this period soared to $33,947 million USD, making up 47.3% of the total FDI inflows.

The global financial crisis of 2008 had a significant impact on Bulgaria's FDI inflows, leading to a sharp decline, particularly in speculative sectors like real estate, which had previously been a major driver of FDI growth. The economy underwent a period of adjustment to the new global economic realities, with FDI being volatile. The table shows that FDI inflows during this period amounted to $20,838 million USD, accounting for 29.1% of the total FDI, signifying the broader caution in global financial markets during this time.

Following the global financial crisis, Bulgaria's economy gradually recovered, supported by EU structural funds and improved macroeconomic conditions. From 2015 to 2022, FDI inflows stabilized, with a shift toward more sustainable investments in sectors such as manufacturing, IT, and business process outsourcing (BPO). The inflows during this period totaled $15,843 million USD, representing 22.1% of the total FDI inflows. Figure 10.1 highlights this period of stabilization and modest recovery, though at much lower levels compared to the precrisis peak.

Looking ahead, Bulgaria is expected to align its investment strategies with broader EU objectives concerning green and digital transitions. While this period extends beyond the scope of the figure and table, it is anticipated that future FDI will increasingly focus on renewable energy, digital infrastructure, and industries aligned with sustainability (UNCTAD, 2023). This new phase of investment is likely to emphasize upgrading existing facilities and integrating advanced technologies, in line with the EU's Green Deal and digital transformation initiatives. Furthermore, the pandemic accelerated reshoring trends, with companies bringing operations closer to their home countries to mitigate supply chain disruptions. This could have positively impacted Bulgaria, which offers a strategic location within the EU and a relatively low-cost environment for businesses looking to establish or expand operations within the region.

10.3.2 Recent Trends

While the previous section discussed the broader shifts in Bulgaria's FDI trajectory, this section delves into the specific trends observed over the last 10 years, with a focus on the types of investments and the economic sectors that have attracted the most FDI. The period was characterized by various external factors such as geoeconomic confrontation, COVID-19 pandemic, and the war in Ukraine, which brought about subdued investor's confidence and significant volatility across this period. However, it should be noted that in 2023, there was a significant rise in the volume of inward FDI, underscoring Bulgaria's resilience in attracting FDI amidst global uncertainties.

Figure 10.2 illustrates inward FDI flows to Bulgaria from 2014 to 2023, broken down into debt instruments, reinvested earnings, and equity. These different types of investments carry distinct implications for the host economy.

Reinvested earnings, which have been negative in 2014, have shown a marked increase ever since that. The sharp increase particularly in 2023 with a peak of €3.3 billion suggests that foreign investors are increasingly confident in the Bulgarian market, choosing to reinvest profits rather than repatriate them. This trend is beneficial for the host economy as it signals stability and long-term commitment from investors. The growth of reinvested earnings has fully compensated for the debt instrument's volatility with instances of negative outflows.

Equity investments, while fluctuating, have remained positive overall, indicating ongoing interest in acquiring or expanding ownership stakes in Bulgarian enterprises. Such investments often lead to new business ventures, expansions, and job creation, which are crucial for economic growth.

Figure 10.3 presents FDI inflows by economic sector, highlighting which areas have attracted the most investment from 2014 to 2023. Financial and insurance activities emerged as the leading sector, particularly in 2023 with €1.515 billion in inflows, consistently drawing substantial investment. Manufacturing also stands out, despite net disinvestments in 2014, 2018, and 2021. In 2023, it has registered a peak of €1.3 billion after €985 million in FDI inflows an year earlier. This recent upward trend indicates a renewed focus on industrial production, positioning Bulgaria as a potential hub in the regional realignment of global supply chains. Wholesale and retail trade similarly attracted strong FDI, signifying the attractiveness of the local market. Real estate, traditionally a strong FDI sector, shows more stable yet moderate inflows, suggesting a move toward more strategic and long-term investments.

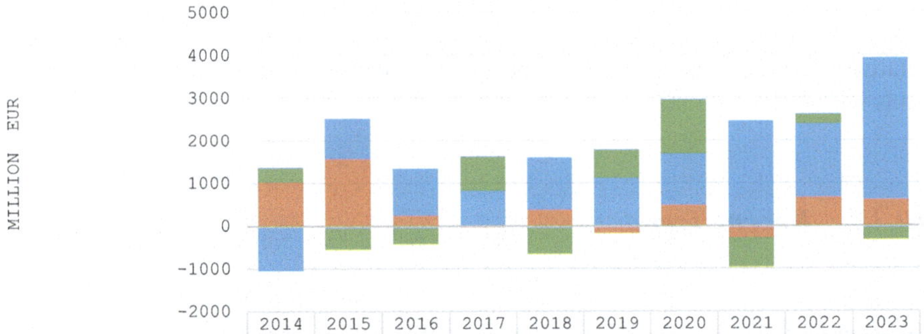

	2014	2015	2016	2017	2018	2019	2020	2021	2022	2023
Debt instruments	349	-526	-407	770	-637	637	1255	-674	200	-313
Reinvested earnings	-1036	939	1091	861	1214	1159	1221	2468	1750	3309
Equity	1035	1586	255	-25	390	-157	498	-277	681	623

Fig. 10.2 Inward FDI flows to Bulgaria by investment type (2014–2023, in million EUR). (Source: Bulgarian National Bank, date accessed: 01.08.2024)

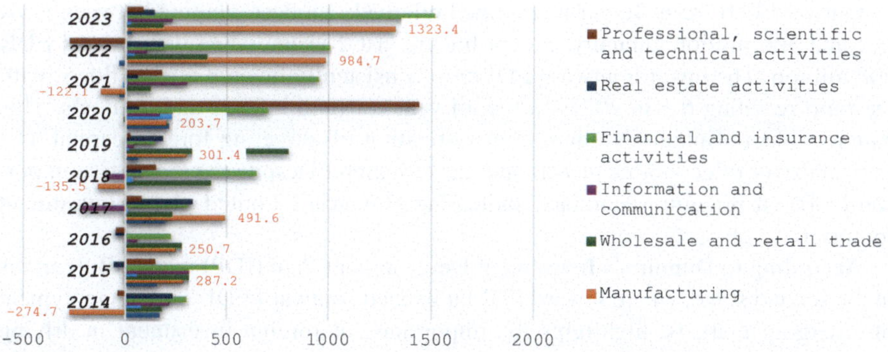

Fig. 10.3 Inward FDI flows to Bulgaria by top performing economic activity (2014–2023, in million EUR). (Source: Bulgarian National Bank, date accessed: 01.08.2024)

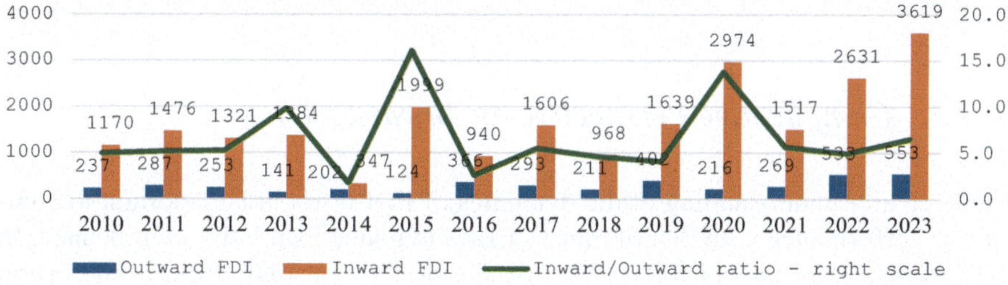

Fig. 10.4 Inward and outward FDI flows in Bulgaria and their ratio (in million EUR, 2010–2023). (Source: Bulgarian National Bank, date accessed: 01.08.2024)

Information and communication and professional, scientific, and technical activities attracted significant FDI further, reflecting Bulgaria's evolving position as a center for knowledge-based industries. This trend aligns with the global shift toward digitalization and innovation, which has accelerated due to the COVID-19 pandemic, as businesses increasingly rely on digital solutions and advanced technical services.

10.4 Importance of FDI for the Bulgarian Economy

10.4.1 Inward vs. Outward FDI: Understanding Bulgaria's Investment Priorities

Figure 10.4 illustrates the dynamics of inward and outward FDI in Bulgaria from 2010 to 2023, highlighting the country's investment priorities. Over this period, inward FDI consistently outpaced outward FDI, underscoring Bulgaria's role as a typical net recipient of foreign investment.

Outward FDI from Bulgaria remained relatively modest, ranging between EUR 124 and 366 million annually, except for the last 2 years, when it surpassed EUR 500 million. The inward/outward FDI ratio consistently favored inward flows, with the ratio reaching 6.5 in 2023—a record year for both inflows and outflows. This pattern reflects Bulgaria's ongoing prioritization of attracting foreign capital as a critical driver of economic growth and development. Despite the recent rise in outward FDI, it remains secondary, indicating Bulgaria's limited global investment footprint.

According to Dunning's Investment Development Path (IDP) model, Bulgaria is in the second stage, where inward FDI far exceeds outward FDI. This stage, typical of emerging markets, highlights the importance of foreign investment in driving industrial growth, technological advancement, and economic modernization. While Bulgaria's outward FDI is gradually increasing, it remains a smaller part of the country's economic activity, reflecting its ongoing emphasis on leveraging inward FDI for development.

10.4.2 Comparative Perspective on Inward FDI

With a clearer understanding of the dynamics of FDI flows, it is important to compare its performance with that of other CEECs to gauge its relative significance. In 2022, Bulgaria accounted for 0.13% of the world's total FDI stock, a proportion comparable to Slovakia but notably higher than smaller countries like Latvia and Lithuania (Table 10.2). At the same time, Bulgaria's FDI stock is substantial when evaluated relative to its GDP, standing at 63.6%.

Table 10.2 Inward FDI stock indicators in Bulgaria and selected CEECs (latest data)

Country	% of world total, 2022	Per capita in USD, 2022	% of GDP, 2022	% of gross fixed capital formation, 2022	Value added in foreign-controlled enterprises in the business economy (% of total), 2020	Employment in foreign-controlled enterprises in the business economy (% of total), 2021
Bulgaria	0.13	8460	63.6	372.8	32.0	18.4
Croatia	0.09	9506	53.6	272.6	27.5	21.0
Czechia	0.46	19314	69.8	258.1	42.3	27.9
Estonia	0.07	22605	78.8	311.1	26.6	25.2
Hungary	0.24	10460	58.8	207.5	46.5	23.0
Latvia	0.06	13019	58.9	270.9	32.7	21.7
Lithuania	0.06	10015	38.9	180.2	27.0	16.6
Poland	0.61	6770	39.2	233.1	30.9	20.0
Romania	0.26	5900	38.6	154.5	42.5	26.6
Slovakia	0.13	10167	49.8	247.2	45.8	27.2
Slovenia	0.05	9955	35.2	162.7	27.8	22.6

Source: UNCTAD and Eurostat, Date of access: 01/08/2024

Per capita, Bulgaria's inward FDI stock of USD 8460 is moderate in a regional context, surpassing only Poland (USD 6770) and Romania (USD 5900). This suggests a middle-tier status within the region, indicating potential for growth but also highlighting the competitive pressures from more affluent peers.

Bulgaria's FDI as a percentage of gross fixed capital formation (GFCF) is remarkably high at 372.8%, the highest among the selected CEECs. This indicator underscores the pivotal role of foreign capital in Bulgaria's investment landscape, suggesting a heavy dependence on external financing to sustain investment activities.

The contribution of foreign-controlled enterprises to Bulgaria's business economy is also notable. These enterprises account for 32% of value added, a figure that is comparable with the regional average. Employment in foreign-controlled enterprises in Bulgaria constitutes 18.4% of the total, which is on the lower end compared to other CEECs like Slovakia (27.2%) and Czechia (27.9%). This reflects a relatively lower degree of foreign influence on the labor market, possibly due to the sectoral composition of FDI which we will discuss in the next section.

10.4.3 Sectoral Structure of FDI

Having established Bulgaria's comparative standing, it is essential to examine the sectoral composition of inward FDI to understand which industries are driving foreign investment in the country as they tend to have different effects on the long-term economic development.

The sectoral composition of FDI in Bulgaria has undergone significant changes over the past two decades, reflecting broader structural shifts in the economy (Table 10.3). In the 1990s, manufacturing was the dominant recipient of FDI, accounting for 42.2% of the inward stock in 2000. This pattern was in line with Bulgaria's broader economic strategy of privatizing state-owned enterprises and integrating into global production networks, where manufacturing played a central role.

However, the mid-2000s marked a pivotal shift as non-tradable sectors began to dominate FDI inflows. By 2007, real estate, renting, and business activities had surged to 20.8%, becoming the most attractive sector for foreign investors. In contrast, manufacturing, traditionally a sector concentrated on technological progress and export competitiveness, saw its share drop more than twofold to 18.6%. This interest in real estate was driven by easy access to credit on a global scale, forthcoming EU membership of the country, and to a large extent had speculative characteristics. The global recession triggered an exodus of such investments, leading to a sharp decline in FDI inflows in the subsequent years. However, the sectoral structure of FDI remained largely unchanged. As of 2019, real estate continued to be the leading sector (23.1%), and together with financial and insurance activities (16.5%), and wholesale and retail trade (16.4%), non-tradable activities dominated the investment landscape, accounting for over half of the FDI stock.

Table 10.3 Inward FDI stock structure in Bulgaria by economic activity (% of total, 2000–2023 selected years)

2000		2007		2014		2019		2023	
Manufacturing	42.2	Real estate, renting, and business activities	20.8	Real estate, renting, and business activities	21.6	Real estate activities	23.1	*Manufacturing*	20.1
Financial intermediation	18.3	*Manufacturing*	18.6	*Manufacturing*	17.3	*Manufacturing*	19.4	Real estate activities	20.0
Wholesale and retail trade; repair	14.9	Financial intermediation	16.9	Financial intermediation	17.1	Financial and insurance activities	16.5	Financial and insurance activities	19.9
Transport, storage, and communication	7.4	Transport, storage, and communication	15.4	Wholesale and retail trade; repair of motor vehicles	14.3	Wholesale and retail trade; repair	16.4	Wholesale and retail trade; repair	14.7
Real estate, renting, and business activities	7.1	Wholesale and retail trade; repair	13.8	Construction	8.2	Electricity, gas, steam supply	6.1	Professional, scientific, and technical activities	6.3
Construction	2.7	Construction	7.3	Electricity, gas, and water supply	7.8	Professional, scientific, and technical activities	4.0	Information and communication	5.7
Electricity, gas, water supply	2.3	Electricity, gas, water supply	3.8	Transport, storage, and communication	6.3	Information and communication	3.3	Electricity, gas, steam supply	5.1
Other	5.1	Other	3.4	Other	7.4	Other	11.3	Other	8.2

Note: In 2015, there was a revision in the categorization of economic activities
Source: Bulgarian National Bank, accessed on: 02.08.2024

This structure has been widely evaluated as unfavorable for Bulgaria's long-term economic development. The dominance of non-tradable sectors, particularly real estate and wholesale and retail trade, has limited the potential for FDI to drive technological advancement, enhance export competitiveness, and contribute to sustainable economic growth (Zhelev & Kussainova, 2024; Mihaylova, 2019).

In recent years, however, this trend has begun to shift. The disruptions caused by the COVID-19 pandemic, the geoeconomic tensions, and the subsequent global economic realignments have led to a resurgence in manufacturing FDI. By 2023, manufacturing had regained its position as a leading sector, accounting for 20.1% of total FDI. This recovery suggests a renewed interest in Bulgaria as a manufacturing hub, likely driven by global trends toward reshoring and nearshoring, where Bulgaria's geographic location and competitive costs offer significant advantages.

Additionally, the increasing FDI in professional, scientific, and technical activities (6.3% in 2023) and information and communication (5.7% in 2023) indicates a gradual shift toward higher value-added sectors. This trend is promising for the diversification and upgrading of Bulgaria's economic structure, as these sectors are crucial for fostering innovation, improving productivity, and enhancing Bulgaria's competitive position in the global economy.

Manufacturing not only already leads Bulgaria's inward FDI but also dominates its outward FDI, underscoring its pivotal role in the country's economy. Bulgaria's outward FDI exhibits a diverse sectoral composition, with manufacturing at the forefront, accounting for 22% of total investments (Fig. 10.5). This reflects the increasing efforts by Bulgarian companies to expand their production capabilities internationally. Significant investments in professional, scientific, and technical activities (18%) highlight a rising focus on higher value-added sectors. Meanwhile, wholesale and retail trade (14%), along with financial and insurance activities (9%), demonstrate Bulgaria's deeper integration into regional markets and its pursuit of new business opportunities abroad. This varied investment portfolio signals Bulgaria's gradual emergence as an investor on the global stage.

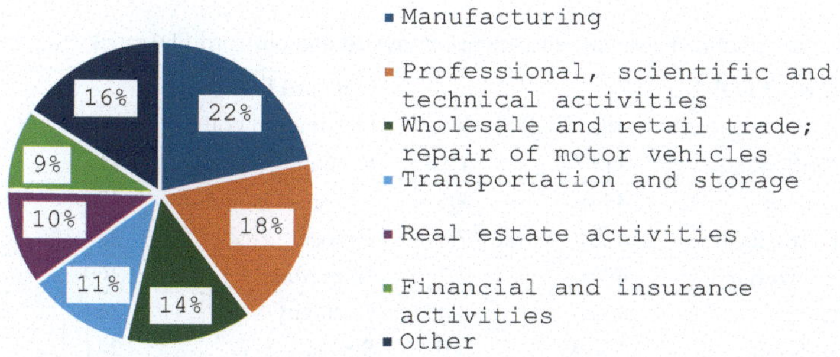

Fig. 10.5 Structure of Bulgarian outward FDI stock (%, 2023)

10.4.4 Geographical Structure of FDI

Beyond sectoral analysis, the geographical origins and destinations of FDI provide further insights into Bulgaria's economic relationships and strategic partnerships. Table 10.4 shows that Bulgaria's inward FDI is heavily concentrated in EU countries, with the Netherlands leading as the top source, accounting for nearly 13% of the total. This dominance is partly due to favorable tax regimes, with the Netherlands serving as a hub for investments from non-EU countries like Russia and the USA. Austria and Germany follow, reflecting strong economic ties within the EU, while Switzerland is the only non-EU investor in the top 10. The presence of major investors like the Netherlands, Switzerland, Luxembourg, and Cyprus—often associated with offshore or favorable tax regimes—has implications for Bulgaria, as these investments may be driven more by tax optimization than by long-term economic commitment, potentially leading to a more volatile investment base.

On the other hand, Bulgaria's outward FDI is strategically focused on neighboring and regional markets, with Romania as the largest recipient, accounting for 10.7% of the total. This highlights close economic ties within the region. Other significant destinations include Greece and Germany, indicating a focus on reinforcing existing EU partnerships. The presence of the Marshall Islands and Netherlands as major destinations also underscores the role of tax optimization in Bulgaria's outward FDI strategies, reflecting a broader pattern of regional expansion combined with strategic financial management.

Finally, the regional distribution of inward FDI within Bulgaria reveals how foreign investments are shaping economic development across different parts of the country.

The regional distribution of inward FDI in Bulgaria is highly imbalanced, with a pronounced concentration in the southwestern region, particularly in Sofia, the capital city. As shown in Table 10.5, the southwestern region, which includes Sofia City, has attracted 60.2% of the country's total inward FDI, amounting to nearly EUR

Table 10.4 Geographical structure of Bulgarian inward and outward FDI stock (%, 2023)

	Inward FDI			Outward FDI		
Rank	Source country	mln. EUR	%	Destination country	mln. EUR	%
1	Netherlands	7177	12.8	Romania	416	10.7
2	Austria	4748	8.5	Marshall Islands	306	7.8
3	Germany	4218	7.5	Greece	273	7.0
4	Switzerland	4046	7.2	Netherlands	269	6.9
5	Greece	3570	6.4	Germany	244	6.3
6	Belgium	3369	6.0	Serbia	241	6.2
7	Italy	3255	5.8	Moldova	233	6.0
8	Luxembourg	3048	5.4	N. Macedonia	172	4.4
9	Cyprus	2738	4.9	Italy	171	4.4
10	Hungary	2394	4.3	Malta	167	4.3

Source: Bulgarian National Bank, accessed on: 02.08.2024

Table 10.5 Regional distribution of inward FDI stock in Bulgaria (mln. EUR and %, 2022)

Statistical region (districts)	mln. EUR	%
Northwestern		
(Vidin, Vratsa, Lovech, Montana, Pleven)	677	2.3
Northcentral		
(V. Tarnovo, Gabrovo, Razgrad, Ruse, Silistra)	1503	5.1
Northeastern		
(Varna, Dobrich, Targovishte, Shumen)	2598	8.8
Southeastern		
(Burgas, Sliven, St. Zagora, Yambol)	3128	10.6
Southwestern		
(Blagoevgrad, Kyustendil, Pernik, Sofia, Sofia City)	17,688	60.2
Southcentral		
(Kardzhali, Pazardzhik, Plovdiv, Smolyan, Haskovo)	3782	12.9

Source: National statistical institute, date accessed: 02.08.2024

17.7 billion. Remarkably, Sofia City alone accounts for approximately EUR 14.97 billion, or over 50% of the national total, making it more attractive to foreign investors than all other regions combined.

This stark concentration of FDI exacerbates rather than alleviates regional disparities. The northwestern region, which is one of the least economically developed areas in the EU, has attracted only 2.3% of FDI, underscoring the urgent need for a realignment of the national FDI attraction policy to better address regional inequalities and foster more balanced economic growth across the country.

10.5 Government Policy and FDI in Bulgaria: Evolution and Challenges

Building on earlier analysis (Zhelev & Kussainova, 2024), this section examines Bulgaria's evolving approach to FDI, which has long prioritized *quantity*—through a low-tax environment and cost competitiveness—over *quality*, such as high-value sectors or innovation-driven projects. Initial reforms in the 1990s emphasized liberalization, with the 1992 *Encouragement and Protection of Foreign Investment Act* granting foreign investors full ownership rights and equal treatment, distinguishing Bulgaria from its restrictive post-Soviet peers (Petranov, 2003). Subsequent laws, including the 2004 *Investment Promotion Act (IPA)*, further eliminated distinctions between foreign and domestic investors but retained a passive, volume-driven strategy, lacking targeted incentives, focusing instead on broad deregulation.

The institutional framework mirrored this passive approach. The Invest Bulgaria Agency (IBA), established in 1995, focused on marketing Bulgaria's cost advantages abroad rather than targeting strategic investors. Chronic underfunding and bureaucratic fragmentation further limited its capacity to prioritize high-quality projects (Milanov, 2014). Critics argued for merging the IBA with the Bulgarian Small and Medium Enterprises Promotion Agency (BSMEPA) to consolidate resources and align trade and investment policies—a proposal reflecting broader debates about administrative efficiency in CEE economies.

Fiscal levers became central to Bulgaria's FDI appeal. A flat 10% corporate tax rate (introduced in 2007) and EU-low labor costs initially positioned the country as a cost-competitive destination. While these measures attracted FDI inflows, they disproportionately favored low-value sectors like assembly-line manufacturing and back-office services, failing to address structural weaknesses such as lack of technological modernization and regional disparities.

The consequences of this quantity-over-quality focus became starkly apparent: stagnant tax revenues, mass emigration (reducing the population by ~2 million since the 1980s), and regional labor shortages. Post-2008 reforms sought to address these gaps through infrastructure-focused measures, such as state-managed industrial zones under the National Company "Industrial Zones" (NCIZ). However, delayed implementation limited their impact, as major transnational corporations had already relocated production to earlier adopters in Central Europe.

Later amendments to the IPA (adopted in 2013 and 2015) introduced tiered incentives linked to job creation and sectoral priorities (Table 10.6). Projects in manufacturing, ICT, and R&D received preferential terms, including social security reimbursements and infrastructure subsidies. Yet, rigid thresholds (e.g., €50 million for "Priority" projects) and opaque funding mechanisms undermined uptake. Very few projects qualified as "Priority," underscoring the mismatch between policy design and investor needs. Territorial incentives, such as tax retention in

Table 10.6 Incentives under the Bulgarian Investment Promotion Act, amended in 2015

	Priority Class	Class A	Class B
Threshold Incentives	€ 50M 50–150 jobs	€ 1–5 M 25–150 jobs	€ 0.5–2.5 M 10–100 jobs
Shortcut on administrative terms	√	√	√
No tender-no competition for acquisition of state/municipal land	√	√	√
Financing vocational training	√	√	√
Social security cash back	√	√	√
Individual services	√	√	
Financing technical infrastructure	√	√	
Public-private partnerships	√		
No tax on changing land status	√		
Buying public land on favorable prices	√		
Grants for R&D	√		

Source: Invest Bulgaria Agency (IBA, n.d.)

high-unemployment regions, also failed to curb deepening economic disparities—a testament to the misalignment between policy design and regional realities.

Recent reforms signal a tentative shift toward strategic selectivity. Proposed amendments to the IPA aim to phase out support for low-value activities (e.g., warehousing, hospitality) and redirect incentives to advanced manufacturing and high-tech sectors (Council of Ministers, 2022). This reflects belated recognition that Bulgaria's historical reliance on passive, cost-based attraction—while successful in boosting FDI volumes—has done little to enhance economic complexity or retain skilled labor.

These efforts coincide with broader EU-level priorities. In response to growing concerns over national security and the influence of foreign capital from non-EU countries, the EU adopted a regulation in March 2019 for screening FDI on grounds of public order and security. As an EU member state, Bulgaria aligned with this framework by introducing a national screening mechanism, effective from March 2024. Managed by an Interagency Council, the system evaluates non-EU investments in critical sectors like energy, defense, and communications, with decisions mandated within 45 days and penalties for noncompliance. This marks a decisive break from Bulgaria's historically unregulated approach, which left strategic sectors—notably energy, where Russian investments were pervasive—exposed to geopolitical risks (CSD, 2022). By adopting stricter controls and automatic screening for high-risk jurisdictions, Bulgaria now balances its liberal investment tradition with proactive safeguards, signaling a dual commitment to attracting FDI while protecting strategic interests.

10.6 Conclusion

Bulgaria's experience with FDI over the past three decades offers critical insights into the opportunities and pitfalls of leveraging FDI as a driver of economic transformation. Initially hailed as a regional pioneer for its liberal regulatory framework and horizontal fiscal incentives, the country succeeded in attracting significant capital inflows, particularly around the EU accession years. However, as this chapter has demonstrated, Bulgaria's overreliance on passive, cost-based strategies—centered on low corporate taxes and cheap labor—has yielded diminishing returns. While FDI volumes were substantial, their qualitative impact remained uneven, perpetuating structural imbalances that undermine long-term competitiveness.

The spatial and sectoral distribution of FDI exemplifies these shortcomings. Foreign capital has concentrated overwhelmingly in Sofia and a few other urban centers, exacerbating regional disparities and leaving peripheral areas reliant on dwindling public resources. Sectorally, FDI has clustered in low-value-added activities such as non-tradable services and labor-intensive manufacturing, with limited spillovers into technology transfer, innovation, or high-skilled employment. This pattern, as argued elsewhere (Zhelev & Kussainova, 2024), reflects a policy framework that prioritized rapid capital accumulation over strategic alignment with national development goals. The result is an FDI landscape that has amplified, rather than alleviated, Bulgaria's dual economy: dynamic urban enclaves contrast starkly with underdeveloped regions starved of infrastructure and human capital.

The Bulgarian case holds broader lessons for emerging economies navigating the complexities of globalization. First, it underscores the risks of conflating FDI *quantity* with *quality*. While tax competition and deregulation may boost short-term inflows, they often fail to catalyze sustainable growth without complementary policies—such as targeted R&D incentives, workforce upskilling, or infrastructure upgrades—to channel investments into productive sectors. Second, the absence of proactive spatial policies risks entrenching geographic inequalities, as market forces alone rarely direct capital toward marginalized regions.

Looking ahead, Bulgaria's FDI strategy requires a paradigm shift. Rather than competing solely on cost, which is no longer possible, policymakers must cultivate comparative advantages rooted in innovation, sustainability, and institutional resilience. This entails closer collaboration between the public sector, academia, and industry to align FDI with sectors like renewable energy, advanced manufacturing, and digital services. Strengthening the Invest Bulgaria Agency's mandate—equipping it with adequate funding and regional offices—could enhance its capacity to attract high-value projects while addressing local needs. Finally, integrating FDI policy with broader developmental agendas, such as the EU's Green Deal or digital transition frameworks, would position Bulgaria as a strategic partner for multinational firms seeking alignment with global trends.

In conclusion, FDI remains a vital tool for economic modernization, but its benefits are not automatic. Bulgaria's journey illustrates that maximizing FDI's transformative potential demands more than laissez-faire openness; it requires visionary governance, strategic targeting, and institutional agility. For emerging economies, the challenge lies not merely in attracting capital, but in harnessing it as a catalyst for inclusive, sustainable progress.

References

Center for the Study of Democracy (CSD). (2022, December). Investment screening in Bulgaria: Challenges and policy options. Policy Brief No. 123.

Colliers. (2023). Exceeding borders—Technology as a remedy for ageing office supply, CEE 2023/2024 edition. https://www.colliers.com/download-article?itemId=05157d3d-96a6-47e7-ac49-6edf798fe079#page=58.05

Council of Ministers of the Republic of Bulgaria. (2022). Draft resolution of the council of ministers on amendments and supplements to the regulations for implementation of the Investment Promotion Act. https://www.strategy.bg/PublicConsultations/View.aspx?lang=bg-BG&Id=6958

Enache, C. (2024). Corporate Income Tax Rates in Europe—2024. Tax Foundation. https://taxfoundation.org/data/all/eu/corporate-tax-rates-europe-2024/

European Commission. (n.d.). About the connecting Europe facility. https://cinea.ec.europa.eu/programmes/connecting-europe-facility/about-connecting-europe-facility_en

Eurostat. (2024). Electricity price statistics. https://ec.europa.eu/eurostat/statistics-explained/index.php?title=Electricity_price_statistics

Eurostat. (n.d.). Government deficit/surplus, debt and associated data. https://ec.europa.eu/eurostat/databrowser/view/gov_10dd_edpt1__custom_11061165/default/table

Geenhuizen, M. (2014). Which role for foreign direct investment? Active space development in Central and Eastern Europe. In M. van Geenhuizen & R. Ratti (Eds.), *Gaining advantage from open borders: An active space approach to regional development* (pp. 173–192). Taylor and Francis Inc.

Günther, J., & Kristalova, M. (2016). No risk, no fun? Foreign direct investment in Central and Eastern Europe. *Intereconomics, 51*, 95–99. https://doi.org/10.1007/s10272-016-0583-1

Invest Bulgaria Agency. (n.d.). Bulgaria presentation. https://investbg.government.bg/about-the-investor/

Kalotay, K. (2008). FDI in Bulgaria and Romania in the wake of EU accession. *Journal of East-West Business, 14*(1), 5–40. https://doi.org/10.1300/J097v14n01_02

Koparanova, M. S. (1998). Overview of foreign direct investments in Bulgaria in the middle of the 1990s. *Eastern European Economics, 36*(4), 5–14. https://doi.org/10.1080/00128775.1998.11648664

Lungu, A. (2024). Foreign direct investments in the post-socialist economies of Central and Eastern Europe. In A. M. Dima & S. Vâlcea (Eds.), *Reshaping power dynamics between sustainable growth and technical disruption. Springer proceedings in business and economics*. Springer. https://doi.org/10.1007/978-3-031-58967-6_8

Marinova, S., & Marinov, M. (2019). Motives and strategies for foreign direct investment in Central and Eastern Europe. In S. Marinova (Ed.), *Foreign direct investment in Central and Eastern Europe* (pp. 93–116). Routledge.

Mehic, E., Silajdzic, S., & Babic-Hodovic, V. (2013). The impact of FDI on economic growth: Some evidence from Southeast Europe. *Emerging Markets Finance and Trade, 49*(suppl), 5–20. https://doi.org/10.2753/REE1540-496X4901S101

Mihaylova, S. (2019). Analysis and assessment of the policy towards foreign direct investment in Bulgaria in the period 1990–2018. *Dialog E-Journal of Tsenov Academy, 1*(2019) https://www2.uni-svishtov.bg/dialog/title.asp?title=1376

Milanov, R. (2014). Izsledvane na vzmozhnostite za nasrchavane na prekite chuzhdestranni investitsii v Blgariya [Study on the possibilities for the promotion of foreign direct investment in Bulgaria]. http://pods-bg.org/?p=1810

Molnar, M., Abendschein, M., & Zhelyazkova, Z. (2023). Better jobs and incomes in Bulgaria. OECD Economics Department Working Papers No. 1759. OECD Publishing. https://doi.org/10.1787/38d07f99-en

Moraliyska, M. (2023). Bulgaria's trade and investment position in 2023. In the membership of Bulgaria in the European Union: Sixteen Years Later. UNWE.

OECD. (2009). *OECD benchmark definition of foreign direct investment 2008: Fourth edition*. OECD Publishing. https://doi.org/10.1787/9789264045743-en

OECD. (2023). *Public investment in Bulgaria: Planning and delivering infrastructure*. OECD Publishing. https://doi.org/10.1787/b73ef3b4-en

Pavlínek, P. (2004). Regional development implications of foreign direct investment in Central Europe. *European Urban and Regional Studies, 11*(1), 47–70. https://doi.org/10.1177/0969776404039142

Petranov, S. (2003). *Foreign direct investments to Bulgaria*. Agency for Economic Analysis & Forecasting.

Rodionova, T., Yakubovskiy, S., & Kyfak, A. (2019). Foreign capital flows as factors of economic growth in Bulgaria, Czech Republic, Hungary and Poland. *Research in World Economy, 10*(4), 48–57.

Sohinger, J. (2005). Growth and convergence in European transition economies: The impact of foreign direct investment. *Eastern European Economics, 43*(2), 73–94. https://doi.org/10.1080/00128775.2005.11041099

UNCTAD. (2023). *World Investment Report: Investing in sustainable energy for all*. United Nations.

US Department of State. (2023). 2023 Investment climate statements: Bulgaria. https://www.state.gov/reports/2023-investment-climate-statements/bulgaria/

Zavarská, Z. (2022). Global value chains in the post-pandemic World: How can the Western Balkans Foster the potential of nearshoring? Policy Notes and Reports No. 58. The Vienna Institute for International Economic Studies (wiiw), Vienna.

Zhelev, P., & Kussainova, A. (2024). The experience of Bulgaria in attracting foreign direct investment—Lessons for emerging economies. *Economy of Regions, 20*(1), 305–320.

Chapter 11
Bulgaria's Participation in the International Labor Migration

11.1 Introduction

International migration[1] is a key driver of global economic dynamics, shaping countries both at the source and the destination. According to the latest available data, there were 280.6 million international migrants in 2020 (i.e., around 3.6% of the world population lived abroad), up from 153 million in 1990 (2.9% of the total population).[2] This increase in international migrants reflects both the growing interconnectedness of the world and the persistent challenges and disparities that prompt migration. Besides a complex mix of factors including family reunification, education, asylum seeking, and fleeing from conflict or environmental issues, a significant number of people leave their home countries in search of better economic opportunities. The economic aspect is the dominant driver behind the decision to migrate, in line with the historical perspective provided by Ravenstein's laws of migration, formulated in the late nineteenth century.[3] In 2019, the number of international migrant workers was estimated to be 169 million or almost 5% of the labor force of destination countries (ILO, 2021, p. 20).

For Bulgaria, international labor migration has been particularly impactful phenomenon. Bulgaria's engagement in it represents a story deeply rooted in its specific historical, political, and economic conditions. The transition to a market economy and the integration into the European Union with the ensuing liberalization of its borders marked a significant turning point in the country's migration history. This period not only welcomed a diverse range of skills and economic opportunities for

[1] The United Nations has defined international migration as the relocation from one nation to another, resulting in a shift in the individual's usual place of living (UN, 2020).

[2] United Nations Department of Economic and Social Affairs, Population Division (2024). International Migrant Stock (2021)

[3] One of Ravenstein's laws explicitly states that economic reasons are a predominant motive for people's migration and relocation choices (Ravenstein, 1885).

P. Zhelev, *Bulgaria in the Global Economy*, Societies and Political Orders in Transition, https://doi.org/10.1007/978-3-031-87923-4_11

Bulgarians but also led to a notable outflow of labor from the country. These demographic shifts have significantly altered Bulgaria's demographic status and socio-economic dynamics, creating a subtle balance between gains and losses.

The Guardian's observation, "Opening of the borders was both the best and the worst thing that has happened to Bulgarian society after the fall of the Berlin Wall" (Krastev, 2015), expressively captures the dual nature of Bulgaria's experience with labor migration, a central theme of this chapter. From an individual viewpoint, the free movement of labor following the EU accession represents a blessing giving huge opportunities for better living but from the perspective of the national economy that is not necessarily the case. Being uncompetitive to retain talent, the country has experienced an exodus of young and qualified people leading to a demographic crisis and jeopardizing its future development prospects.

Nevertheless, with a better-designed migration policy, Bulgaria can try to attract more returnees, who bring valuable skills and investments, and better leverage its diaspora abroad. This, along with the country's emerging status as a destination for foreign workers, can mitigate the effects of earlier brain drain and catalyze economic revitalization.

11.2 International Labor Migration: Drivers and Effects

When it comes to economic migrants, which serve as a broader term encompassing labor migrants, there is no universally acknowledged definition (Mitterbacher, 2021). The lack of consensus on the definition highlights the complexity inherent in understanding migration dynamics and the diverse factors influencing migration decisions.

In the realm of economic thought surrounding the phenomenon of international labor migration, a multitude of theories have been developed to elucidate the underlying motivations and mechanisms driving this complex process. The neoclassical economic theory, a cornerstone in the study of international labor migration, posits that movement of workers is primarily driven by the differentials in wage rates between countries. It suggests that individuals are motivated to migrate from countries with low wages to countries with higher wages. This wage differential is viewed as a result of differences in the capital-labor ratios creating variations in labor demand and thus influencing migration patterns. Regions with a relative surplus of labor (typically developing and emerging economies) will have lower wages, while regions with a shortage of labor (typically developed countries) will offer higher wages. The international labor migration will lead to equalization of wages and will benefit both the sending and the destination countries as the production factor will be more efficiently utilized. The host economies will increase their output by having more labor force available, while the source economies will be compensated by receiving remittances. Furthermore, the workers staying in their home countries will benefit from reduced labor-to-capital ratio and increasing wages, while those in the destination countries will see a downward pressure on their incomes. The migration motives will disappear in the long run with the decrease in the wage disparities.

The perspective of the neoclassical economists is largely criticized because of its emphasis on higher wages as the primary motivations for individuals to become migrants. However, it is equally important to acknowledge that migration decisions are rarely driven by a single factor. Migration is a complex process influenced by a myriad of economic, social, political, and personal considerations. This broader perspective of the "push" and "pull" factors, known as the dominant model in migration literature, recognizes that individuals may migrate for a combination of reasons, taking into account the multifaceted determinants of migration decision-making. Push factors, which can include high unemployment rates, low wages, political unrest, conflicts, civil wars, and natural disasters, are conditions within the country of origin that drive individuals to leave. Pull factors are the appealing aspects of the destination country that attract migrants such as better living standards and access to quality education and healthcare, family reunification, and social networks. While able to integrate theoretical insights from other models, it encounters challenges in explaining why certain regions produce more migrants than others and why migration flows exhibit diverse directions (Gheasi & Nijkamp, 2017).

Intriguingly, the "new economics of migration" broadens the scope of migration analysis by incorporating the household, rather than the individual, as a key decision-making unit. It argues that households use migration as a strategy to diversify risk and overcome constraints on income and investment (Stark, 1991). Families diversify their resource allocation by sending physically able members abroad for work while investing in the education of others. This approach views returnees as successful rather than failures, as they bring back accumulated savings or knowledge. Although criticized for its supply-side focus and applicability to poorer regions, this theory underscores the importance of families in managing migration-related risks.

Additionally, the dual labor market theory, developed by Piore (1979), posits that pull factors in developed countries, rather than push factors in developing countries, drive international migration. Developed countries, facing labor market changes and demographic shifts, necessitate unskilled and cheap migrant labor. These jobs, often low-paying and undesirable to natives, are frequently filled by low-skilled and often undocumented migrants. The theory highlights the intrinsic demand for foreign workers in modern industrial societies.

Migration systems theory integrates many of the factors outlined above and emphasizes the importance of networks, institutions, and inter-state relationships in shaping migration. It views migration not merely as an outcome of economic disparities but as a process influenced by historical, political, and social ties between sending and receiving countries. The theory highlights how migration patterns are sustained and transformed over time through feedback mechanisms.

In response to the evolving landscape of globalization and technological advancements, newer perspectives like transnationalism have emerged. The transnationalism theory recognizes migrants as individuals with transnational lives and identities, enabled by advancements in transportation, telecommunications, and remittance transfer. Transnationalism challenges traditional migration models and nation-state concepts. Migrants increasingly maintain ties to both their countries of origin and destination, blurring the lines between "origin" and "destination" and redefining categories like "permanent" and "temporary" migration (De Haas, 2010). This shift indicates that migrants' integration in host countries and connections to their homelands are complementary, not mutually exclusive. This new perspective reveals that migrants continue to contribute to their home countries through remittances, communication, and visits, challenging the assumption that permanent migration results in a loss for the origin country.

An effective way to present a balanced and comprehensive view of the complex issue of the international labor migration effects in a structured way is by summarizing the associated advantages and disadvantages. Table 11.1 encapsulates the multifaceted impacts of migration on sending countries, highlighting both the potential benefits and the challenges that need to be managed.

Table 11.1 Advantages and disadvantages of international labor migration for the sending economies

Advantages	Disadvantages
Remittances	*Brain drain*
Economic benefit from remittances sent home by migrants, contributing to national income, poverty alleviation, reduction of regional inequality	Loss of skilled and educated workers, potentially leading to a shortage of critical skills in key sectors
Labor market adjustment	*Dependency on remittances*
Eases unemployment pressures, especially in oversaturated job markets	Economic reliance on remittances can lead to vulnerability to global economic fluctuations
Skill acquisition and transfer	*Social costs*
Migrants often acquire new skills abroad which can be beneficial if transferred back to the home country	Disruption of family structures and potential social problems due to long-term separation of family members
International networks and partnerships	*Demographic challenges*
Enhances global networks, opening doors for trade, investment, and diplomatic relationships	Long-term demographic challenges due to the emigration of working-age individuals
Innovation and entrepreneurship	*Cultural and social brain drain*
Returning migrants may bring innovative ideas and entrepreneurship, boosting the local economy	Loss of cultural vibrancy and social capital as a result of emigration of dynamic and ambitious individuals
Diaspora engagement	*Potential for political instability*
Strong diaspora communities can advocate for the country's interests abroad and assist in development projects	Discontent among those left behind or returnees facing reintegration challenges may lead to social and political tensions

11.3 Historical Context of Bulgarian Labor Migration

Bulgaria's participation in international labor migration after WWII can be segmented into four distinct phases, each reflecting the country's political, economic, and social conditions and its unique challenges shaping the country's socioeconomic landscape:

- The socialist era (post-WWII to 1989): a period of state-controlled labor migration.
- Political and economic transformation (early 1990s to early 2000s): a stage, characterized by an emigration surge due to political and economic instability and mostly push factors.
- Diversification of migration patterns during the pre-accession period (early 2000s to 2007): increase in economic migration, often for seasonal or informal work.
- Post-EU accession (2007 onward): free movement of labor within the single European market. The European period can be further divided into three additional specific subperiods: transitional measures on free movement of workers (2007–2014), the European refugee crisis (2014–2016), and the COVID-19 pandemic (2020–2022).

What stands out in the entire post-WWII era is the distinct positioning of Bulgaria as a typical sending economy. This term captures the consistent pattern where the inflow of people into the country has been persistently outstripped by the outflow. As illustrated in Fig. 11.1 depicting the crude rate of net migration from 1950 to 2022, this enduring trend underscores a complex interplay of factors that have encouraged a steady outward flow of the population. This visual representation not only highlights the intensity of this dynamic but also signals the profound demographic and economic implications that have come to shape Bulgaria's development trajectory throughout the outlined distinct phases of migration.

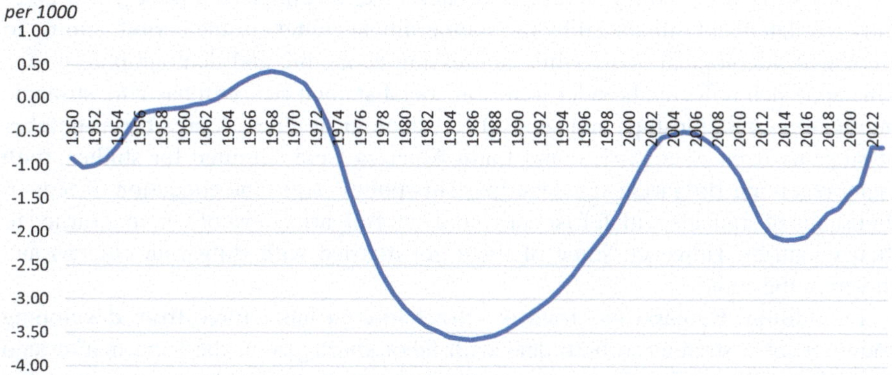

Fig. 11.1 Crude rate of net migration in Bulgaria, per thousand persons (1950–2022). (Source: United Nations, Department of Economic and Social Affairs, Population Division (2024))

Having established the overarching migration trends, it becomes crucial to delve into the specific historical contexts that have influenced these patterns, beginning with the socialist period, which presents its unique set of circumstances and policy decisions impacting migration flows.

The establishment of a communist regime in Bulgaria after the WWII heralded an era, characterized by stringent state control over the labor force and its mobility. During this period, the Bulgarian government severely restricted citizens' free movement by implementing strict border controls and a complex passport system, designed to discourage citizens from leaving the country (Markova, 2010). These measures were part of a broader strategy of the Soviet-aligned Eastern Bloc nations to limit Western influences and maintain full control over their populations.

Socialist Bulgaria regulated labor supply through bilateral agreements with other COMECON countries and with nations in the Arab world such as Syria, Libya, Tunisia, and Iraq that had political associations with communist principles (Ibid.). These agreements allowed for a managed outflow of labor, particularly in sectors that aligned with the state's economic and political interests. Given the predominantly banned emigration landscape, Bulgarians who managed to leave the country typically did so as refugees. Between the late 1950s and 1989, an estimated 20,000 Bulgarians left the country, constituting a relatively modest emigration figure, compared to some other Central and Eastern European nations (Staikova, 2013).

Besides political factors, ethnicity played a significant role in Bulgarian emigration during the socialist period. Bulgarian Turks were particularly affected, with substantial numbers migrating to Türkiye in response to ethnic and political pressures. The 1980s saw the largest outflow of Bulgarian Turks, precipitated by the government's assimilation policies and the forced change of Turkish names to Bulgarian Slavic ones. This culminated in the mass exodus of 1989, shortly before the fall of the communist government, with approximately 360,000 ethnic Turks leaving for Türkiye (Guentcheva et al., 2003). The emigration waves of Bulgarian Turks represent the highest contribution to the negative net migration rates of Bulgaria, outlined on Fig. 11.1.

The immigration policy of Bulgaria, much like its emigration policy, was carefully regulated and influenced by the sociopolitical context of the period, aiming to align with ideological goals while addressing economic and demographic needs. This approach reflected broader trends in socialist countries, emphasizing strategic international relationships and support for ideological allies. A significant number of students from Asia, Africa, and Latin America were admitted for studies, with many receiving Bulgarian scholarships. This policy led to the education of tens of thousands of students with leftist convictions in Bulgaria, most of whom returned to their countries. However, some of them got married with Bulgarian citizens and stayed in the country.

In addition, Bulgaria has tried to attract foreign labor force from developing countries, as a strategy to both deal with labor shortages on the local market and strengthen political ties. The agreement between Bulgaria and Vietnam, initiated in 1967, facilitated the influx of Vietnamese workers and students to Bulgaria for vocational training and employment in various sectors, notably industry and construction. This collaboration, repeatedly renewed until 1991, significantly contributed to the demographic and economic landscape of Bulgaria. Estimates of the number of Vietnamese in Bulgaria during the 1980s range from 15,000 to nearly 30,000, indicating the scale and success of this program, which stood out compared to similar initiatives with other countries (Muchinov, 2022).

Interestingly, in the late 1980s, Bulgaria's approach to managing its foreign debt led to a distinctive policy. Vietnamese workers in Bulgaria were subjected to a 10% salary tax for debt repayment. This tax illustrates Bulgaria's unique strategy in handling economic challenges with its foreign workforce, signifying a shift from mutual benefit to economic pragmatism in international labor agreements (Apostolova, 2017).

Bulgaria's immigration policy during the socialist period also extended support to citizens from the USSR and Eastern Bloc countries, facilitating their settlement in Bulgaria. This was part of the efforts toward Soviet-style transformation, under which Soviet specialists assumed leading roles in various sectors in the Bulgarian economy. This period saw a notable increase in the exchange of specialists, students, and workers, leading to numerous mixed marriages and a significant rise in Soviet immigrants in Bulgaria, from about 10,000 in the mid-1950s to nearly 20,000 by the end of the period (Muchinov, 2022).

Overall, the effectiveness of Bulgaria's immigration policy during the socialist era on its demographic development was constrained. Ideological limitations and the temporary residence of many of the immigrants in the country meant that the influx of people did not significantly offset ethnic outflows, thus having a limited impact on changing the country's demographic composition.

The collapse of the socialist system and the subsequent transition to a market economy opened up new avenues and challenges for labor migration. This period was a critical phase in shaping Bulgaria's contemporary labor migration landscape, with long-lasting effects on its economy, society, and the global Bulgarian diaspora.

In the immediate aftermath of the transition, Bulgaria experienced a surge in emigration. This was primarily driven by the economic upheaval, high unemployment rates, and the desire for better living standards and opportunities abroad. Many Bulgarians sought employment in Western Europe and North America, regions that were previously inaccessible due to the closed borders of the socialist regime. This wave of emigration was marked by a significant brain drain, as skilled and educated individuals left the country in search of better prospects. Conversely, immigration into Bulgaria during this period was limited. The country became less attractive to foreign workers due to its economic struggles and political instability. Any immigration that did occur was largely from neighboring countries and often linked to ethnic and historical ties rather than economic opportunities (Krasteva, 2006).

During the early 2000s, Bulgaria underwent a period of economic stabilization and a significant shift in its labor migration trends. With the easing of travel restrictions, including the removal of visa requirements for most EU countries and the implementation of economic and legal reforms, the landscape of migration began to change. The overall net migration from Bulgaria decreased during this time. However, the nature of migration evolved, with Bulgarians increasingly engaging in temporary migration, often for seasonal or informal work, rather than seeking permanent relocation.

Following Bulgaria's accession to the European Union in 2007, the country entered a new phase of labor migration, characterized by the principle of free movement of labor within the single European market. However, this transition was moderated by the implementation of transitional measures on the free movement of workers, which were in place from 2007 to 2014 according to the "2+3+2" formula. Initially, these measures allowed existing EU countries to maintain certain controls, such as requiring work permits or imposing quotas on Bulgarian workers, to manage their integration into the labor markets of host countries. These controls were designed to be revisited and potentially relaxed or extended in stages over a maximum of 7 years, providing a safeguard against potential labor market disruptions in receiving countries. Despite these restrictions, Bulgarian citizens began to explore and utilize the opportunities presented by the broader European labor market more actively. The period saw a diversification in the destinations of Bulgarian migrants, with an increasing number seeking temporary or seasonal employment across the EU. Concurrently, Bulgaria's EU membership, coupled with its improving macroeconomic situation, began to make the country an attractive destination for foreign workers as well. This dual dynamic of outward and inward migration reflects the complex interplay of labor mobility within the EU, highlighting Bulgaria's evolving role in the European labor market.

11.4 Recent Trends in Bulgarian Labor Migration

In recent years, Bulgaria's participation in labor migration has undergone significant transformations, reflecting broader socioeconomic factors such as the impact of the EU membership, the global financial and economic crisis, the European immigration crisis, the global pandemic, and the war in Ukraine. This section delves into the recent trends in Bulgarian labor migration from 2007 to 2022, offering a comprehensive analysis through various data points.

Contrary to expectations, the immediate years after joining the EU did not see a significant surge in emigration. Instead, it was the onset of the global economic and financial crisis that intensified emigration, as deteriorating economic conditions within Bulgaria amplified "push" factors, compelling many to seek opportunities abroad.

Figure 11.2 shows that emigration numbers remained relatively modest initially but experienced a sharp increase in 2009, coinciding with the peak of the global crisis. This spike reflects the challenging economic climate at the time, driving Bulgarian workers to migrate in search of more stable employment. After a drop in 2011, Bulgarian emigration figures display a resurgence, more pronounced after 2014 when all the remaining transitionary restrictions of EU countries elapsed, and the freedom of movement together with the lure of higher wages made thousands of Bulgarians to leave the country. Their number peaked in 2019 with emigrants

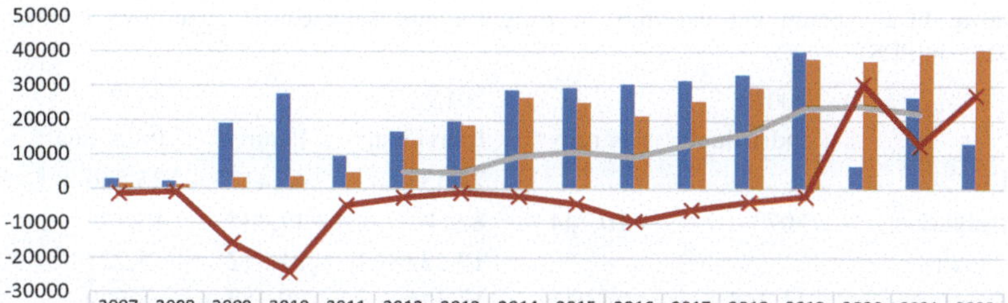

	2007	2008	2009	2010	2011	2012	2013	2014	2015	2016	2017	2018	2019	2020	2021	2022
Emigrants	2958	2112	19039	27708	9517	16615	19678	28727	29470	30570	31586	33225	39941	6649	26755	13175
Immigrants	1561	1236	3310	3518	4722	14103	18570	26615	25223	21241	25597	29559	37929	37364	39461	40619
Return migrants						4964	4682	9502	10722	9254	13060	16169	23555	24007	22087	
Net migration	-1397	-876	-15729	-24190	-4795	-2512	-1108	-2112	-4247	-9329	-5989	-3666	-2012	30715	12706	27444

Emigrants Immigrants Return migrants Net migration

Fig. 11.2 Emigration, immigration, return migration, and net external migration in Bulgaria, number of people (2007–2022). (Source: National Statistical Institute of Bulgaria)

reaching almost 40,000 people. However, in the last few years, the data shows that emigration rates significantly declined.

Immigration to Bulgaria, on the other hand, showed a gradual increase over time, with notable upticks in 2012 and a more pronounced rise from 2019 onward. This could suggest a strengthening of Bulgaria's economy and an improved perception of Bulgaria as a destination for migrants. Simultaneously, return migration displayed an interesting pattern with an overall upward trend particularly notable in the latter years. These movements could be related to improved conditions for Bulgarians abroad to return, as well as the global trend toward remote working which the pandemic accelerated, allowing people to relocate back to Bulgaria while maintaining employment elsewhere.

The trajectory of net migration, following a nadir in 2010, displays fluctuating patterns in the ensuing years. Notably, a shift toward positive net migration emerges in the latter years of the dataset, signifying a departure from the prevalent trend of emigration. This noteworthy reversal implies that Bulgaria may be experiencing a transition wherein it retains a greater portion of its population while concurrently drawing in migrants. However, the underlying causes of this phenomenon are multifaceted and could stem from alterations in the socioeconomic landscapes of other nations. Yet, the sustainability of this trend remains uncertain, necessitating further scrutiny to discern its long-term viability.

The examination of annual net earnings in Bulgaria in comparison with selected EU countries can offer valuable insights into the socioeconomic dynamics potentially influencing this migration trend. The data presented in Table 11.2, which outlines annual net earnings in Bulgaria and selected EU countries, provides a tangible metric to assess economic progress and its possible impact on migration. The data reveals a significant increase in both individual and family net earnings in Bulgaria over the studied period. Specifically, individual net earnings increased from 5073 PPS in 2008 to 15,125 PPS in 2022, and family net earnings rose from 10,744 PPS to 31,906 PPS. This substantial growth in earnings reflects improvements in the

Table 11.2 Annual net earnings in Bulgaria and selected EU countries (2008, 2015, and 2022, in PPS)

	2008		2015		2022	
	Individual*	Family**	Individual*	Family**	Individual*	Family**
EU-27	...	...	21,334	45,417	25,596	54,508
Bulgaria	5073	10,744	8724	17,448	15,125	31,906
Croatia	...		12,233	25,872	15,227	32,694
Czechia	11,268	24,741	13,476	29,357	18,770	40,189
Hungary	8166	18,140	10,921	24,782	17,194	37,653
Romania	6531	13,519	9279	19,417	16,316	34,789
Slovakia	9910	21,066	11,922	25,369	13,114	28,658
Germany	22,505	49,120	26,540	58,022	31,955	69,600
Netherlands	27,614	57,929	30,259	64,034	35,789	75,730
Spain	19,353	39,666	21,971	44,963	22,878	46,968
Greece	19,280	45,470	17,714	38,476	17,463	38,172

Note: * a single person without children, earning 100% of the average earning; ** a two-earner couple with two children, both earning 100% of the average earning
Source: Eurostat

economic conditions within Bulgaria, potentially contributing to the reversal in migration trends. Higher earnings can enhance the attractiveness of the Bulgarian labor market, both for retaining its citizens and attracting migrants from other regions.

When comparing Bulgaria's earnings growth to other selected EU countries, it is evident that while Bulgaria started from a lower base in 2008, the rate of increase in its earnings outpaces many of its peers. For instance, countries like Greece experienced a decrease in net earnings from 2008 to 2022, highlighting the economic challenges they face, which may, in turn, affect migration patterns toward or away from these countries. At the same time, the comparison with countries like Germany and the Netherlands shows there still exist a large disparity in income possibilities that in addition to factors like quality of life, social services, and better infrastructure still preserve a large stimulus for Bulgarians to emigrate.

As Bulgaria's economic landscape evolves, it concurrently shapes the migration preferences of its citizens, influencing the distribution of its diaspora and the attractiveness of various host economies. This dynamic interplay is reflected in Fig. 11.3 providing data on the Bulgarian-born population in OECD countries, which reveals shifting migration patterns over time.

For instance, Spain, which saw a sharp increase in the Bulgarian-born population by 2011, experiences a plateau and subsequent decline. This could be attributed to the economic downturn Spain faced, particularly after the 2008 financial crisis, which likely impacted job opportunities and quality of life for immigrants. Italy also shows a reduction in the Bulgarian-born population between 2016 and 2021. Conversely, despite the political and economic uncertainties precipitated by Brexit, the UK has seen a steady increase in Bulgarian migrants. This suggests that the UK's overall economic and social environment retains some appeal for Bulgarian migrants. Other countries, such as Germany, Belgium, and the Netherlands, have

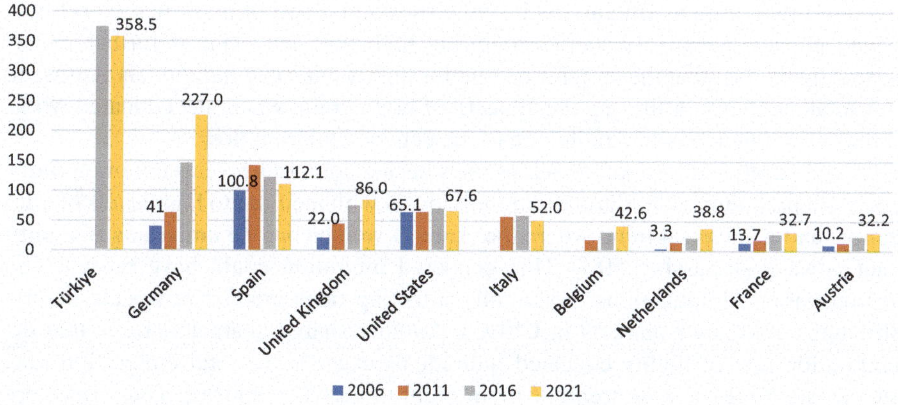

Fig. 11.3 Top 10 OECD countries with largest stock of Bulgarian-born population, thousand people (2006, 2011, 2016, 2021). (Source: OECD)

Table 11.3 Characteristics of emigrants and emigration rates to OECD countries for Bulgaria and selected comparator countries (2015/2016)

	Distribution by level of education (%)			Share of women (%)	Emigration rates to OECD countries (%)		
	Low	Medium	High		Total	Women	Highly educated
Bulgaria	41.3	33.3	25.4	54.2	15.1	15.7	15.3
Croatia	32.9	46.8	20.3	51.5	14.1	13.9	15.4
Czechia	24.0	42.5	33.5	59.4	4.0	4.6	6.7
Hungary	19.3	44.5	36.2	52.1	6.6	6.5	9.6
Romania	30.3	47.5	22.2	53.9	17.1	17.7	17.9
Serbia	40.4	39.2	20.4	50.8	8.2	8.1	8.9
Slovakia	17.8	49.0	33.2	55.7	6.8	7.4	10.4

Source: Database on Immigrants in OECD Countries (DIOC), 2015/2016

also recorded consistent growth in their populations of Bulgarian-born individuals, indicative of their strong and enduring economic draw.

When analyzing the labor migration patterns, it is important to look at the emigration profile of Bulgaria. Table 11.3 presents the educational composition of emigrants from selected CEECs to OECD nations, alongside gender distribution and emigration rates.

The data portrays Bulgaria as a nation experiencing substantial emigration to OECD countries across all educational levels. Among the comparator countries, Bulgaria exhibits the highest share of emigrants with low educational attainment (41.3%). However, the significant portion of highly educated emigrants (25.4%) cannot be overlooked, as it represents a quarter of the emigration cohort. This figure, when juxtaposed with the total emigration rate[4] (15.1%), signals a concerning

[4] Percentage of a country's native people living abroad at present.

trend of brain drain as Bulgaria is losing a substantial part of its skilled workforce, which impacts negatively sectors requiring high-skill sets. This is further underscored by the fact that the emigration rate for highly educated individuals is close to this total, at 15.3%, affirming the concern of brain drain, where the educated workforce is leaving at a comparable rate to the general emigrant flow.

A comparative examination across the selected countries reveals common traits, such as a predominant emigration of individuals with medium to high levels of education, and a universal trend where the share of women among emigrants is significant, always surpassing 50%. This gendered migration could have far-reaching socioeconomic implications, potentially affecting demographic prospects, family structures, and labor markets in CEECs. Another shared characteristic is that the emigration rate of highly educated individuals exceeds the total emigration rate, suggesting a region-wide trend of brain drain to OECD countries. These developments necessitate a multifaceted policy strategy that tackles not just the economic drivers pushing emigration but also the educational and gender dimensions, with the goal of mitigating the negative consequences of brain drain while maximizing the potential advantages of a gender-diverse emigration pattern.

Notable trends in Bulgaria's participation in international labor migration can be inferred from data on personal remittances, constituting of personal transfers (transfers between residents and nonresidents of a country) and compensation of employees (mostly payments to border and seasonal workers). Over the previous 10 years, their yearly inflows have averaged 3.02% of the country's GDP, which is comparable to the magnitude of FDI inflows and demonstrates their importance to the national economy.

Figure 11.4 shows there is a resounding predominance of personal transfers and compensation of employees received over those paid out, reflecting Bulgaria's status as a net exporter of labor. Despite a slight fluctuation in 2021, a robust inflow of funds from Bulgarians living abroad is indicated by the upward trajectory in the amount of personal transfers received, peaking in 2020 at 1.3 billion euro. The compensation of employees received has also seen a rise reaching 873 million euro in 2019, but the seasonal and cross-border work was severely hit by the restrictions related to the COVID pandemic and dropped substantially in 2020 yet not reaching the prior levels.

The remittances paid, both as personal transfers and compensation of employees, have remained relatively low compared to the inflows, reflecting that Bulgaria is currently less integrated into the international labor market as a host country. Although their value remained negligible (25.6 million euro in 2022), personal transfers paid registered a more than fourfold increase from 2013 to 2022. At the same time, compensation of employees paid showed a gradual increase throughout the last decade. The growing presence of foreign workers in Bulgaria is indicative of the evolving economic landscape and signals an increase in the demand for foreign expertise and seasonal workers in certain sectors.

The growing value of the personal remittances paid reflects that over the last 10 years, Bulgaria has experienced a substantial increase in its foreign-born population, both in absolute numbers (from 96.1 thousand to 220.8 thousand) and as a

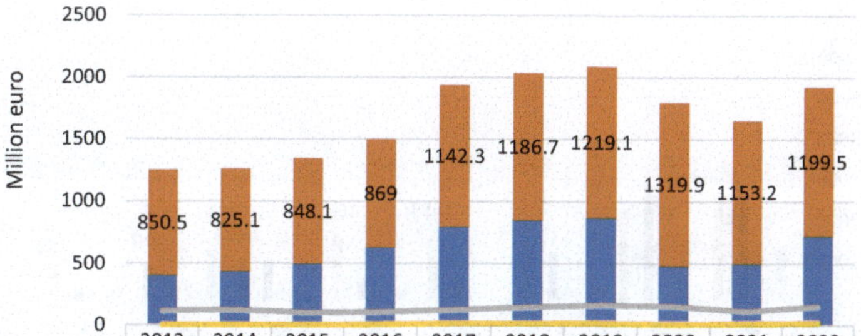

	2013	2014	2015	2016	2017	2018	2019	2020	2021	2022
Personal transfers (received)	850.5	825.1	848.1	869	1142.3	1186.7	1219.1	1319.9	1153.2	1199.5
Compensation of employees (received)	406.8	440.3	499.9	633	799.9	851.9	873.4	483.7	504	728.2
Compensation of employees (paid)	116.1	123	99.2	105.5	124.3	145.2	162.1	151.6	112.3	152.8
Personal transfers (paid)	5.9	4.3	4.3	9	19.7	20.2	20.7	14.2	20	25.6

Fig. 11.4 Personal remittances received and paid by Bulgaria, in million euro, 2013–2022. (Source: Eurostat)

Table 11.4 Foreign-born population in Bulgaria and selected CEECs (thousand people and in % of the total population)

	2013		2017		2022	
	Thousands	%	Thousands	%	Thousands	%
Bulgaria	96.1	1.3	145.4	2.1	220.8	3.4
Czechia	387.3	3.7	465.1	4.4	453.4	4.2
Croatia	574.4	13.5	539.6	13.1	472.3	12.1
Hungary	423.3	4.3	513.6	5.2	612.6	6.3
Romania	182.9	0.9	419.2	2.1	316.1	1.7
Slovakia	158.2	2.9	186.2	3.4	213.2	3.9

Source: Eurostat

percentage of the total population (from 1.3% to 3.4%) (see Table 11.4). Nevertheless, in spite of this notable expansion, Bulgaria continues to have one of the lowest percentages of foreign-born people in the EU. Even while foreign migration to Bulgaria is increasing, compared to other EU members, it still has a little impact on the demographic makeup of the nation, which calls for a supportive policy framework that could make Bulgaria a more attractive work destination for foreign talent.

Figure 11.5 shows that countries sending migrants to Bulgaria over the last decade encompass a diverse mix, reflecting a variety of economic, geopolitical, and social factors influencing migration patterns.

Immigration from traditional sources such as Türkiye has remained consistently high, though with some fluctuations, indicating sustained ties and continuous movement. Eastern European countries like Russia and Ukraine contribute significantly to the migrant population in Bulgaria. The cultural and historical bonds that Bulgaria shares with these nations, along with the search for economic opportunities, are key factors driving this trend.

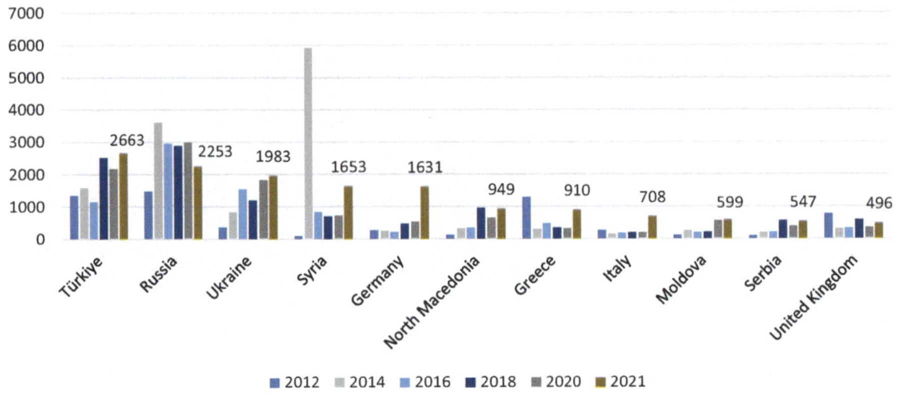

Fig. 11.5 Immigration flows to Bulgaria by country of birth, 2012–2021. (Source: Eurostat)

Syria stands out as an example of migration driven by conflict, with many individuals fleeing to Bulgaria in the quest for a safe haven. Bulgaria's response to this crisis reflects its role as a sanctuary for those seeking refuge from the instability and danger in their native countries.

The migration flow from within the European Union—from countries such as Germany and Italy—showcases the dynamics of intra-EU mobility. Citizens of these countries choose Bulgaria for various reasons, including but not limited to retirement plans, lifestyle shifts, or employment opportunities that arise from the country's participation in the EU's single market.

11.5 Bulgaria's Labor Migration Policy

As outlined in the previous sections, Bulgaria faces significant challenges in its migration landscape, primarily driven by the emigration of skilled labor, demographic decline, and the insufficient integration of migrants. The departure of young, educated Bulgarians in search of better opportunities abroad has led to a brain drain, weakening the country's potential for economic growth and innovation, raising regional disparities. Concurrently, demographic decline due to low birth rates and high emigration rates poses a threat to the sustainability of Bulgaria's social security systems and labor market stability. The integration of returning migrants remains a critical issue, with existing policies insufficiently addressing the barriers to effective labor market integration, even for the highly educated (Bakalova, 2021).

Bulgaria's Migration Strategy 2021–2025 aims to address these challenges through a comprehensive framework focusing on the management of migration flows, integration of migrants, and the engagement of the Bulgarian diaspora. However, a critical analysis reveals gaps in the strategy's approach to leveraging migration for economic development and addressing the underlying causes of brain drain and demographic decline.

One of the strategy's key areas is the regulation of migration flows to ensure security and compliance with EU standards. While necessary, this focus on regulation does not fully address the economic and social dimensions of migration. The strategy's measures for integrating migrants into the labor market and society are steps in the right direction but lack the depth and resources required for significant impact. Furthermore, the strategy underutilizes the potential of the Bulgarian diaspora as a resource for economic investment and development. The Strategy identifies returning migration as a key solution but lacks specific policies for effective implementation to attract and integrate returnees.

The Strategy indicates that its activities will be funded through the national budget via the approved annual budgets of the relevant institutions, European Union financial instruments, and other international funds and programs. While these funds provide a financial framework, the Strategy does not detail specific budget allocations or project costs. Furthermore, the Strategy lacks tangible targets, specific policy measures, and implementation timelines. Without this level of detail, the Strategy may be perceived mostly as a declarative document that cannot prompt actionable change and address the critical challenges it identifies.

A notable aspect of Bulgaria's migration policy is its participation in the EU Blue Card scheme, designed to attract highly skilled workers from outside the EU. The issuance of EU Blue Cards allows Bulgaria to tap into a global talent pool, addressing skill shortages in critical sectors such as IT, engineering, and healthcare. However, the effectiveness of the Blue Card scheme in Bulgaria has been limited by bureaucratic hurdles, stringent eligibility criteria, and a lack of awareness among potential applicants and employers. To fully leverage the Blue Card scheme, Bulgaria needs to streamline application processes, enhance promotion efforts, and ensure that the scheme is aligned with the country's specific labor market needs.

Over this decade, Bulgaria issued a total of 2270 EU Blue Cards, with a notable increase in the number of cards issued each year, culminating in 922 cards in 2022 alone. This trend indicates a growing openness and demand for highly skilled labor from non-EU countries within the Bulgarian labor market.

The data reveals significant disparities in the distribution of EU Blue Cards among nationals from different countries. Russian nationals represent the largest group, receiving 928 cards, which accounts for approximately 40.9% of all cards issued during this period. This high percentage underscores the strong presence of Russian professionals in Bulgaria's skilled labor market, possibly reflecting cultural and linguistic affinities, as well as professional networks that facilitate migration flows from Russia to Bulgaria.

Ukrainian nationals are the second largest group, with 304 cards issued, representing 13.4% of the total. The presence of Ukrainian professionals in Bulgaria may be attributed to geographical proximity and shared historical and cultural ties, which ease the integration process for these migrants (Table 11.5).

Table 11.5 EU Blue Cards granted by Bulgaria by citizenship of the holder (number of persons), 2013–2022

	2013	2014	2015	2016	2017	2018	2019	2020	2021	2022	Total (2013–2022)	%
World	14	21	61	115	121	126	268	299	323	922	2270	100
Russia	3	2	8	54	23	14	68	115	80	561	928	40.9
Ukraine	:	7	36	25	22	31	45	87	29	22	304	13.4
Türkiye	1	1	:	4	6	10	26	30	34	49	161	7.1
Belarus	:	:	2	1	3	3	4	1	29	84	127	5.6
India	1	1	1	3	10	9	24	7	20	38	114	5.0
Cuba	:	:	:	:	:	1	28	9	29	33	100	4.4
China	:	:	5	11	21	11	16	1	9	9	83	3.7
N. Macedonia	:	6	3	3	8	13	7	1	6	10	57	2.5
Serbia	3	:	1	4	6	7	14	8	11	3	57	2.5
Tunisia	:	:	:	:	1	2	3	1	23	22	52	2.3

Source: Eurostat

To address the identified gaps and enhance the effectiveness of Bulgaria's migration policies, the following recommendations are proposed:

- *Strengthen economic focus of diaspora engagement*: Develop targeted programs to facilitate the economic integration of the Bulgarian diaspora, including incentives for investment, entrepreneurship, and the transfer of knowledge and skills back to Bulgaria.
- *Expand and enhance integration programs*: Broaden the scope of integration programs to include comprehensive career counseling, mentorship opportunities, and partnerships with the private sector to facilitate employment matching for migrants and returning Bulgarians.
- *Policies that maximize the developmental impacts of remittances* flows, such as through investment in local enterprises or savings schemes that could further stimulate economic growth
- *Develop sector-specific strategies*: Identify and target sectors most affected by skill shortages with specific strategies, including targeted recruitment of foreign workers and incentives for returning Bulgarians with relevant skills.
- *Implement policies to retain talent:* Introduce measures aimed at retaining young and skilled individuals, such as improving working conditions, offering competitive salaries, and creating opportunities for professional growth within Bulgaria.
- *Enhance policy coherence and coordination:* Ensure that migration policies are coherently integrated with economic, labor market, and social policies. This requires close coordination between various government agencies, the private sector, and civil society organizations.
- *Monitor and evaluate policy impact:* Establish mechanisms for the regular monitoring and evaluation of migration policies to assess their effectiveness and make necessary adjustments. This should include feedback from migrants, the diaspora, employers, and other stakeholders.

11.6 Conclusion

Bulgaria's participation in international labor migration is multifaceted, reflecting its geopolitical location, economic transitions, and demographic shifts. While the country experiences challenges such as brain drain and demographic decline, it has also become an emerging destination for migrants due to regional dynamics and EU integration. The National Strategy on Migration (2021–2025) acknowledges these issues and aims to attract and reintegrate the Bulgarian diaspora. However, critiques highlight the need for concrete policies and measures to effectively harness the potential of returnees and the foreign-born workforce. Embracing a balanced view of migration that recognizes not only its challenges but also its opportunities is crucial for Bulgaria to maximize the benefits of its involvement in international labor migration.

References

Apostolova, R. (2017). Duty and debt under the ethos of internationalism: The case of the Vietnamese workers in Bulgaria. *Journal of Vietnamese Studies, 12*(1), 101–125.

Bakalova, M. (2021). Education and migration: The (non)return of better educated migrants to Bulgaria, *Ikonomicheski Izsledvania, 30*(4), 166–186.

De Haas, H. (2010). Migration and development: A theoretical perspective. *International Migration Review, 44*(1), 227–264. https://doi.org/10.1111/j.1747-7379.2009.00804.x

Gheasi, M., & Nijkamp, P. (2017). A brief overview of international migration motives and impacts, with specific reference to FDI. *Economies, 5*(3), 31. https://doi.org/10.3390/economies5030031

Guentcheva, R., Kabakchieva, P., & Kolarski, P. (2003). Migration trends in selected EU applicant countries: Bulgaria: the social impact of seasonal migration. International Organization for Migration.

International Labour Organization (ILO). (2021). *ILO Global Estimates on International Migrant Workers—Results and Methodology*. ILO. https://www.ilo.org/wcmsp5/groups/public/@dgreports/@dcomm/@publ/documents/publication/wcms_808935.pdf

Krastev, I. (2015, March 24). Britain's gain is Eastern Europe's brain drain. *The Guardian*. https://www.theguardian.com/commentisfree/2015/mar/24/britain-east-europe-brain-drain-bulgaria

Krasteva, A. (2006). Post-communist discovery of immigration: The case of Bulgaria. *SEER: Journal for Labour and Social Affairs in Eastern Europe, 9*(2), 25–34.

Markova, E. (2010). Effects of migration on sending countries: Lessons from Bulgaria. Hellenic Observatory Papers on Greece and Southeast Europe, GreeSE Paper No. 35.

Mitterbacher, K. (2021). Motives for economic migration: A review. University of Graz, School of Business, Economics and Social Sciences, Working Paper 2021-07.

Muchinov, V. (2022). The immigration policy of Bulgaria in the period 1944–1989. *Bulgarian Historical Review, 1–2*, 129–147.

National Statistical Institute. (n.d.). https://infostat.nsi.bg/infostat/pages/reports/query.jsf?x_2=120

Piore, M. (1979). *Birds of passage: Migrant labour and industrial societies*. Cambridge University Press.

Ravenstein, E. (1885). The laws of migration. *Journal of the Statistical Society of London, 48*(2), 167–235. https://www.jstor.org/stable/pdf/2979181

Staikova, E. (2013). Emigration and immigration: Bulgarian dilemmas. *SEER Journal for Labour and Social Affairs in Eastern Europe, 4*, 403–415.

Stark, O. (1991). *The Migration of Labour*. Basil Blackwell.

United Nations. (2020). Revised overarching conceptual framework and concepts and definitions on international migration produced by the Expert Group on Migration Statistics. Background document for Item 3(g), 52nd Session of the Statistical Commission. Statistics Division, United Nations. https://unstats.un.org/unsd/statcom/52nd-session/documents

United Nations, Department of Economic and Social Affairs, Population Division. (2024). Data portal. United Nations. Retrieved January 7, 2024, from https://population.un.org/DataPortal/

Chapter 12
Technological Advancement of the Bulgarian Economy in the Era of Digitalization

12.1 Introduction

In today's global economy, technological advancement and digitalization are crucial drivers of growth, productivity, and innovation across all sectors. The Fourth Industrial Revolution—characterized by artificial intelligence (AI), the Internet of Things (IoT), big data analytics, and automation—has revolutionized traditional business models and unlocked new opportunities for economic development (Heavey et al., 2024). Countries that effectively leverage these technologies gain a competitive edge, attract foreign investment, and enhance their citizens' quality of life.

For Bulgaria, embracing digital technologies is vital to its economic transformation, promoting increased productivity, economic diversification, and growth in key sectors such as manufacturing, information technology, and services. Digitalization also boosts public-sector efficiency through e-government initiatives, streamlined administration, and improved public services, creating a more favorable environment for business and investment. By integrating digital technologies, Bulgaria can ascend the value chain, innovate its products and services, and compete more effectively on the global stage.

This chapter aims to evaluate the current state of technological development and digitalization in Bulgaria, providing a detailed analysis of key indicators and benchmarking its performance against other EU countries. By using a structured methodology that includes a different set of indicators, the chapter assesses Bulgaria's technological capabilities, innovation outputs, and the digital readiness of its population and businesses, exploring how these foundations support the adoption of new technologies. Additionally, it presents the government policies and initiatives aimed at promoting digital transformation, including investments in infrastructure, education, and innovation ecosystems.

Ultimately, this examination demonstrates that technological advancement and digitalization are essential for Bulgaria's sustained economic development and

P. Zhelev, *Bulgaria in the Global Economy*, Societies and Political Orders in Transition, https://doi.org/10.1007/978-3-031-87923-4_12

global competitiveness. It underscores the importance of prioritizing digital transformation as a cornerstone of Bulgaria's economic strategy.

12.2 Analyzing Technological Development on a National Level

Technology has always been a key determinant of the competitive advantage of nations, but in the era of the Fourth Industrial Revolution, digital transformation, and the knowledge-based economy, technological development turns into a critical enabler of sustainable economic growth, competitiveness, and societal well-being. In this context, nations that invest in emerging technologies such as artificial intelligence (AI), robotics, and advanced manufacturing techniques gain a substantial edge in global markets, as these technologies drive productivity gains and innovation (OECD, 2024). Furthermore, digitalization enables the integration of advanced technologies into business processes, improving efficiency and allowing firms to quickly adapt to market changes, thereby enhancing national economic competitiveness (Di & Xuefeng, 2024). Research shows that countries prioritizing digital infrastructure development and technology-driven education systems are more likely to achieve long-term growth and competitiveness (World Economic Forum, 2023). As industries and markets evolve rapidly, the ability of nations to leverage these technological advancements effectively becomes a decisive factor in sustaining economic prosperity and securing a leading position in the global economy (UNCTAD, 2021).

The study of technological development at the national level requires a comprehensive, multidimensional approach that effectively captures the complex and interrelated factors driving innovation and technological adoption. Traditional analysis based on individual indicators—such as R&D spending or patent filings—offers important but often fragmented insights. To overcome these limitations, composite indicators like the EU Innovation Union Scoreboard (IUS) have been developed. The IUS aggregates multiple dimensions, including R&D inputs, human capital, high-tech exports, and digital skills, to provide an encompassing view of a country's innovation capacity (European Commission, 2021). This approach enables policymakers and researchers to benchmark and monitor innovation performance, offering a clear and comparable measure of innovation ecosystems across countries.

Similarly, the Digital Economy and Society Index (DESI) assesses digital competitiveness by integrating various components such as connectivity, digital skills, Internet usage, and digital public services (European Commission, 2023). By considering these diverse aspects, DESI reflects the multidimensional and interconnected nature of technological progress, highlighting not just technological outputs but also the infrastructure and digital skills required to sustain and amplify technological advancements.

While these composite indicators provide systematic and valuable tools for cross-country comparison and policy intervention design, they are not without criticism. Various scholars have pointed out the limitations and biases inherent in such indices. For instance, the Summary Innovation Index (SII), a key component of the IUS, has been questioned for its effectiveness in accurately measuring innovation performance (Edquist et al., 2018). Criticisms focus on the oversimplification of innovation as a single, aggregated score, which can obscure important differences in how innovation systems function and evolve across countries and regions. Furthermore, the selection and weighting of indicators within these indices may not fully capture the qualitative and contextual aspects of innovation activities, potentially leading to misleading conclusions (Adam, 2014; Vértesy, 2016).

To address these criticisms and enhance the robustness of the analysis, it is necessary to complement composite indicators like the IUS and DESI with individual, targeted measures that delve into specific aspects of technological development. For instance, Gross Expenditure on R&D (GERD) as a percentage of GDP provides a clear view of the resources a country allocates to innovation, while the number of researchers per million inhabitants offers insights into the availability of human capital essential for scientific advancement. Similarly, output measures such as patent applications per million inhabitants and the share of high-tech exports as a percentage of total exports allow for a detailed examination of the tangible results of a nation's innovation efforts. Enabling indicators like broadband penetration rates and population digital skills also provide a nuanced understanding of the conditions necessary for digital and technological engagement, thus complementing the broad, aggregated insights offered by composite indices.

The theoretical foundation of this approach is rooted in Endogenous Growth Theory and the National Innovation Systems (NIS) framework. Endogenous Growth Theory underscores the importance of investments in R&D, human capital, and knowledge as fundamental drivers of technological progress and economic growth (Romer, 1990). Complementing this, the NIS framework emphasizes the collaborative interactions among institutions, firms, and governments that stimulate innovation (Freeman, 1987; Lundvall, 1992). By incorporating input, output, and enabling indicators, the methodology effectively captures the multidimensional and systemic nature of technological development, aligning with these theories to offer a comprehensive view of innovation capacity. Applied to Bulgaria's context, the combined use of composite and individual indicators, as presented in Table 12.1, allows for a granular understanding of its technological landscape. This approach helps pinpoint strengths and weaknesses, facilitating targeted policy interventions and comparative analysis crucial for advancing in the digital era.

Table 12.1 Indicators for evaluating technological development in the digitalization era

Category	Indicator	Description	Data source
Input indicators	Gross Expenditure on R&D (GERD) as % of GDP	Measures the resources allocated to research and development	World Bank, Eurostat
	Number of Researchers per Million Inhabitants	Indicates the availability of human capital for innovation	Eurostat, OECD
Output indicators	Patent Applications per Million Inhabitants	Assesses technological output through the number of patent filings	World Intellectual Property Organization (WIPO), Eurostat
	High-Tech Exports as % of Total Exports	Reflects the commercialization and export of technology-based products	World Bank, Eurostat
Enabling indicators	Broadband Internet Penetration Rate (Population %)	Measures the accessibility of broadband Internet infrastructure	Eurostat, DESI
	Digital Skills (Population with at least basic digital skills)	Evaluates the population's readiness to engage with digital technologies	DESI, European Commission
Composite indicators	EU Innovation Scoreboard	Aggregates innovation-related metrics for comparative analysis	European Commission
	Digital Economy and Society Index (DESI)	Assesses digital competitiveness, covering connectivity, skills, and digital public services	European Commission

Source: Own compilation

12.3 Current State of Technological Development in Bulgaria

Bulgaria's technological development, amidst the ongoing wave of digitalization, has shown gradual improvement over the past decade. However, the country continues to lag significantly behind the EU average, revealing deep-rooted structural challenges in fostering innovation and embracing digital technologies. Despite some progress, Bulgaria consistently falls short of EU benchmarks across most key indicators, underscoring the need for more robust science and technology policies to close the gap and drive sustainable advancement.

R&D spending, a critical input for technological development, has seen some progress but remains an area where Bulgaria diverges significantly from the EU. In 2022, Bulgarian businesses allocated 0.51% of GDP to R&D, a modest improvement, yet still far below the EU average of 1.52% (Fig. 12.1). Overall R&D expenditure, including public-sector contributions, reached 0.75%, showing gradual progress but remaining significantly lower than the EU average of 2.27%. This slow pace of investment reflects an ongoing lack of financial commitment to innovation,

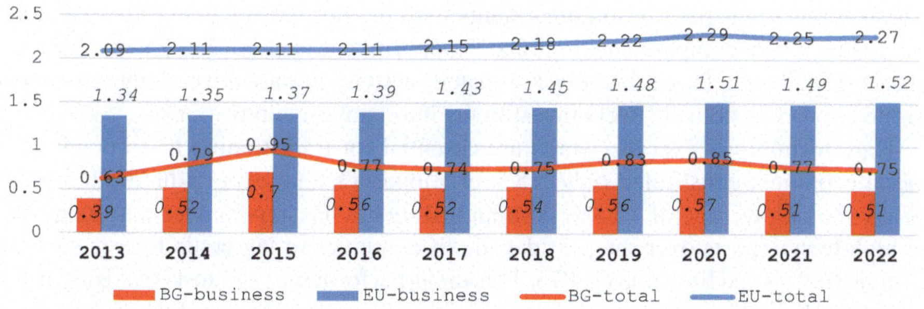

Fig. 12.1 R&D expenditure by the business sector and all sectors in Bulgaria and the EU-27 (2013–2022, % of GDP). (Source: Eurostat)

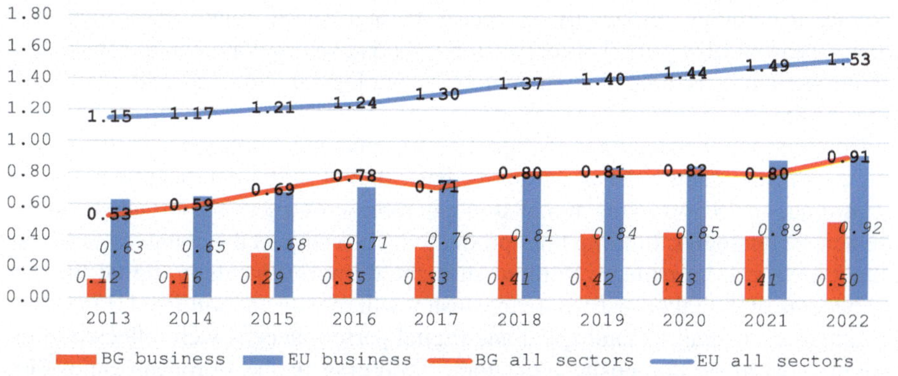

Fig. 12.2 R&D personnel by the business sector and all sectors in Bulgaria and the EU-27 (2013–2022, % of population in the labor force). (Source: Eurostat)

limiting Bulgaria's ability to compete in high-tech sectors. A positive shift from the 2000s, when public spending dominated R&D, is that businesses now recognize its importance, accounting for 68% of total R&D expenditure in 2022. However, growth remains too slow to drive transformative change across the economy. Without faster, sustained efforts—especially in scaling up private-sector investment—Bulgaria risks missing opportunities to fully integrate into high-value global supply chains. Public-sector efforts, while improving, still require greater focus and resources to foster collaboration with industry and academia, which is essential for long-term technological progress.

R&D personnel, a key indicator of innovation capacity, continues to highlight Bulgaria's lag compared to the EU. In 2022, R&D personnel accounted for only 0.9% of the labor force, much lower than the EU-27 average of 1.5% (Fig. 12.2). However, there has been a modest but steady increase in R&D personnel over the past decade, particularly in the business sector, reflecting a gradual improvement in Bulgaria's innovation landscape.

Output indicators such as patent applications and high-technology exports offer a glimpse into Bulgaria's innovation outcomes. In 2023, Bulgaria recorded 6.2

patent applications per million inhabitants with the European Patent Office, a modest figure when compared to regional leaders like Czechia (22.3) and Hungary (10.7) (Fig. 12.3). This relatively low patent activity is indicative of the country's limited ability to convert R&D investments into tangible innovations.

High-technology exports, which are essential for transitioning to a knowledge-based economy, constituted only 5.5% of Bulgaria's total exports in 2022, starkly below the EU average of 17.3%. Although Bulgaria has experienced a gradual rise in high-tech exports over the past decade, it continues to lag behind peers such as Croatia (6.9%) and Slovakia (7.4%). This underperformance suggests that Bulgaria's industrial base has not yet shifted significantly toward high-value, technology-driven production (Table 12.2).

Digital infrastructure, as a key enabling factor, has shown significant improvement in recent years. By 2023, Bulgaria had made strides in increasing broadband Internet penetration, especially in access to high-speed connections (over 100 Mbps), nearing EU levels. This expansion is a positive development, as robust digital infrastructure is crucial for enabling technological diffusion and innovation (Fig. 12.4).

However, the development of digital skills remains a bottleneck. In 2023, only 35.52% of Bulgarians had basic or above-basic digital skills, significantly below the EU average of 55.56%. This digital skill gap represents a serious obstacle to adopting new technologies, limiting both productivity growth and the country's ability to attract high-tech investment. Without substantial improvements in digital literacy, the benefits of digital infrastructure expansion will remain underutilized (Fig. 12.5).

Bulgaria's overall technological and digital performance is well reflected in the rankings based on composite indicators. According to the European Innovation Scoreboard (EIS), Bulgaria is classified as an "emerging innovator," with the Summary Innovation Index (SII) showing only slight improvement, rising from 47.9% of the EU's 2017 level to 50.6% by 2024 (Fig. 12.6). This confirms Bulgaria's long-standing position as one of the lower-performing EU countries in innovation. On the Digital Economy and Society Index (DESI), Bulgaria has made more noticeable progress. DESI scores increased from 70.9% of the EU's 2017 baseline to

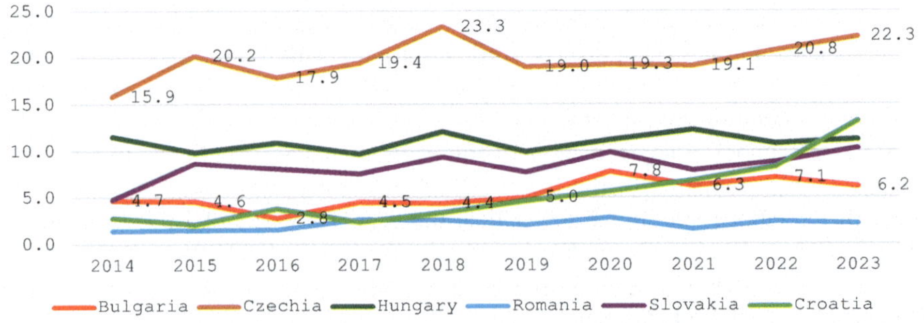

Fig. 12.3 Patent applications to the European Patent Office by applicants' country of residence in selected CEECs (2014–2023, per million inhabitants). (Source: Eurostat)

Table 12.2 High-technology product exports (2013–2022, % of total exports)

	2013	2014	2015	2016	2017	2018	2019	2020	2021	2022	2013–2022 av.
EU	14.6	14.8	16.0	16.5	16.7	16.9	17.9	17.7	17.7	17.3	16.6
Bulgaria	4.0	3.9	4.4	5.1	5.4	6.0	6.3	6.8	6.4	5.5	5.4
Czechia	15.1	15.3	15.6	15.1	16.1	17.9	19.0	20.6	18.4	19.2	17.2
Hungary	16.3	14.5	15.3	15.9	16.0	15.5	16.3	16.8	14.9	14.8	15.6
Romania	5.6	6.4	7.3	8.3	7.9	8.4	9.1	9.9	9.0	8.9	8.1
Slovakia	9.7	9.9	10.0	9.8	10.7	9.7	9.1	9.2	8.2	7.4	9.4
Croatia	7.9	6.6	7.1	9.7	9.2	8.0	8.1	9.3	7.8	6.9	8.0

Source: Eurostat

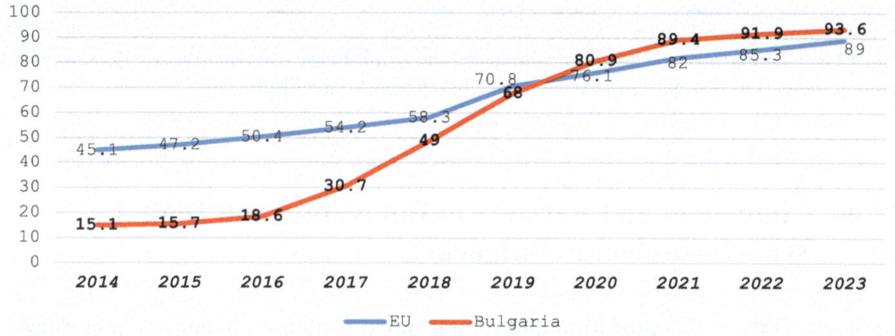

Fig. 12.4 Broadband Internet penetration rate (2014–2023, > 100 Mbps, % of households). (Source: Eurostat)

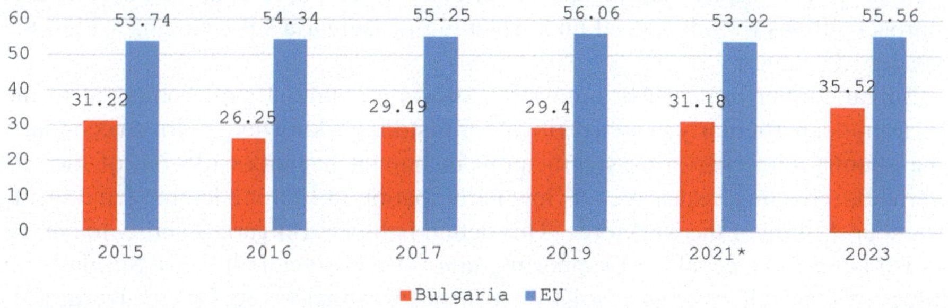

Fig. 12.5 Individuals with basic or above-basic overall digital skills (2015–2023, % of all). (Note: * break in the series. Source: Eurostat)

111.9% in 2022, indicating significant improvement in digital integration. However, the EU overall has advanced at a faster pace, reaching 155.2% in 2022. Together, these indicators highlight the persistent systemic challenges Bulgaria faces in advancing its technological and digital sectors, underscoring the need for comprehensive policy reforms and targeted investments to close the gap with more advanced EU economies.

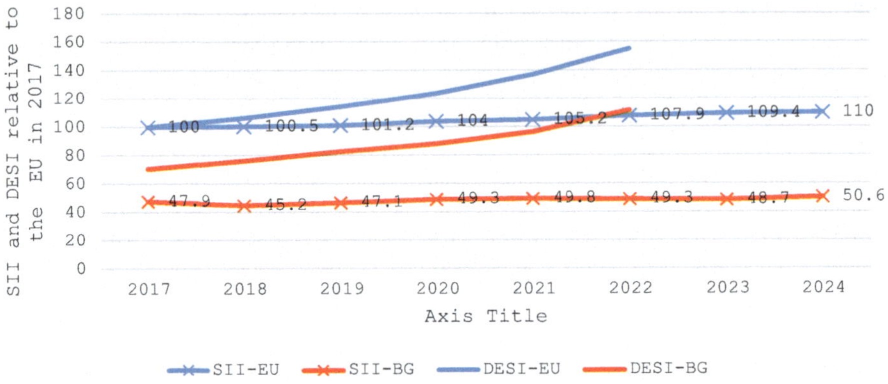

Fig. 12.6 Comparison of Bulgaria's Summary Innovation Index (SII) and Digital Economy and Society Index (DESI) relative to the EU (2017 baseline). (Source: Eurostat)

12.4 Challenges and Barriers to Innovation and Digital Transformation in Bulgaria

To assess Bulgaria's innovation and digital transformation challenges, a comparative analysis of the country's performance relative to the EU average is essential. By identifying key areas where Bulgaria lags significantly behind the EU, we can highlight the structural weaknesses impeding progress. Conversely, recognizing relative strengths provides a foundation upon which further advancements can be built. This approach allows for a balanced understanding of Bulgaria's positioning within the broader EU context.

Bulgaria's performance in innovation shows substantial gaps compared to the EU average, particularly in areas critical for fostering a knowledge-driven economy. The country underperforms significantly in human resources (38.7% of the EU average), reflecting issues such as low participation in lifelong learning and insufficient upskilling of the workforce. This deficit hampers Bulgaria's ability to build a skilled labor force capable of supporting innovation-driven industries. Similarly, in attractive research systems (30.4%) and firm investments (36.7%), Bulgaria falls well below the EU average (Fig. 12.7). These low scores indicate weaknesses in research collaboration and inadequate private-sector R&D investment, which are essential for creating an environment conducive to technological advancements and innovation (European Commission, 2024).

Despite these challenges, Bulgaria demonstrates relative strength in intellectual assets (91.9%) and employment impacts (59.7%). The strong performance in intellectual assets, particularly trademarks and design applications, suggests that Bulgaria has a solid foundation for protecting and leveraging intellectual property. However, these achievements are not mirrored across other innovation dimensions, with the Innovators score at only 29.4%, reflecting the low rate of product and

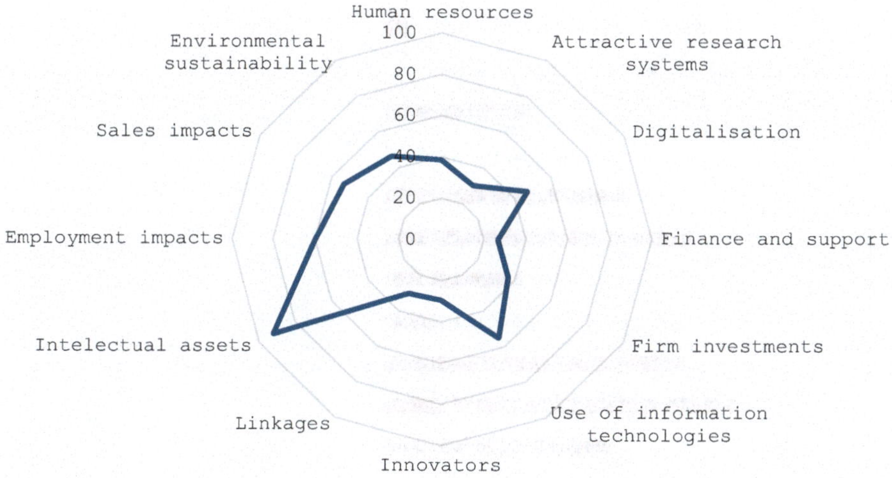

Fig. 12.7 Bulgaria's performance according to the indicators of the Summary Innovation Index relative to the EU in 2024. (Source: European Commission)

business process innovations among SMEs. Additionally, the Linkages score of 30.2% highlights poor collaboration between enterprises and research institutions, a critical barrier to advancing innovation through knowledge sharing and joint projects (European Commission, 2024).

Turning to digital transformation, Bulgaria's 2023 performance, measured against the Digital Decade KPIs, reveals significant barriers in both infrastructure and digital skills. While Bulgaria surpasses the EU average in Fibre to the Premises (FTTP) coverage by 24.6 percentage points and has made progress in Fixed Very High-Capacity Networks (VHCN) (9.8 points above the EU average), it still lags substantially in key areas that are crucial for a competitive digital economy. Overall 5G coverage is 18.4 percentage points below the EU average, limiting the country's ability to fully integrate advanced mobile technologies across sectors. Moreover, the proportion of SMEs with at least a basic level of digital intensity is 29.3 percentage points below the EU average, indicating that many businesses lack the necessary digital tools and capabilities to compete in the modern economy.

The gap in digital skills further compounds these challenges. The proportion of the population with at least basic digital skills is 20.1 percentage points lower than the EU average, which severely restricts the country's ability to develop a digitally literate workforce capable of supporting innovation. Similarly, Bulgaria is behind in the adoption of advanced technologies such as cloud (24.7 points below the EU average) and data analytics (11.3 points below), which are critical for modern business operations and decision-making. Even though the country is close to the EU average in terms of ICT specialists (−0.5), the overall digital skill gap remains a major obstacle to further development (Fig. 12.8).

In terms of digital public services, Bulgaria shows mixed results. While digital public services for businesses exceed the EU average by 6.5 percentage points,

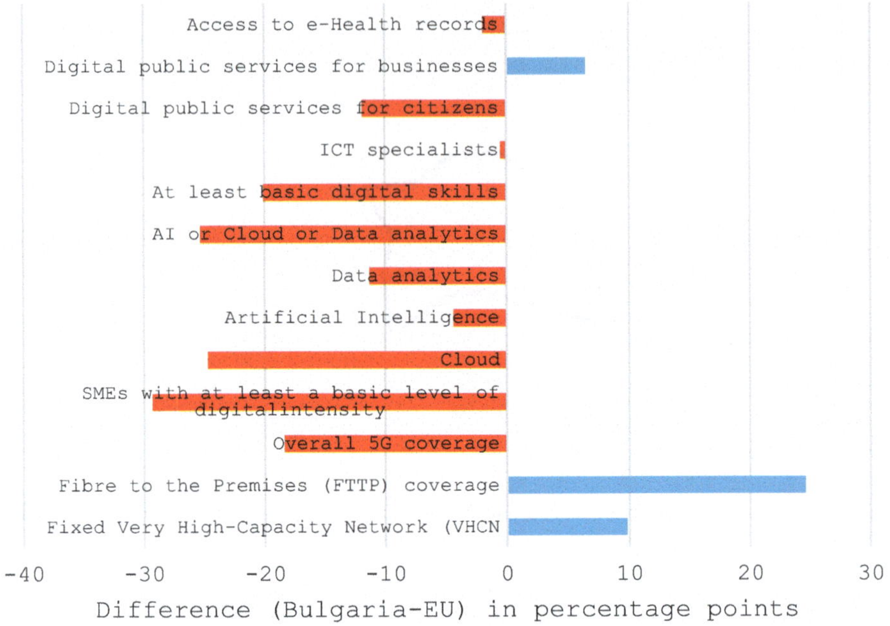

Fig. 12.8 Bulgaria's performance vs. EU average in digital transformation according to Digital Decade KPI (2023). (Source: Digital Decade)

services for citizens are 11.9 points below, suggesting inefficiencies in the digital infrastructure supporting individuals. Access to e-Health records is also slightly below the EU average (−1.9), indicating that the country still has room for improvement in providing digital healthcare services.

Based on the analysis, it can be concluded that the key barriers to Bulgaria's innovation and digital transformation are structural weaknesses such as inadequate R&D investment, poor research collaboration, low digital skills, and insufficient SME digitalization. Addressing these challenges will require targeted policies to boost public- and private-sector investment in innovation, expand digital skills training, and improve digital infrastructure, particularly in areas like 5G coverage and advanced technologies like cloud and artificial intelligence.

12.5 Government Strategies and Initiatives for Innovation, Technological Modernization, and Digitalization in Bulgaria

Bulgaria's long-term strategic framework for sustainable economic growth and modernization is encapsulated in the *National Development Program BULGARIA 2030*. One of the key priorities in this plan is fostering innovation and digital transformation, aiming to boost the competitiveness of the Bulgarian economy. This program provides a broad policy framework that emphasizes innovation as a driving force for growth, promoting the green transition, and improving digital infrastructure. It also prioritizes inclusive growth by addressing regional disparities and supporting the development of human capital through education and skills enhancement.

Complementing this broader strategic framework is the *National Strategy for the Development of Scientific Research 2017–2030: "Better Science for a Better Bulgaria."* This strategy seeks to enhance Bulgaria's research ecosystem by increasing public investment in research, fostering international collaboration, and improving the linkages between research institutions and industries. The strategy focuses on modernizing research infrastructure, stimulating technological advancements, and aligning the Bulgarian scientific community with European standards. However, a persistent challenge remains in ensuring consistent funding for scientific research, particularly in fields such as engineering and technical sciences, where Bulgaria has historically lagged behind the EU (ARC Fund, 2023).

Bulgaria's *Innovation Strategy for Smart Specialization (S3) 2021–2027* serves as the country's cornerstone policy for driving innovation and modernization while also laying the foundation for other national strategies, such as the *National Strategy for SMEs* and the *Strategy for Industrial Zones Development*. Marking a significant departure from earlier approaches, this strategy prioritizes clean technology, circular economy, and low-carbon economy as both horizontal and vertical pillars, promoting sustainable development across all sectors. These sustainability-focused investments are supported nationwide, while four additional thematic areas—informatics and ICT, mechatronics and microelectronics, industries for a healthy life (bioeconomy and biotechnology), and new technologies in creative and recreational industries—are strategically tailored to regional strengths through specialization at the NUTS III level. This shift from the broader NUTS II level, used in the 2014–2020 strategy, reflects a more localized approach, essential for addressing Bulgaria's socioeconomic diversity (Ministry of Innovation and Growth, 2022).

In addition to the innovation efforts, the country has focused on digital transformation and artificial intelligence as crucial drivers of modernization. Bulgaria's *Digital Transformation Strategy for 2020–2030* sets clear priorities for the integration of digital technologies across public and private sectors. This includes expanding broadband infrastructure, enhancing cybersecurity, and improving digital literacy. Significant emphasis is placed on e-government and e-health systems to streamline public services.

Complementing the digitalization strategy, the *National AI Strategy* (2020) outlines Bulgaria's roadmap for artificial intelligence development, especially in fields such as healthcare, agriculture, and public administration. The strategy promotes the creation of AI hubs, strengthens research capacities, and encourages collaboration between public institutions and private enterprises. Although the AI ecosystem is still developing, the strategy lays a foundation for long-term growth by aligning Bulgaria's regulatory framework with EU standards (Ministry of Transport and Communications, 2020). Together, these digitalization and AI initiatives are

Table 12.3 Key funding mechanisms supporting innovation and digitalization in Bulgaria (2021–2027)

Fund name	Est.	Managed by	Purpose	Details	Annual budget (approx.)
National Innovation Fund (NIF)	2004	Ministry of Economy and Industry	Support innovation projects	Focuses on smart specialization and SMEs	€10 million
Bulgarian National Science Fund (BNSF)	2008	Ministry of Education and Science	Promote scientific research	Supports world-class research and scientific capacity development	€20 million
OP "Innovation and Competitiveness in Enterprises"	2021	Ministry of Economy and Industry	Foster SME competitiveness through innovation	Supports clean technologies, digitalization, and industrial competitiveness	€2.5 billion (2021–2027)
OP "Scientific Research, Innovation and Digitalization for Intelligent Transformation"	2021	Ministry of Innovation and Growth	Promote digitalization and scientific research	Focuses on AI development, smart technologies, and digital economy initiatives	€2.14 billion (2021–2027)
OP "Human Resources Development"	2021	Ministry of Labour and Social Policy	Improve human capital for innovation and digitalization	Supports digital skills training, vocational education, and workforce adaptability	€1.5 billion (2021–2027)
EU Recovery and Resilience Facility (RRF)	2022	European Commission and Bulgarian Govt.	Support post-COVID recovery and green/digital transition	Invests in green energy, digitalization, infrastructure, and public services modernization	€6.2 billion (2022–2026)

Source: Ministries of Economy, Education, Innovation and Labour in Bulgaria, European Commission

essential for driving the country's broader goals of technological modernization and integration into the global digital economy (Table 12.3).

Bulgaria's innovation and digitalization strategies face significant implementation challenges, primarily due to fragmentation and lack of cohesive coordination. The strategies often remain aspirational rather than operational, with multiple ministries managing distinct parts of the innovation ecosystem, leading to disjointed efforts (Kandilarov, 2020; World Bank Group, 2020). This lack of integration between public and private sectors has resulted in underutilized R&D potential, insufficient funding, and limited private-sector involvement. Despite growth in the ICT sector, Bulgaria remains a modest innovator, and without addressing institutional weaknesses, the country risks falling behind in adopting advanced technologies and realizing its full innovation potential (ARC Fund, 2023).

Despite the fragmentation in strategy implementation, Bulgaria has several funding mechanisms and substantial support for innovation and digitalization. Key instruments, such as the National Innovation Fund (NIF) and the Bulgarian National Science Fund (BNSF), are designed to promote research and innovation, with a focus on sectors like ICT and clean technologies. Additionally, operational programs like Innovation and Competitiveness and Scientific Research, Innovation, and Digitalization provide resources to drive SME growth and digital transformation.

The EU Recovery and Resilience Facility (RRF) provides the largest financial boost, with €6.2 billion allocated to support Bulgaria's post-COVID recovery and long-term economic resilience. However, these investments come with the requirement of key reforms to accelerate digital and green transitions. Reforms in education, the labor market, and innovation are central, with a focus on higher education, vocational training, and STEM development to address the misalignment between labor market needs and educational outcomes. The effectiveness of these funding mechanisms is closely tied to the successful implementation of reforms, such as improving research and innovation policy coordination and addressing skills mismatches. As detailed in the Council's assessments, a unified approach to policy execution is crucial to fully leverage these substantial investments (Council of the EU, 2022).

12.6 SWOT Analysis of Bulgarian Innovation System

Bulgaria's innovation system presents a mix of significant opportunities and persistent challenges. While the country has made progress through strategic frameworks and growing sectors like ICT, weaknesses in implementation and structural issues continue to hinder its full potential. Below is a SWOT analysis that outlines the key strengths, weaknesses, opportunities, and threats within Bulgaria's innovation ecosystem (Table 12.4).

Table 12.4 SWOT analysis of Bulgaria's innovation system

Strengths	**Weaknesses**
– Macroeconomic stability, EU membership, and strategic location strengthen Bulgaria's integration into global markets	– Skills shortages, particularly in STEM fields, and low attractiveness of research careers
– Comprehensive strategies like S3 to guide STI activities, supported by significant EU funding	– Weak collaboration between academia and industry, limiting innovation and knowledge transfer
– Good Internet infrastructure and expanding ICT sector with strong export potential	– Low domestic demand for R&D, with weak business innovation, especially among SMEs
Opportunities	**Threats**
– EU-led green energy and digitalization initiatives offer substantial growth prospects	– Global economic instability and supply chain disruptions pose risks to innovation-driven growth
– Higher FDI, stronger ties with foreign companies, and leveraging the Bulgarian diaspora can boost technology transfer	– Brain drain and emigration of skilled professionals, exacerbated by global competition for talent
– Increasing awareness of lifelong learning and vocational training helps address skills shortages and enhances workforce adaptability	– Bureaucratic inefficiencies and slow reforms could hinder timely access to EU funds and program implementation

12.7 Conclusion

Bulgaria is at a crucial point in its efforts to modernize its economy through new technologies adoption and digitalization. While progress has been made, especially in the growing ICT sector, challenges like fragmented policies and skill gaps still need to be addressed. However, with significant EU funding and rising foreign investment, the potential for innovation-driven growth is undeniable, particularly in areas like digital and green technologies.

Looking ahead, Bulgaria's success will hinge on its ability to fully integrate reforms, strengthen ties with foreign companies, nurture and retain talent, and effectively engage its diaspora. By addressing structural weaknesses, particularly in education and R&D capacity, and capitalizing on its strategic location and growing ICT sector, Bulgaria can enhance its competitiveness and position itself as a leader in the digital economy within the region. The path forward involves fostering a culture of innovation, improving public-private collaboration, and ensuring the workforce is equipped with the necessary skills to thrive in the rapidly evolving technological landscape.

References

Adam, F. (2014). Measuring national innovation performance—The innovation union scoreboard revisited. SpringerBriefs in economics. Springer Berlin: Heidelberg.

ARC Fund. (2023). Innovation.bg 2023: Innovation and sustainable growth. Applied Research and Communications Fund.

Council of the European Union. (2022). Addendum to the council implementing decision on the approval of the assessment of the recovery and resilience plan for Bulgaria. Document ST 8091/22 ADD 1. https://data.consilium.europa.eu/doc/document/ST-8091-2022-ADD-1/en/pdf

Di, W., & Xuefeng, S. (2024). Research on the impact of digital transformation on the production efficiency of manufacturing enterprises: Institution-based analysis of the threshold effect. *International Review of Economics & Finance, 91*, 883–897. https://doi.org/10.1016/j.iref.2024.01.046

Edquist, C., Zabala-Iturriagagoitia, J. M, Barbero, J., & Zofío, J. L. (2018). On the meaning of innovation performance: Is the synthetic indicator of the innovation union scoreboard flawed? *Research Evaluation, 27*, 196–211.

European Commission. (2021). EU Innovation Scoreboard. [Online]. https://ec.europa.eu/growth/industry/innovation/facts-figures/scoreboards_en

European Commission. (2023). Digital Economy and Society Index (DESI). [Online]. https://ec.europa.eu/digital-strategy/desi_en

European Commission. (2024). European Innovation Scoreboard 2024—Country Profile Bulgaria.

Freeman, C. (1987). *Technology policy and economic performance: Lessons from Japan*. Pinter.

Heavey, C., Simsek, Z., & Fox, B. (2024). The fourth industrial revolution technologies and strategic leadership: New research directions and a Clarion call for creating shared understanding. In *Handbook of research on strategic leadership in the fourth industrial revolution* (pp. 62–87). Edward Elgar Publishing Ltd.

Kandilarov, E. (2020). Bulgaria economy briefing: Bulgarian national innovation system—Condition and weaknesses. *China-CEE Institute Weekly Briefing, 32*(2).

Lundvall, B. (1992). *National systems of innovation: Toward a theory of innovation and interactive learning*. Pinter Publishers.

Ministry of Innovation and Growth. (2022). Innovation strategy for smart specialisation (S3) of Bulgaria. https://www.mig.government.bg/wp-content/uploads/2022/12/isis-2021-2027.pdf

Ministry of Transport and Communications. (2020). Concept for the development of artificial intelligence in Bulgaria until 2030. https://www.mtc.government.bg/sites/default/files/conceptforthedevelopmentofaiinbulgariauntil2030.pdf

OECD. (2024). *OECD digital economy outlook 2024 (Volume 1): Embracing the technology frontier*. OECD Publishing. https://doi.org/10.1787/a1689dc5-en

Romer, P. M. (1990). Endogenous technological change. *Journal of Political Economy, 98*(5), 71–102.

UNCTAD. (2021). Technology and Innovation Report 2021: Catching technological waves: Innovation with equity. United Nations. https://unctad.org/publication/technology-and-innovation-report-2021

Vértesy, D. (2016). A critical assessment of quality and validity of composite indicators of innovation. OECD Blue Sky III Forum on Science and Innovation Indicators, Ghent.

World Bank Group. (2020). Bulgaria—Country needs and STI policy mix assessment.

World Economic Forum. (2023). Annual Report 2022–2023. World Economic Forum. https://www.weforum.org/publications/annual-report-2022-2023/in-full/

Chapter 13
Green Transformation: Bulgaria's Path in the Energy Transition Process

13.1 Introduction

The global shift toward decarbonization and the development of green economies has become a defining feature of contemporary economic policy, driven by the urgent need to address climate change and promote sustainable development. Within Europe, this shift is embodied in the European Green Deal, which seeks to position the continent as a leader in the global fight against climate change by achieving carbon neutrality by 2050 (Tkachuk, 2024). For Bulgaria, this ambitious agenda presents a mix of challenges and opportunities, given its current economic structure and energy dependence.

Bulgaria's economy, with its reliance on fossil fuels and energy-intensive industries, faces significant hurdles in aligning with the European Green Deal's targets. The green transition in Bulgaria is often perceived as an external imposition from Brussels rather than a domestic priority. This perception has contributed to Bulgaria being classified as a less ambitious member state in terms of its commitment to green policies (ECFR, 2020). Nonetheless, the potential benefits of the green transition—such as economic modernization, enhanced energy security, and improved environmental quality—make it a crucial agenda for the country's future development.

The objective of this chapter is to analyze Bulgaria's trajectory toward green energy transitioning within the context of the European Green Deal. By examining Bulgaria's current position and the challenges it faces, the chapter sets the stage for a deeper exploration of how the country can navigate its green transition, leveraging opportunities while addressing the critical obstacles that lie ahead.

P. Zhelev, *Bulgaria in the Global Economy*, Societies and Political Orders in Transition, https://doi.org/10.1007/978-3-031-87923-4_13

13.2 The European Green Transition Framework

The green transition refers to the shift from carbon-intensive practices to sustainable, low-carbon systems (Serrano & Zaveri, 2020), with the energy sector at its core due to its significant contribution to global greenhouse gas (GHG) emissions. Achieving this transition requires replacing fossil fuels with renewable energy sources like wind, solar, and hydroelectric power, coupled with improvements in energy efficiency and technologies such as carbon capture (IEA, 2021). This transition is driven by the urgent need to combat climate change, which, fueled by human activity, is disrupting ecosystems, human health, and economies globally.

In response to this crisis, global frameworks such as the 2015 Paris Agreement were established to guide nations in reducing GHG emissions. The Paris Agreement aims to limit global warming to well below 2 °C above preindustrial levels and encourages countries to commit to Nationally Determined Contributions (NDCs) to mitigate and adapt to climate impacts. Additionally, the United Nations' 2030 Agenda for Sustainable Development links climate action with broader social and economic goals, reinforcing the necessity of the green transition.

The European Union, recognizing both the environmental urgency and economic opportunity, has embraced the green transition, adopting a comprehensive and ambitious framework to transform its economy into one that is sustainable, competitive, and climate-neutral. In 2015, the Energy Union was established advancing the green transition by ensuring secure, sustainable, competitive, and affordable energy across the EU. It was conceived in response to energy crises and the growing geopolitical risks linked to dependence on external suppliers, particularly in the wake of disruptions to natural gas supplies from Russia. The Energy Union framework aims to integrate energy markets, improve energy efficiency, promote the use of renewable energy, and enhance energy security by reducing reliance on fossil fuel imports (Stefanova & Zhelev, 2022). Central to the Energy Union is the balance between energy security, environmental sustainability, and affordability, often referred to as the "energy trilemma." This balance is especially relevant for member states like Bulgaria, which face the challenge of transitioning from coal-dependent energy systems while maintaining reliable and affordable energy supplies.

The cornerstone of the EU's green transition efforts is the European Green Deal, introduced in December 2019, marking a major escalation in the EU's climate ambitions. The European Green Deal outlines a roadmap to make the EU's economy sustainable by turning climate and environmental challenges into opportunities across all policy areas and making the transition just and inclusive for all (European Commission, n.d.). Key targets of the European Green Deal include achieving climate neutrality by 2050, reducing GHG emissions by at least 55% by 2030 (compared to 1990 levels), and decoupling economic growth from resource use. To reach these goals, the EU has introduced several initiatives, including the EU Climate Law, which legally enshrines the 2050 climate neutrality target, and the Fit for 55 package, which comprises legislative proposals to align the EU's climate and energy policies with the new 2030 target.

The EU is also focusing on transforming its energy system, which is responsible for over 75% of the EU's GHG emissions. The EU Renewable Energy Directive sets binding targets for renewable energy production, and the Energy Efficiency Directive aims to make energy consumption more efficient across the Union. Furthermore, the Circular Economy Action Plan promotes sustainable resource use by designing waste out of the economy and keeping products and materials in use.

To support the financial aspects of the green transition, the EU has established the Just Transition Mechanism (JTM), which provides financial resources and technical assistance to the regions and sectors most affected by the transition to a green economy. This mechanism is a critical component of ensuring that the green transition is equitable, leaving no one behind, especially in regions heavily dependent on fossil fuels or carbon-intensive industries.

However, not all countries in the EU are in favor of ambitious decarbonization policies which create political tensions and threaten the integration process. While countries like Sweden, Denmark, and Germany are strong supporters of renewable energy, some new member states find it too volatile and expensive to replace fossil fuels. Perez et al. (2019) identify two clusters of countries within the EU which based on their location, natural resources, and history have different perception of energy security, and accordingly their positions differ on common European initiatives. The green clusters comprising of most Western member states perceive the green transition policies as a tool to combat climate change and consider renewables a business opportunity that simultaneously decreases the import dependence. The blue cluster, consisting mostly of East European countries which are more vulnerable to supply disruptions and have limited renewable sources in their energy mix, tends to prioritize security of supply and the diversification of sources over ambitious climate targets and resists shifting from traditional power sources to renewables in a short time frame (Perez et al., 2019).

For member states like Bulgaria, the Green Deal presents both challenges and opportunities. On one hand, it requires significant structural changes, particularly in phasing out coal and transitioning to renewable energy. On the other hand, the Green Deal provides financial support, helping countries navigate the socioeconomic impacts of the reduction of carbon emissions. This green transition brings opportunities for modernization and enhanced competitiveness, but careful planning and investment are essential to avoid undermining energy security and affordability.

13.3 Tracking Bulgaria's Green Energy Transition

Bulgaria's green energy transition has been relatively slow compared to the EU average. Despite improvements in renewable energy deployment, the country remains heavily reliant on fossil fuels in its energy mix. This is especially pronounced in the electricity generation, which, as of 2022, consists predominantly of solid fossil fuels (43%) and nuclear power (33%), with renewables making up only

19%, whereas the EU, on average, derives 38% of its energy from renewables (Fig. 13.1). This disparity highlights Bulgaria's slower progress in transitioning to cleaner energy sources.

Bulgaria has seen gradual improvements in renewable energy adoption since 2005, with its overall renewable energy share growing from 9.2% in 2005 to 19.1% in 2022, though this is still below the EU's 23% (Table 13.1). Bulgaria made significant strides in renewable heating and cooling, increasing from 14.3% in 2005 to 31.7% in 2022. However, renewable electricity generation peaked at 23.6% in 2020 and has since slightly declined, indicating a need for more consistent growth. Renewable energy in transport also lags behind the EU average.

Bulgaria faces significant challenges with energy efficiency. Its primary energy intensity in 2022 stood at 340 toe/M€'15, a modest improvement from 376 toe/M€'15 in 2013 (Fig. 13.2). In contrast, the EU average dropped to 91 toe/M€'15 in 2022, showing a much steeper improvement. This gap underscores Bulgaria's slower pace in enhancing energy efficiency, making it one of the most energy-intensive economies in Europe, reflecting inefficiencies in energy use across sectors.

Another area of concern is the GHG emissions intensity which has followed a downward trend but remains extremely high. From 1251 tons CO2 eq./M€'15 in 2013, it decreased to 1062 tons CO2 eq./M€'15 in 2022. However, this is still over four times the EU average, which dropped to 253 tons CO2 eq./M€'15 in 2022. The high carbon intensity is primarily due to Bulgaria's reliance on fossil fuels, particularly in the electricity generation sector.

A useful tool to assess Bulgaria's advances in green technology is the *European Clean Tech Tracker*, which provides data on the EU countries' progress in renewable energy deployment, and clean tech manufacturing (Tagliapietra et al., 2024). It highlights Bulgaria's slow adoption of solar PV and wind energy technologies, which are key to achieving further decarbonization of the energy sector. It further underscores that Bulgaria has limited clean tech manufacturing capacity compared

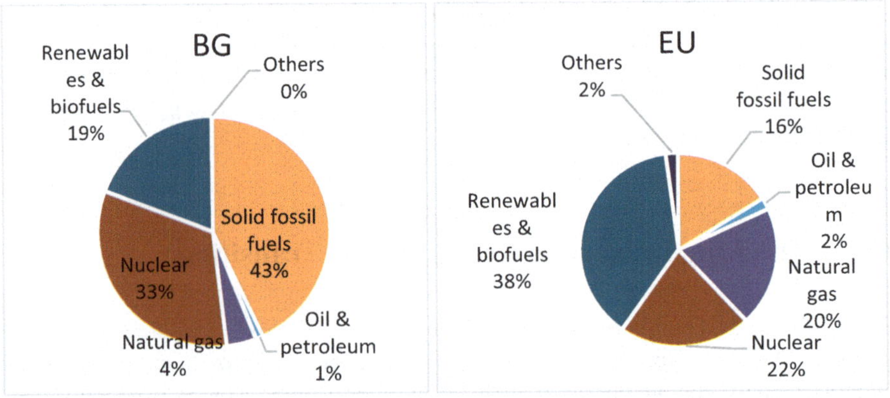

Fig. 13.1 Share of main energy products in gross electricity generation in Bulgaria and the EU (2022, %). Source: Eurostat, EU energy statistical pocketbook and country datasheets

Table 13.1 Renewable energy share in gross final energy consumption in Bulgaria and in the EU (2005–2022 select years, %)

	Bulgaria							EU						
	2005	*2010*	*2015*	*2019*	*2020*	*2021*	*2022*	*2005*	*2010*	*2015*	*2019*	*2020*	*2021*	*2022*
Overall renewable share	9.2	13.9	18.3	21.5	23.3	19.4	19.1	10.2	14.4	17.8	19.9	22.0	21.9	23.0
Renewable energy in transport	0.9	1.5	6.5	7.9	9.1	7.6	7.7	1.8	5.5	6.8	8.8	10.3	9.1	9.6
Renewable electricity generation	8.7	12.4	19.0	23.5	23.6	21.4	20.2	16.4	21.3	29.7	34.1	37.4	37.8	41.2
Renewable heating and cooling	14.3	24.3	28.9	35.4	37.2	30.0	31.7	12.4	17.0	20.3	22.4	23.0	22.9	24.9

Source: Eurostat, EU energy statistical pocketbook and country datasheets

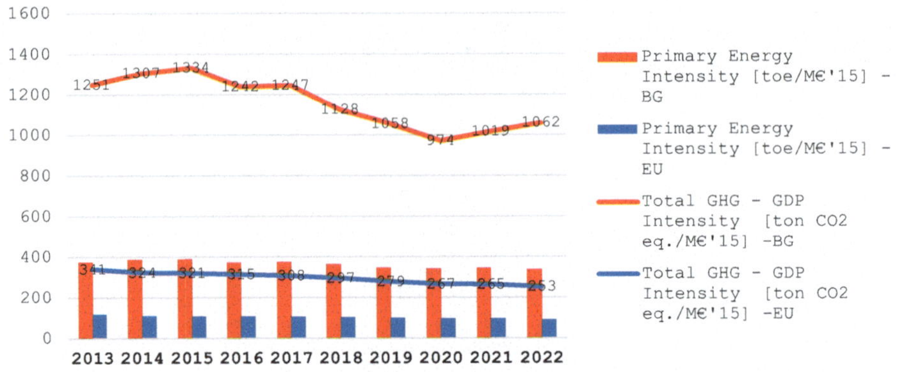

Fig. 13.2 Trends in primary energy intensity and GHG emissions intensity per GDP for Bulgaria and the EU (2013–2022). Source: Eurostat, EU energy statistical pocketbook and country datasheets

to leading EU nations. Unlike countries such as Germany and the Netherlands, where significant investments in clean tech manufacturing (e.g., solar panels, wind turbines, and battery components) have bolstered green growth, Bulgaria has not yet emerged as a manufacturing hub in the green economy. This gap limits the country's ability to domestically produce key components for renewable energy systems, instead relying heavily on imports of green technologies. The lack of a robust clean tech manufacturing sector also impacts Bulgaria's potential for job creation and economic growth tied to the green transition.

Bulgaria's slow progress in the adoption of electric vehicles (EVs) is another issue. The European Clean Tech Tracker highlights that Bulgaria has one of the lowest rates of EV adoption in the EU. This is due in part to inadequate infrastructure, such as insufficient charging stations, and a lack of strong government incentives to promote EVs. While wealthier EU countries are seeing rapid growth in the EV market, Bulgaria lags behind in creating the conditions for widespread EV adoption. This slower uptake of EVs is a missed opportunity in terms of reducing transport sector emissions, which are a major contributor to Bulgaria's greenhouse gas output.

While Bulgaria has made some progress in renewable energy deployment, it still faces significant challenges in scaling up renewable electricity generation and developing clean tech manufacturing. The slow integration of electric vehicles and green technologies further impedes Bulgaria's energy transition. Expanding solar PV, wind energy, and EV adoption will be crucial for Bulgaria to align with the EU's green transition. This underscores the need for greater investment, infrastructure development, and stronger policy frameworks.

13.4 Challenges in Bulgaria's Green Transition

Bulgaria's green transition faces multiple challenges that impede the country's ability to meet its decarbonization targets. These include financial, socioeconomic, and systemic hurdles.

One of the major barriers in Bulgaria's green transition is the limited availability of financing for clean energy projects. The European Clean Tech Tracker indicates that Bulgaria has lagged in fully accessing EU funding mechanisms like the Innovation Fund and the Just Transition Fund, which could support the deployment of renewable energy and energy efficiency measures. Additionally, Bulgaria's underutilization of financial instruments such as green bonds and sustainable finance initiatives has hampered investment in large-scale clean tech projects (Petrov et.al., 2024). The lack of public-private partnerships further exacerbates these challenges, limiting the country's ability to attract the necessary capital to scale up its renewable energy production and infrastructure.

Bulgaria's energy infrastructure is outdated and ill-equipped to handle the increasing share of renewable energy sources. There are significant delays in the deployment of grid-scale renewable projects due to complex administrative procedures and a lack of grid capacity. Upgrades to the country's transmission and distribution networks are essential for integrating new generation capacities from renewable sources like solar PV and wind power. Furthermore, investments in energy storage technologies are crucial for ensuring system balancing, especially as Bulgaria seeks to phase out fossil fuels like coal by 2038 (European Commission, 2023). Without modernizing its energy infrastructure, Bulgaria will struggle to accommodate its growing renewable energy capacity and meet its decarbonization targets.

Public awareness and societal adaptation are critical components of the green transition. However, Bulgaria faces challenges in these areas, particularly in terms of education and public engagement. The low rate of participation in adult learning programs focused on green skills development poses an obstacle to preparing the workforce for a low-carbon economy. The EU Commission country report for 2023 further suggests that many Bulgarians remain uninformed or unconvinced about the benefits of renewable energy and energy efficiency measures. There is a lack of broad public support for green policies, and education and cultural shifts toward sustainability are needed to foster societal acceptance of renewable energy technologies (European Commission, 2023).

The green transition in Bulgaria is compounded by the high energy poverty in the country, with the proportion of Bulgarians unable to afford adequate heating consistently above the EU average. In 2023, 20.7% of Bulgarians struggled to heat their homes, compared to 10.6% in the EU (Fig. 13.3). Although the figure has decreased from a high of 40.5% in 2014, it still underscores the difficulties many Bulgarians face in accessing affordable energy, reflecting broader socioeconomic vulnerabilities and the social dimension of Bulgaria's energy transition. Addressing energy

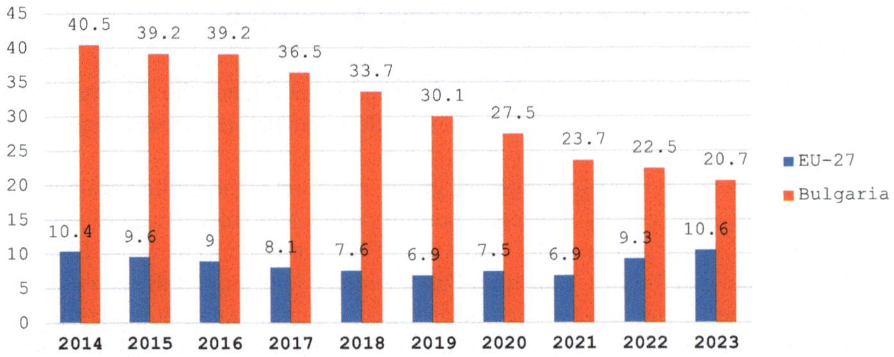

Fig. 13.3 Energy poverty in Bulgaria and the EU measured as the proportion of people who are unable to keep their homes adequately warm (2014–2023, %). Source: Eurostat

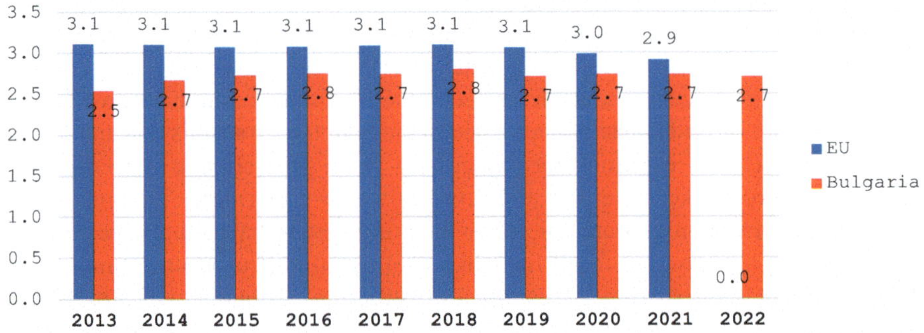

Fig. 13.4 Employment share in energy-intensive industries (Based on the NACE, these include mining and quarrying (NACE B), chemicals (C20), minerals (C23), metals (C24), and automotive (C29)) in Bulgaria and the EU (2013–2022, %). Source: Eurostat

poverty will require targeted measures to increase access to affordable renewable energy while protecting vulnerable groups from the impacts of rising energy costs.

Another socioeconomic challenge is the employment share in energy-intensive industries, where Bulgaria's share of 2.7% in 2022 is lower than the EU's 3.1% (Fig. 13.4). While Bulgaria has a smaller proportion of its workforce in these industries, the potential disruption caused by the green transition still poses risks for workers in sectors dependent on high energy consumption. This is especially pronounced in the coal mines and fossil fuel based thermal power plants that are concentrated in few regions in the country (see Box 13.1). Ensuring a just transition by reskilling workers and creating new opportunities in green industries is crucial for mitigating the negative impacts on employment.

Box 13.1 The Human Cost of Bulgaria's Green Transition: Job Losses in the Fossil Fuel

The European Green Deal, with its ambitious climate neutrality targets, has placed Bulgaria's fossil fuel industries under immense pressure. The country's dependence on lignite coal, particularly in the regions of Stara Zagora, Pernik, and Kyustendil, means that the transition to greener energy sources comes at a steep social and economic cost. It is estimated that between 11,900 and 16,000 jobs in the coal mining and energy sectors will be lost by 2030 as coal plants are decommissioned, leaving entire communities vulnerable (Zheleva & Markov, 2024).

The response to these impending job losses has been marked by widespread protests, particularly from workers in the coal industry who face an uncertain future. Despite promises of support from the Just Transition Mechanism, many workers and regional stakeholders express frustration with the lack of a clear strategy on how to manage the shift away from coal. The absence of concrete plans for retraining and reemployment exacerbates fears that the green transition will deepen regional inequalities, particularly in Bulgaria's coal-dependent areas (Apostolopoulos et al., 2023).

In addition to social unrest, the slow pace of planning and the government's unclear approach have further heightened tensions. While the EU's Green Deal sets clear environmental goals, the roadmap for managing the labor transition remains vague. Without immediate and robust policies to address these job losses, Bulgaria risks not only economic downturns in its coal regions but also prolonged social instability.

13.5 Opportunities for Bulgaria in the Green Economy

The global green transition presents not only challenges but also unprecedented opportunities for Bulgaria to reshape its economic landscape. As countries shift toward sustainable development, Bulgaria stands at a critical juncture where it can leverage the green transition to foster economic growth, technological innovation, and job creation. By embracing this shift, Bulgaria has the potential to transform from a fossil fuel-dependent economy into a leader in the renewable energy sector, and green technology innovation, positioning itself favorably in the global economy of the future.

The European Union's Green Deal is the framework under which Bulgaria can capitalize on its green potential. With its ambitious target of achieving climate neutrality by 2050, the EU offers a comprehensive support mechanism to member states, including Bulgaria, through various financial tools, such as the Just Transition Fund, the Recovery and Resilience Facility, and the Modernisation Fund. These mechanisms collectively provide billions of euros to help Bulgaria accelerate its green transition, restructure its energy sector, and make critical investments in renewable energy, energy efficiency, and sustainable agriculture.

The EU's Green Deal also fosters opportunities for Bulgaria to diversify its economy. With EU funds earmarked for green innovation, research and development in clean technologies, and support for small and medium-sized enterprises (SMEs), Bulgaria can enhance its competitiveness and create a more resilient economic model. This shift is not only about adopting cleaner energy but also about adopting sustainable business models, circular economies, and fostering green entrepreneurship (Zhelyazkova, 2020).

Bulgaria's geographic and climatic conditions make it highly suited to expand its renewable energy capacity, particularly in solar, wind, and hydroelectric power. The transition offers an opportunity for Bulgaria to tap into this potential and reduce its dependence on imported energy. Recent EU reports indicate that Bulgaria could significantly increase its renewable energy share, potentially reaching 27% of its energy mix by 2030 (Apostolopoulos et al., 2023). Investments in solar and wind farms not only promise cleaner energy but also can provide thousands of new jobs, helping to offset job losses in the fossil fuel sectors.

Moreover, Bulgaria has the opportunity to modernize its energy infrastructure and improve energy efficiency, which will reduce costs for businesses and households alike. By adopting new smart-grid technologies and energy storage solutions, Bulgaria could become a regional leader in energy security, integrating more renewable sources into its grid while enhancing stability.

Bulgaria stands to benefit from the green transition by tapping into sectors like renewable energy technologies, including solar photovoltaics and wind turbines, as well as energy storage technologies like lithium-ion batteries and fuel cells. These sectors offer significant job opportunities in the production and maintenance of electric vehicles, bioplastics, and energy-efficient building materials. Furthermore, the growing need for smart-grid design and advanced energy management services opens up new roles in engineering, environmental monitoring, and eco-industrial park development (Altenburg & Rodrik, 2017). As outlined in Box 13.2, local companies are already taking advantage of these opportunities. For instance, Solar MD has established a manufacturing facility in Rousse to produce lithium-iron-phosphate (LiFePO4) batteries, critical for energy storage in renewable energy systems. Similarly, Dynamo-Sliven is leveraging its expertise in electric motor production to meet the growing demand for electric vehicles and wind turbines, positioning itself as a key player in the green technology supply chain.

To fully capitalize on these opportunities, Bulgaria must also focus on reskilling its labor force. Programs aimed at reskilling workers, particularly those from declining industries, can help foster a new generation of workers skilled in renewable energy technologies, electric vehicle production, energy efficiency retrofitting, and more (Apostolopoulos et al., 2023). These initiatives will enable Bulgaria to not only boost its domestic economy but also to expand its market reach in the growing global green economy.

Beyond the manufacturing and energy sectors, Bulgaria's agri-food industry can also benefit from green innovations. The push for sustainable agriculture, coupled with EU support for green practices, opens opportunities for the country to develop eco-friendly farming techniques, organic production, and sustainable land use. This not only promises increased agricultural productivity but also bolsters Bulgaria's exports to environmentally conscious markets.

The shift to organic farming is gaining momentum as a way to enhance environmental security and improve rural life. Bulgaria's rich agricultural heritage and growing demand for organic products offer significant potential (Georgieva, 2023). Integrated organic models can optimize outputs while conserving energy and protecting soil fertility, fostering sustainable rural development (Nikolova et al., 2019).

Biogas production from agricultural waste offers Bulgaria a crucial opportunity to lower its carbon footprint and boost energy security. Environmentally sustainable and economically viable biogas technologies benefit both households and industries. With legislation aligned to European standards, Bulgaria is well-positioned to adopt biogas as a renewable energy source, supporting EU goals to reduce greenhouse gas emissions (Ganev et al., 2022).

Box 13.2 Harnessing the Green Economy: Opportunities for Companies in Bulgaria

The transition to a green economy is creating substantial opportunities for Bulgarian companies to innovate and expand their market reach. Recent developments in Rousse and Sliven highlight how local industries are beginning to capitalize on this shift.

In Rousse, Solar MD, a South African company specializing in energy storage, has established a new manufacturing facility to produce lithium-iron-phosphate (LiFePO4) batteries. These batteries are crucial for energy storage in renewable energy systems, such as solar and wind power installations. The facility, which is Solar MD's first outside of South Africa, aims to meet the growing demand for efficient, reliable energy storage across Europe. Initially, the plant will produce 60 MWh of batteries annually, with plans for significant expansion. This venture not only provides local employment opportunities but also positions Rousse as a key player in the European green energy supply chain, offering Bulgaria a foothold in the rapidly expanding market for renewable energy technologies.

In Sliven, Dynamo-Sliven, a company with a long history of producing electric motors, is strategically placed to benefit from the growing global demand for green technologies. As the world moves toward electric vehicles (EVs) and renewable energy, Dynamo-Sliven's expertise in electric motor manufacturing becomes increasingly relevant. Electric motors are essential components in both EVs and wind turbines, making Dynamo-Sliven's entry into these markets highly promising. By leveraging their established manufacturing capabilities and adapting to the needs of the green economy,

(continued)

Dynamo-Sliven could play a crucial role in supplying key components for these technologies, not only within Bulgaria but also to international markets.

These examples from Rousse and Sliven show how Bulgaria can engage with the green economy. Foreign investments like Solar MD's battery facility in Rousse bring new technologies, while local companies like Dynamo-Sliven can leverage their expertise to enter the green technology sector. Together, these developments demonstrate Bulgaria's potential as both a destination for green investment and a source of sustainable solutions.

Ultimately, the green transition offers Bulgaria the chance to not only align with the EU's ambitious climate goals but to embark on a path of long-term economic sustainability. The modernization of energy infrastructure, the adoption of renewable technologies, and the development of green industries could create a more competitive economy, better jobs, and an improved quality of life for Bulgarian citizens.

13.6 Conclusion

Bulgaria's path toward green transitioning and sustainable development, as explored in this chapter, is fraught with significant challenges, primarily driven by socioeconomic consequences, political dynamics, and institutional constraints. The country's reliance on fossil fuels and its energy-intensive industries make the transition particularly difficult, with substantial social and economic impacts expected in regions heavily dependent on coal.

One of the major obstacles is the lack of political will, which has slowed the pace of reforms and investment in green technologies. This is compounded by a lack of institutional capacity, where bureaucratic inefficiencies and limited coordination have hindered the effective implementation of green policies. Additionally, there is considerable industry and public opposition to the transition, stemming from concerns over job losses and economic instability in traditional sectors.

Despite these challenges, the green transition offers Bulgaria a crucial opportunity for economic modernization and sustainable growth. The green agenda should be seen not merely as a requirement but as a strategic imperative for national development. Overcoming the obstacles of political inertia, institutional weaknesses, and public resistance will require a concerted effort. By strengthening political commitment, building institutional capacity, and addressing the socioeconomic concerns of affected communities, Bulgaria can navigate these challenges and fully participate in Europe's broader vision for a sustainable future in the new global architecture.

References

Altenburg, T., & Rodrik, D. (2017). *Green industrial policy: Accelerating structural change towards wealthy green economies*. Copy at https://tinyurl.com/yxb23bkz

Apostolopoulos, N., Kakouris, A., Liargovas, P., Borisov, P., Radev, T., Apostolopoulos, S., Daskou, S., & Anastasopoulou, E. (2023). Just transition policies, power plant workers and green entrepreneurs in Greece, Cyprus and Bulgaria: Can education and retraining meet the challenge? *Sustainability, 15*, 16307. https://doi.org/10.3390/su152316307

European Commission. (2023). *Bulgaria - 2023 country report*. Commission Staff Working Document, SWD (2023) 602 final, Brussels.

European Commission. (n.d.) *The European Green Deal - striving to be the first climate-neutral continent*. Retrieved from https://commission.europa.eu/strategy-and-policy/priorities-2019-2024/european-green-deal_en

European Council on Foreign Relations (ECFR). (2020). *Europe's green moment: How to meet the climate challenge*. Available at ECFR.

Ganev, I. K., Gieva, E., Filipov, K., & Дімітров, Л. (2022). Possibility for production of biogas from manure in Bulgaria. *IOP Conference Series: Earth and Environmental Science, 1006*(1), 012010. https://doi.org/10.1088/1755-1315/1006/1/012010

Georgieva, M. (2023). Development of organic farming as a prospective way to environmental security of the Bulgarian Village. *European Historical Studies, 24*, 33–46. https://doi.org/10.17721/2524-048x.2023.24.3

International Energy Agency (IEA). (2021). *Net zero by 2050: A roadmap for the global energy sector*. IEA.

Nikolova, M., Velkovski, V., & Tsenov, D. A. (2019). Structural measures in the agricultural lands – Condition and factor for the functioning of organic agriculture in the Republic of Bulgaria (by the example of expert study). New stages of development of modern science in Ukraine and EU Countries. https://doi.org/10.30525/978-9934-588-15-0-128.

Perez, M., Scholten, D., & Stegen, K. (2019). The multi-speed energy transition in Europe: Opportunities and challenges for EU energy security. *Energy Strategy Reviews, 26*, 100415.

Petrov, S., Aleksandrova, S., Kirova, S. (2024). Environmental Effects of Green Bonds and Other Forms of Financing in the European Union. *International Journal of Economic Sciences, XIII*(1), 81–105.

Serrano, P. V., & Zaveri, A. (2020). Venturing the definition of green energy transition: A systematic literature review. *Environmental Science*. https://doi.org/10.48550/arXiv.2004.10562

Stefanova, B., & Zhelev, P. (2022). Testing the premises of International Society in the European Energy Union: The pluralism/solidarism nexus. *JCMS: Journal of Common Market Studies, 60*(5), 1255–1271.

Tagliapietra, S., McWilliams, B., Trasi, C., & Keliauskaitė, U. (2024). European clean tech tracker. *Bruegel*. Available at https://www.bruegel.org/dataset/european-clean-tech-tracker

Tkachuk, O. (2024). The European Union in its pursuit of being a global leader in climate neutrality. *Global Policy, 15*(S8), 69–74.

Zhelyazkova, V. (2020). Circular Economy: International Policies and Practices. Izvestiya. *Journal of Varna University of Economics, 64*(3), 239–255.

Zheleva, V., & Markov, N. (2024). Socio-economic challenges in the transition to a low-carbon economy at regional level in Bulgaria. *Scientific Papers Series Management, Economic Engineering in Agriculture and Rural Development, 24*(2), 975–982.

Chapter 14
Conclusion

Bulgaria's integration into the global economy represents a multifaceted journey marked by significant transformations, enduring challenges, and emergent opportunities. This monograph, after providing historical context, has focused on tracing Bulgaria's post-socialist economic trajectory, examining its EU integration, role in regional economic cooperation, global trade in goods and services, foreign direct investment, international labor migration, and the twin transitions toward digitalization and sustainability.

Bulgaria's accession to the European Union in 2007 marked a pivotal milestone in its economic evolution, providing access to broader markets, structural funds, and regulatory frameworks. While EU membership has catalyzed significant infrastructural development and trade growth, it has not automatically guaranteed economic convergence with more advanced member states. Persistent regional disparities, governance challenges, and income inequality underscore the need for sustained national efforts to fully leverage EU integration's potential.

Strategically located at the crossroads of Europe and Asia, Bulgaria serves as a vital bridge between the EU and emerging markets. This geopolitical positioning however is both an asset and a liability. While it facilitates economic exchanges and political cooperation, it also places Bulgaria in the midst of regional tensions and competing global interests, particularly in the Black Sea region. Building on its EU integration, Bulgaria has sought to strengthen its position through regional cooperation in the Black Sea. Bulgaria's participation in initiatives like the Black Sea Economic Cooperation (BSEC) and the EU's Black Sea Synergy reflects its efforts to enhance regional connectivity and economic collaboration. However, ongoing geopolitical tensions and shifting alliances necessitate a balanced approach that promotes stability and fosters economic integration with neighboring countries.

These regional and European connections have had a profound impact on Bulgaria's foreign trade in goods and services, a cornerstone of the country's international economic engagement. While goods exports have diversified, structural challenges such as a chronic trade deficit and reliance on low-value-added products persist. Conversely, the service sector has witnessed faster, positive transformations, particularly with a notable shift of comparative advantage from traditional manufacturing services on physical inputs owned by others to ICT. This transition has not only strengthened Bulgaria's position in high-value service sectors but also

P. Zhelev, *Bulgaria in the Global Economy*, Societies and Political Orders in Transition, https://doi.org/10.1007/978-3-031-87923-4_14

contributed to a positive trade balance that largely offsets the deficits observed in goods trade.

Closely linked to trade is Bulgaria's role in global value chains (GVCs). Bulgaria's integration into GVCs has increased, but its role remains predominantly downstream, focusing on assembly and processing activities. This positioning limits the potential for higher value-added contributions. To move up the value chain, Bulgaria should attract higher-quality foreign direct investment (FDI).

FDI has played a critical role in Bulgaria's economic transformation. However, much of the investment has concentrated in low-value, non-tradable sectors, limiting its long-term benefits. Recent trends show a shift toward manufacturing and knowledge-intensive industries, but governance issues and regional disparities remain barriers.

The other form of production factors migration presents a much more dual narrative. While remittances have contributed to the economy, the exodus of skilled workers—or brain drain—poses ominous long-term developmental challenges. Recent trends of declining emigration rates and increasing return migration offer opportunities to leverage returning talent. However, effective migration policies are urgently needed to balance these dynamics, as our analysis has shown that one of the most daunting challenges in Bulgaria is its shrinking and aging population.

Conversely, Bulgaria's burgeoning tech sector and potential for energy diversification present significant opportunities. The rise of digital entrepreneurship and the country's strategic investments in technology infrastructure could position Bulgaria as a regional innovation hub. Energy diversification, particularly in the context of EU's green transition, offers avenues to reduce dependency on external suppliers and foster sustainable development.

One of the main takeaways from the monograph is that benefits from integration in the global economy do not come automatically but require active national policies. Bulgaria's future hinges on forging a balanced, long-term strategy that harnesses global opportunities in a manner attuned to local capacities and needs.

A critical first step is the *creation of broad-based consensus* among political institutions, the private sector, and civil society. Too often, Bulgaria has experienced abrupt policy swings tied to electoral cycles or external pressures, hindering consistent progress. By establishing an inclusive forum where stakeholders can negotiate priorities—from infrastructure development to educational reforms—Bulgaria can craft a shared vision of economic modernization. Such a consensus requires transparent communication of policy objectives, predictable regulatory frameworks, and rigorous public scrutiny to ensure that measures align with national goals rather than short-term political interests.

Equally important is adopting *a long-term policy horizon*. Although immediate economic concerns must be addressed, the structural changes required for sustaining growth—such as upgrading human capital, investing in research and development, and modernizing industrial sectors—demand planning that extends beyond the electoral cycle. Ensuring continuity in key initiatives, such as digital infrastructure and green transition projects, can help Bulgaria remain competitive amid shifting global forces.

Strengthening *institutions and the rule of law* forms the bedrock of any robust economic strategy. In practice, this entails bolstering regulatory agencies, reducing corruption, and guaranteeing judicial independence to create an environment where domestic firms and foreign investors can operate with confidence. Transparent procurement processes, consistent enforcement of regulations, and judicial reform are especially vital for attracting higher-value foreign direct investment and spurring technology transfers.

Within this strengthened institutional framework, *well-designed structural policies* can proactively foster Bulgaria's latent comparative advantages. Whether focusing on technology-intensive exports, niche agribusiness, tourism, or specialized services, policy interventions should target clear bottlenecks and leverage the country's geographic advantages and human capital. Incentivizing private research and development, building partnerships between academia and industry, and supporting start-up ecosystems can help expand Bulgaria's technological frontier. By identifying specific sectors where Bulgaria holds an unrealized competitive edge—such as advanced information technologies, renewable energy solutions, or value-added agricultural products—public support and targeted incentives can catalyze private-sector growth.

Finally, Bulgaria's success will depend on diversifying economic ties and strengthening global partnerships. Although European Union integration remains a primary anchor of Bulgaria's economic policy, engagement with markets beyond the EU can help reduce dependency and expose domestic firms to broader opportunities. The strategic cultivation of economic relations with regional partners, the USA, China, and other economic players can not only broaden export destinations but also incentivize domestic innovation and capacity-building.

In weaving these elements together—consensus-building, long-term strategic thinking, robust institutions, carefully crafted structural policies, and diversified partnerships—Bulgaria can more effectively navigate the complexities of the global economy. The challenges ahead are real, especially given intensifying geopolitical pressures and rapid technological change. Yet Bulgaria also possesses distinct strengths: a heritage of adaptability, a favorable geographic position, and an emerging cohort of technology-savvy entrepreneurs. By channeling these assets through stable, future-oriented policies, the country can move beyond reactive cycles of dependence and instead craft a resilient model of sustainable development—one that not only secures its competitiveness on the global stage but also enhances the welfare of its citizens for generations to come.

The manufacturer's authorised representative in the EU is Springer Nature Customer Service Centre GmbH, Europaplatz 3, 69115 Heidelberg, Germany. If you have any concerns regarding our products, please contact ProductSafety@springernature.com

Printed and bound by CPI Group (UK) Ltd, Croydon, CR0 4YY
30/09/2026
02225568-0004